Sion's songs, or hymns: composed for the use of them that love and follow the Lord Jesus Christ in sincerity. By John Berridge, ...

John Berridge

Sion's songs, or hymns: composed for the use of them that love and follow the Lord Jesus Christ in sincerity. By John Berridge, ...

Berridge, John
ESTCID: T173776
Reproduction from John Rylands University Library of Manchester
With a half-title and an index.
London : printed for Vallance and Conder, 1785.
[2],viii,458,[8]p. ; 12°

Eighteenth Century
Collections Online
Print Editions

Gale ECCO Print Editions

Relive history with *Eighteenth Century Collections Online*, now available in print for the independent historian and collector. This series includes the most significant English-language and foreign-language works printed in Great Britain during the eighteenth century, and is organized in seven different subject areas including literature and language; medicine, science, and technology; and religion and philosophy. The collection also includes thousands of important works from the Americas.

The eighteenth century has been called "The Age of Enlightenment." It was a period of rapid advance in print culture and publishing, in world exploration, and in the rapid growth of science and technology – all of which had a profound impact on the political and cultural landscape. At the end of the century the American Revolution, French Revolution and Industrial Revolution, perhaps three of the most significant events in modern history, set in motion developments that eventually dominated world political, economic, and social life.

In a groundbreaking effort, Gale initiated a revolution of its own: digitization of epic proportions to preserve these invaluable works in the largest online archive of its kind. Contributions from major world libraries constitute over 175,000 original printed works. Scanned images of the actual pages, rather than transcriptions, recreate the works *as they first appeared.*

Now for the first time, these high-quality digital scans of original works are available via print-on-demand, making them readily accessible to libraries, students, independent scholars, and readers of all ages.

For our initial release we have created seven robust collections to form one the world's most comprehensive catalogs of 18th century works.

Initial Gale ECCO Print Editions collections include:

History and Geography
Rich in titles on English life and social history, this collection spans the world as it was known to eighteenth-century historians and explorers. Titles include a wealth of travel accounts and diaries, histories of nations from throughout the world, and maps and charts of a world that was still being discovered. Students of the War of American Independence will find fascinating accounts from the British side of conflict.

Social Science

Delve into what it was like to live during the eighteenth century by reading the first-hand accounts of everyday people, including city dwellers and farmers, businessmen and bankers, artisans and merchants, artists and their patrons, politicians and their constituents. Original texts make the American, French, and Industrial revolutions vividly contemporary.

Medicine, Science and Technology

Medical theory and practice of the 1700s developed rapidly, as is evidenced by the extensive collection, which includes descriptions of diseases, their conditions, and treatments. Books on science and technology, agriculture, military technology, natural philosophy, even cookbooks, are all contained here.

Literature and Language

Western literary study flows out of eighteenth-century works by Alexander Pope, Daniel Defoe, Henry Fielding, Frances Burney, Denis Diderot, Johann Gottfried Herder, Johann Wolfgang von Goethe, and others. Experience the birth of the modern novel, or compare the development of language using dictionaries and grammar discourses.

Religion and Philosophy

The Age of Enlightenment profoundly enriched religious and philosophical understanding and continues to influence present-day thinking. Works collected here include masterpieces by David Hume, Immanuel Kant, and Jean-Jacques Rousseau, as well as religious sermons and moral debates on the issues of the day, such as the slave trade. The Age of Reason saw conflict between Protestantism and Catholicism transformed into one between faith and logic -- a debate that continues in the twenty-first century.

Law and Reference

This collection reveals the history of English common law and Empire law in a vastly changing world of British expansion. Dominating the legal field is the *Commentaries of the Law of England* by Sir William Blackstone, which first appeared in 1765. Reference works such as almanacs and catalogues continue to educate us by revealing the day-to-day workings of society.

Fine Arts

The eighteenth-century fascination with Greek and Roman antiquity followed the systematic excavation of the ruins at Pompeii and Herculaneum in southern Italy; and after 1750 a neoclassical style dominated all artistic fields. The titles here trace developments in mostly English-language works on painting, sculpture, architecture, music, theater, and other disciplines. Instructional works on musical instruments, catalogs of art objects, comic operas, and more are also included.

The BiblioLife Network

This project was made possible in part by the BiblioLife Network (BLN), a project aimed at addressing some of the huge challenges facing book preservationists around the world. The BLN includes libraries, library networks, archives, subject matter experts, online communities and library service providers. We believe every book ever published should be available as a high-quality print reproduction; printed on-demand anywhere in the world. This insures the ongoing accessibility of the content and helps generate sustainable revenue for the libraries and organizations that work to preserve these important materials.

The following book is in the "public domain" and represents an authentic reproduction of the text as printed by the original publisher. While we have attempted to accurately maintain the integrity of the original work, there are sometimes problems with the original work or the micro-film from which the books were digitized. This can result in minor errors in reproduction. Possible imperfections include missing and blurred pages, poor pictures, markings and other reproduction issues beyond our control. Because this work is culturally important, we have made it available as part of our commitment to protecting, preserving, and promoting the world's literature.

GUIDE TO FOLD-OUTS MAPS and OVERSIZED IMAGES

The book you are reading was digitized from microfilm captured over the past thirty to forty years. Years after the creation of the original microfilm, the book was converted to digital files and made available in an online database.

In an online database, page images do not need to conform to the size restrictions found in a printed book. When converting these images back into a printed bound book, the page sizes are standardized in ways that maintain the detail of the original. For large images, such as fold-out maps, the original page image is split into two or more pages

Guidelines used to determine how to split the page image follows:

• Some images are split vertically; large images require vertical and horizontal splits.
• For horizontal splits, the content is split left to right.
• For vertical splits, the content is split from top to bottom.
• For both vertical and horizontal splits, the image is processed from top left to bottom right.

SION's SONGS,

OR

HYMNS.

[Price 2s. 6d. bound.]

SION's SONGS,

OR

HYMNS:

COMPOSED

For the Ufe of them that love and follow
the Lord Jefus Chrift in Since.ity.

By JOHN BERRIDGE, M. A.

VICAR of EVERTON, near Potton, in Bedfordfhire,
late FELLOW of CLARE-HALL, in Cambridge,
and CHAPLAIN to the EARL of BUCHAN.

LONDON.

Printed for VALLANCE and CONDER, Cheapfide.

M DCC LXXXV.

PREFACE.

MANY volumes of Hymns have been lately publiſhed, ſome of them a new compoſition, others a mere collection; and it may ſeem needleſs to add one more to the number, eſpecially after having publiſhed a collection myſelf. But ill health, ſome years paſt, having kept me from travelling or preaching, I took up the trade of Hymn-making, a handicraft much followed of late, but a buſineſs I was not born or bred to, and undertaken chiefly to keep a long ſickneſs fiom preying on my ſpirit, and to make tedious nights paſs over more ſmoothly. Some tinkling employment was wanted, which might amuſe and not fatigue me.

Beſide, I was not wholly ſatisfied with the collection I had publiſhed. The bells, indeed, had been chiefly caſt in a celebrated Foundery, and in ringing were tunable enough, none more ſo, but a clear goſpel tone was not found in them all. Human wiſdom and ſtrength, perfection and merit, give Sion's bells a Levitical twang, and
drown

drown the mellow tone of the gospel outright.

The book of Psalms seems intended
as a model for Hymns; and after this
model I have copied, as nearly as I could.
There we find instruction, exhortation, caution, and christian experience, blended with
prayer and praise. The thoughts are easy
and free, flowing from the heart; and the
language simple and plain, yet neat and
elegant. And nothing sure can be more
unsuitable, than humble prayer uttered in
pompous expressions.

In composing the Hymns, an easy flow
of words has been sought, with a care to
make the sense end, or nearly end, at proper
pauses. Some text of scripture also has
been taken as a subject for each Hymn,
with a view to keep my thoughts from
rambling, and to explain scripture with a
reference to Christ. He is the *end of the
law*, which was a *shadow of things to come*;
and *Christ is that body*, to which the shadow
belongs. Accordingly he is shadowed forth
by patriarchs, prophets, and kings of Israel,
and by a vast variety of types and simili-
tudes; and must be sought in the book of
Proverbs, as well as in Leviticus, the
clearest book of Jewish gospel.

My

My heart, I think, is open to embrace every one of every sect, who truly loves and follows Jesus Christ. The whole household of faith are my brethren, and some care has been taken not to give any of them a needless offence. In matters, which are not fundamental, let every one see with his own eyes, and judge for himself, as God enables him. The Hymns are upon a catholic plan, not intended to depreciate any set of christians, but to sink the creature to his real standard of worthlessness and helplessness, and to exalt the Saviour in the hearts of his people, that they may trust in him, love and obey him. Man's emptiness, and Christ's fulness, are my general topics, but diversified in a variety of cases; and these topics are not suited to the relish of depraved nature, which loveth gilding and varnish to hide a base metal.

The more we feel our own misery, the more we learn to value Jesus; and the more we know of him, the more we shall trust in him; and the more we can trust him, the more we shall love and obey him. *To know Jesus*, was the top of Paul's ambition, and is the joy and crown of each believer; it is the pinnacle of human glory; and according to the Lord's own account, it *is eternal life.*

Where

Where human pageantry appears in any
shape, Jesus Christ is vailed by it; and
much of this is found among us. Human
wealth, human grandeur, human literature,
all naturally producing human loftiness,
have almost buried Jesus in Great Britain.
The power of godliness is gone, and the
form is scampering after it. The Head of
the Christian body is dishonoured and re-
jected; and the members can have no life,
apart from the Head. These Hymns are
likely to please no one, who is pleased with
himself. They are designed to set a man
at variance with himself, and to shew that
his worst foes are lodged in his own breast.
Nor yet will they satisfy a Laodicean professor, who is neither cold nor hot, and
seemeth to be rich, but is poor, having an
head full of knowledge, and a heart full of
mammon, talking bravely of the doctrines
of faith, but a stranger to holiness and the
life of faith. My kindly readers must be
such, as feel they have no spiritual supplies
in themselves, nor ability to lay up stores
for a future supply, and therefore live as
daily pensioners on the Saviour's bounty;
having vital union with him by faith, producing conformity to him; and centering
all their hope *in* him, while receiving all
supplies from him.

Do

Do you wish to sing as angels sing? Ask of God an heavenly mind. An harp must be tuned, before it makes good music. And when the heart is put in tune, well warmed with the love of God, singing proves delightsome service, and a heavenly feast. But genuine praise cannot be offered unto God, while saucy merit roosts in man. Who thanks another for only paying us what is our due? And if eternal life is not the gift of God, but wages due for service, no need to thank him for his heaven. Since merit has prevailed much among us, Psalm-singing is become a vulgar business in our churches This tax of praise is collected chiefly from an organ, or a solitary clerk, or some bawling voices in a singing loft. The congregation may listen if they please, or talk in whispers, or take a gentle nap. By feeling ourselves monuments of mercy, spared, fed, and redeemed by it, we learn to love and praise the Author of such mercy.

Twelve years ago these Hymns were composed in a six months illness, and have since laid neglected by me; often threatened with the fire, but have escaped that martyrdom. Fatherly mercy prevented that literary death; for authors can seldom prove cruel to their own offspring, how-

ever

ever deformed. But they come into the world naked, neither clothed with recommendation or correction of any friend. Such as they are, I offer them to the Reader, and suppose he may find in them the common lot of human productions, some things to blame, and some to commend.

A few of the following Hymns occasionally rambled into Magazines, under the signature of *Old Everton,* and are now finding their way home again.

Before the Preface shuts up, I must turn to Jesus my Master; and, christian Reader, if thou canst pray, join with me in asking his blessing.

My Saviour and my God, accept this mite of love, which is cast into thy treasury. Give it a blessing, and it shall be blessed. What is water in the Hymns, turn into wine, by giving them a charge to enliven the hearts of the children, and to stir up the wills of aliens to seek thy salvation. Only attend them with an unction of thy Spirit, and whatever be the Hymns, thy glory shall be promoted by them. Amen.

E R R A T A.

Page 24, line 6, read, Guard his breast from harm.
Page 59, line 3, read, Speaks it's worth
Page 384, line 8, read, Are living in pain.

SION's

SONGS or HYMNS.

HYMN 1.

" Behold, I was shapen in iniquity!"
Pfal. li. 5.

1.

HOW shall I come to thee,
O God, who holy art,
And cannot evil see
But with a loathing heart!
I am defil'd throughout by sin,
And by my very birth unclean.

2.

Soon as my heart could beat,
It drank in various woe;
Pride, lust, and self-deceit,
Thro' all it's channels flow;
A captive born, a child of earth,
It knows and craves no higher birth.

B

3.

From this polluted spring
All filthy waters rife;
From this difeafed thing
I date my maladies:
My heart, a moft degenerate root,
Produceth only canker'd fruit.

4.

And what can wafh me clean
But Jefu's precious blood?
This only purgeth fin,
And bringeth nigh to God;
Lord, wafh my fores, and heal them too,
And all my leprofy fubdue.

5.

Thy heavenly image draw
Upon my earthly heart,
And well engrave thy law
Upon the inward part;
My fallen nature upward raife,
And teach me how to love and praife.

HYMN 2.

" I beheld tranfgreffors, and was grieved,"
Pfal. cxix. 158.

1.

JESUS, I long for thee,
   And figh for Canaan's fhore,
Thy lovely face to fee,
And all my warfare o'er;

Here billows break upon my breaft,
And brooding forrows fteal my reft.

2.

I mourn to fee thy blood
So foully trampled on ;
And finners, daring God,
To fwift deftruction run ;
With heedlefs heart and fimp'ring face,
They dance the hell-ward road apace.

3.

Profeffors, too, in name,
Of Jefus make their boaft,
Who put the Lord to fhame,
And yet to fhame are loft ;
Well-fkill'd of faith and grace to prate,
And, Judas like, can kifs and hate.

4.

But when thy fimple fheep
For forms and fhadows fight,
I fit me down, and weep
To fee their fhallow wit,
Who leave their bread to gnaw the ftones,
And fondly break their teeth with bones.

5.

Yet chiefly, Lord, I grieve
For my untoward heart ;
How full of doubts I live,
Though full of grace thou art ;
What poor returns I make to thee
For all the mercy fhewn to me !

6.

And muſt I ever ſmart,
A child of ſorrows here?
Yet, Lord, be near my heart,
To ſooth each riſing tear,
Then at thy bleeding croſs I'll ſtay,
And ſweetly weep my life away.

HYMN 3.

" Thou art my hiding-place," Pſal. xxxii. 7.

1.

WHERE muſt a ſinner fly,
Who feels his guilty load,
And ſtands condemn'd to die
Out of the mouth of God?
Can any door of hope be found?
Not any, ſure, on nature's ground.

2.

What if he mend his life,
And pour out floods of tears,
And pray with fervent ſtrife?
Theſe pay no paſt arrears.
The law, with unrelenting breath,
Declares the wage of ſin is death. [Rom. vi. 23.

3.

Who then ſhall reconcile
Such jarring things as theſe?
Say, how can juſtice ſmile
At mercy on her knees?

Or how can mercy lift her head,
If all the legal debt is paid?

4.

Jesus, thy helping hand
Has made the conteft ceafe,
Paid off each law-demand,
And bought the bleft releafe;
Stern juftice satisfy'd by thee,
Bids mercy bring the news to me.

5.

O tidings fweet of grace
To finners loft and poor,
Who humbly feek thy face,
And knock at mercy's door;
Who tafte the peace thy blood imparts,
And feel the Saviour in their hearts!

6.

All hail! we blefs thee now,
Who bought us with thy blood;
Our gracious Shepherd, thou,
To bring us home to God!
On earth we fing thy bleeding love,
And long to fee thy face above.

HYMN 4.

"I am the Rose of Sharon, and the Lily
of the valleys," Cant. II. 1.

1.

JESUS, thou art the Rose
   That blusheft on the thorn;
Thy blood the semblance shews,
   When on Mount Calv'ry torn;
A rugged tree thou hadft indeed!
But rofes from a thorn proceed.

2.

This Rofe has fragrance fweet,
   And chears a confcience well;
Yet pluck it, as it's meet,
   Or nothing wilt thou fmell;
It's application does impart
The confolation to thy heart.

3.

So lilies low and fair,
   Which in the valley grow,
With Jefus may compare,
   Since it has pleas'd him fo;
Like thefe an humble form he wears,
And on his robe no fpot appears.

4.

A robe fo clean and white
   No Fuller's art can fhew;
Surpaffing even light,
   And purer far than fnow;

Not David's son, on high-days dreſt,
Could ever match this lily-veſt.

·5·

Coupled in ſong we ſee
The roſe and lily are,
And fancy out to me
My ſurety's office clear;
One ſhews his blood to waſh me whole,
And one his robe to clothe my ſoul.

6.

Lord, bring the ſweet'ning roſe
To make my conſcience clean;
And give me lily-clothes
To hide my rags within;
So ſhall thy blood and righteouſneſs
Bring goſpel peace and heavenly dreſs.

7·

Completely thus array'd,
And ſweetly cheared on,
No danger ſhall I dread,
No duty ſhall I ſhun:
The roſe and lily when combin'd,
Afford a peaceful, loving mind.

HYMN 5.

"I fat down under *his* fhadow with great
delight, and his fruit was fweet to my
tafte," Cant. ii. 3.

1.

COME hither, weary foul,
    And drop thy burden here;
If thou wouldft be made whole,
A bleffed tree is near;
Upon the highway-fide it grows,
And fweetly healeth human woes!

2.

It only fuits the foil,
Where broken hearts abound;
Yet vifits every ifle
Where gofpel-truth is found:
'Tis planted for the health of man,
And by an heavenly hufbandman.

3.

Upon the road it ftands
To catch a pilgrim's eye;
And fpreads it's leafy hands
To beckon ftrangers nigh;
Breathes forth a gale of pure delight,
And charms the humble trav'ler's fight.

4.

It's friendly arms afford
A fcreen from heat and blaft;
It's branches well are ftor'd
With fruits of choiceft tafte;

And in the leaf kind juices dwell,
Which fore and ficknefs quickly heal.

[Rev. xxii. 2.

5.

But ftand not gazing on
The branches of the tree,
Go under and *fit* down,
Or fure it helps not thee;
There reft thy feet and aching fide,
And in this refting-place *abide*.

6.

No fooner art thou fat
Beneath it's fhadow there,
But all thy fcalding heat
And all thy fretful care,
And every pain from thee will drop,
As fruit comes tumbling in thy lap.

7.

This is the tree of life
Which firft in Eden grew,
But Adam with his wife
Conceal'd it from our view;
Then was it fix'd on Calvary's top,
And is the pillar of my hope.

HYMN 6.

"Draw me, and I will run after thee,"
Cant. 1. 4.

1.

HOW sluggish is my heart
In search of endless life!
How loth with toys to part
Which only bring me grief!
Small riddance in the race I make,
Yet pant for breath each step I take.

2.

I cannot well abide
The cross's daily load,
It makes me start aside,
And leave the narrow road:
Like some raw bullock not well broke,
My shoulder frets beneath the yoke.

3.

E'erwhile I sit and sigh,
And loathe my folly too;
Then up I get and try
What human might can do,
Lay to mine arm, but all in vain,
No arm of mine can break the chain.

4.

Ah, whither must I go,
Since flesh and reason fail?
No help on earth, I know,
Can o'er my heart prevail;

No man can mend my tardy pace
But he, whofe name is Truth and Grace.

5.

To him I lift mine eyes,
Thou Son of David hear,
And let my feeble cries
Bring thy falvation near;
My froward heart is in thy hand,
And it will move at thy command.

6.

If thou, Lord, quicken me,
And draw me with thy voice,
I will run after thee,
And in thy word rejoice:
Refresh me well with manna fweet,
And I will shew thee nimble feet.

HYMN 7.

" My heart and my flesh crieth out for the
living God," Pfal. lxxxiv. 2.

1.

WITH folemn weekly ftate
The worldling treads thy court,
Content to fee thy gate,
And fuch as there refort;
But, ah, what is the houfe to me,
Unlefs the mafter I can fee.

2.

Whilst formalists admire
The pillars, walls, and roof,
Which bring no heav'nly fire,
And are but weather-proof;
I seek a man, more choice than gold,
That lovely man, whom Judas sold.

3.

Nought will content my heart
But fellowship with him,
And when from him I start,
My life is all a dream;
I seem to eat and take my fill,   ⌈Isai xxix 8.
But wake and feel my hunger still.

4.

In vain I seek for rest
In all created good,
It leaves me yet unblest,
And makes me pant for God,
And restless sure my heart must be,
Till finding all it's rest in thee.

5.

For thee my flesh will cry,
And send a labouring groan;
For thee my heart will sigh,
And make a pensive moan;
And each for thee will daily pine,
And would be always only thine.

6. Lord,

6.

Lord. fix me on thy fide,
A branch in thy true vine,
Nor let me ftraggle wide,
But round thee twine and twine;
And clufters bear of heavenly fruit,
By fap receiv'd from thy rich root.

HYMN 8.

" Having a form of godlinefs, but denying
the power thereof," 2 Tim. iii. 5.

1.

GOOD doctrines in the head,
Which do not mend the heart,
Are windy food indeed,
And make us proud and pert;
Our cymbal tinkles all day long,
And faith is froth upon the tongue.

2.

Some faft by Calvin hold,
And fome for Luther fight,
And each is mighty bold,
And feemeth mighty right;
Well, though with Calvin I agree,
Yet Chrift is all in all to me.

3.

The form of baptifm too
A cloud of duft will raife;
Here fprinkling will not do,
And there will only pleafe;

C

Some wash the child, and some the man,
And some reject the whole as vain.

4.

And while such waspish worms
Each others side devour,
And bury'd are in forms,
Give me, O Lord, the pow'r,
The pow'r to feast upon thy grace,
And live the life of godliness.

5.

May truth direct my tongue,
And grace my heart control,
And Jesus be my song,
While endless ages roll;
To please him well my single aim,
And all my trust in his dear name.

HYMN 9.

" Ephraim shall say, What have I to do any
more with idols?" Hosea xiv. 8.

1.

OUR fancy loves to range
In search of earthly good,
And freely would exchange
A pearl for rotten wood,
Snaps at a shadow thin and vain,
Is fool'd and vex'd, yet snaps again.

2.

Fain would the heart unite
A Chrift with idols bafe,
And link mid-day with night,
Or mammon foul with grace;
And in one bofom, falfe as hell,
Would have the ark and Dagon dwell.

[1 Sam. v. 2, 3.

3.

But Chrift will not allow
A rival near his throne;
A jealous God art thou,
And wilt be king alone!
Dagon fhall fall before thy face,
Or thy fweet ark will leave the place.

4.

Oft have I forc'd the Lamb
To call away his ark,
And reftlefs then I am,
And flutter in the dark;
Some idol rakes my foolifh breaft,
Beguiles my heart, and breaks my reft.

5.

Thefe dagons make me weak,
And damp my chearful fong,
And of them I am fick,
And hate the noify throng;
No foundnefs in my flefh appears,
And on my head are found grey hairs.

[Hofea vii. 9.

6.

Dear Jesus, thou art true,
Though false from thee I slide,
And wilt thou not subdue
And link me to thy side?
I would give all my ramblings o'er;
Speak, Lord, and bid me stray no more.

HYMN 10.

" My tongue shall speak of thy righteousness,
  and of thy praise all the day long," Psal.
  xxxv. 28.

1.

I Leave the fop to boast
  In titles, wealth, and pow'r,
Possest and quickly lost,
Gay phantoms of an hour!
Of Jesus I would make my song,
And love and praise him all day long.

2.

In heroes some delight,
And stile them staunch and good,
Who sturdy battles fight,
And fill the world with blood;
But of that Hero I will tell,
Who conquer'd sin, and death, and hell.

3.

A trumpet oft we hear
Proclaiming charities,
To dry the widow's tear,
And hush the orphan's cries;

But let my tongue a timbrel be,
To sing his love who dy'd for me.

4.

Rever'd and much renown'd
The hoary sage appears,
Who travels nature round,
And sups among the stars;
But let me sing that Sage's art,
Whose tongue can tune and mend my heart.

5.

Erewhile some patriot man
Pleads well his country's cause,
Brings right abroad again,
And wins a vast applause;
But in that Patriot I will trust,
Whose righteousness makes sinners just.

6.

That hero, patriot, sage,
Is Jesus Christ my Lord,
Whose grace from age to age
Believing souls record:
And some few mites my heart would bring,
To shew it's love for Sion's King.

HYMN 11.

"Thou art my portion, O Lord," Pf. cxix. 57.

1.

I Seek and hope to find
A portion for my soul,
To heal a feverish mind,
And make a bankrupt whole,

C 3

A cup of bleſſing for the poor,
That's free, and full, and flowing o'er.

2.

In vain the world invites
Me to it's empty feaſt,
And ſpreads it's gay delights,
But leaves a ſtarved gueſt ;
And ſure a ſoul that feeds on clay
Muſt ſicken, droop, and pine away.

3.

No ſatisfying reſt
Earth's fluttering joys impart ;
The portion of a beaſt
Will not content my heart ;
The God of ſpirits only can
Fill up the vaſt deſires of man.

4.

Then, Jeſus, thou ſhalt be
My portion and my all ;
And I will wait on thee,
A ſervant in thy hall ;
My daily wants thou ſhalt ſupply,
And find me food, and bring me joy.

5.

Thy blood ſhall be my peace,
Thy fleſh my dainty meat,
Thy robe my wedding-dreſs,
Thy breaſt my ſafe retreat,
Thine eye ſhall guide me, leſt I ſtray,
Thine arm uphold me day by day.

6.

Whate'er I wifh or want
Shall come from thee alone,
Thou canft my heart content,
And let thy grace be fhewn;
I chufe thee for my portion, Lord,
Supply me well from mercy's board.

H Y M N 12.

" Pull me out of the net, which they have
laid privily for me, for thou art my
ftrength," Pfal. xxxi. 4.

1.

A Thoufand fnares befet
A pilgrim in his walk,
To trap him by the feet,
Or catch him in his talk;
The creature often proves a bait,
And Satan lays his wily net.

2.

But fure a pilgrim's heart
Brings all his heavy woes;
It acts a traitor's part,
And lets in all his foes;
If fome poor flanting idol come,
The wanton heart fays, " Give it room."

3.

It comes with bafhful face,
And feems a modeft gueft;
Yet meeting one embrace,
It feizeth on the breaft,

And fetting up a wild uproar,
Would turn the Saviour out of door.

4.

A ftubborn gueft is fin,
And makes a rueful rout;
We may let idols in,
But cannot turn them out;
The Saviour's arm is wanted here,
To pluck the finner from a fnare.

5.

And if fome idol now
Thy foolifh heart fubdue,
Go, captive finner, go,
And try what Chrift can do;
Purfue him with an earneft cry,
And he will fet thy feet on high.

6.

What if the tyrant roar,
And of his conqueft boaft?
The Lord will help the poor,
That in his mercy truft;
And he has gained high renown
In bringing proud Goliahs down,

HYMN 13.

" My foul thirfteth for thee in a dry land,
where no water is," Pfal. lxiii. 1.

1.

WHEN Jefu's gracious hand
Has touch'd our eyes and ears,
Oh! what a dreary land
The wildernefs appears!
No healing balm fprings from it's duft,
No cooling ftream to quench the thirft!

2.

Yet long I vainly fought
A refting-place below,
And that fweet land forgot
Where living waters flow;
I hunger now for heavenly food,
And my poor heart cries out for God.

3.

Lord, enter in my breaft,
And with me fup and ftay;
Nor prove an hafty gueft,
Who tarries but a day;
Upon my bofom fix thy throne,
And pull each faucy idol down.

4.

My forrow thou canft fee,
For thou doft read my heart;
It pineth after thee,
And yet from thee will ftart;

Reclaim thy roving child at laft,
And fix my heart, and bind it faft.

5.

I would be near thy feet,
Or at thy bleeding fide;
Feel how thy heart does beat,
And fee it's purple tide,
Trace all the wonders of thy death,
And fing thy love in every breath.

H Y M N 14.

" The fruit of the Spirit is love," Gal. v. 22.

1.

POOR fickly nature wants
   A portion here below;
For earthly food fhe pants,
   And what the mines beftow;
No fpark of heavenly love is found,
Till grace manures the barren ground.

2.

Love is the Spirit's fruit,
Shed in the heart abroad;
And love can only fuit
The children born of God;
The Father fends the heavenly gueft,
To purify the children's breaft.

3.

Oh, that moft precious love,
Which faints and angels know!
It makes their heav'n above,
And makes our heav'n below!
It fparkles in the Saviour's face,
And clafps his heart with keen embrace.

4.

It chears a pilgrim's toil,
And lightens all his load;
And makes him fweetly fmile,
And fing along the road;
Love yields him all his vigour meet,
A tuneful heart, and nimble feet.

5.

Lord, give me love divine,
And let my cup run o'er;
This is the richeft mine,
And yields the choiceft ftore;
It fills the heart with heavenly cheer,
And ftamps thine holy image there.

HYMN 15.

" All that will live godly in Chrift Jefus,
fhall fuffer perfecution." 2 Tim. iii. 12.

1.

THERE is a godly life,
Built on a worldly plan,
Which brings no fcorn or ftrife
Upon the godly man;

3

With credit he may faft and pray,
When *felf* ufurps and bears the fway.

2.

His noble will and wit,
And his courageous arm,
Shall guide his trufty feet,
And guard his feet from harm ;
And fure of merit fuch will boaft,
For good they feem at their own coft.

3.

But he who feeks to live
A godly life in Chrift,
And unto Chrift will give
The praife from firft to laft,
Is furely doom'd to worldly fhame,
And born to bear a fcoundrel name.

4.

Tho' friendly in his will,
And meek his manners are,
Some perfecution ftill
Attends him every where :
Faith in the crofs brings high difdain,
And ufage coarfe from carnal men.

5.

Oh, let the crofs's fcorn
Be welcome to my heart,
And patiently be borne,
Though bringing daily fmart ;
Nor let me turn my head afide,
Through daftard fear, or fretful pride.

6. Yea,

6.

Yea, let me count that pain,
Which Jefu's crofs will bring,
As moft fubftantial gain,
A prefent from the King;
But let the King fmile on my face,
When for his name I meet difgrace.

HYMN 16.

" God be merciful to me, a finner,"
Luke xviii. 13.

1.

TWO people come to pray,
With different views inclin'd;
One righteous in his way,
And one diftreft in mind;
One eyes himfelf with much delight,
And one laments his guilty plight.

2.

One tells the Lord, how good
And how devout he was;
And pertly thanks his God,
It was the very cafe;
But mercy he forgets to crave,
And mercy fays, he none fhall have.

3.

The lowly publican
Stands with a down-caft eye,
And, like a ruin'd man,
Lifts up a doleful cry;

D

His pray'r is found, and would suit thee,
" O God, be merciful to me."

4.

'To such a contrite soul
The Saviour draweth nigh,
And makes the sinner whole,
And sends him home with joy;
Binds up his bones in ev'ry part,
And bids sweet mercy chear his heart.

5.

So, Lord, I would be fed
While waiting at thy board;
I want no better bread
Than mercy can afford;
No sweeter bread I can receive,
No richer bread my God can give.

6.

A pharisee may rooft
On his religious face;
I am a sinner loft,
And only sav'd by grace;
And of my pray'r this is the sum,
Dear Saviour, let thy mercy come.

HYMN 17.

" All things were created by Jesus, that are
in heaven and that are in earth, visible
and invisible: all things were created *by*
him and *for* him," Coloss. i. 16.

1.

ALL things in heav'n above,
  And things on earth below,
All living things that move,
And lifeless matter too,
Created were *by* Jesus Christ,
And *for* his glory they subsist.

2.

The fairest angel seen
  In yonder arched sky,
  Owes all his graceful mien
  And all his dignity
To Jesu's will and powerful word,
And bows to Jesus as his Lord.

3.

The fowls that float the air,
And insects small that creep,
The beasts that hoofed are,
And fish that sail the deep,
Owe all their various kinds of birth
To Jesu's word, which brought them forth.

D 2

4.

In him we live and move
And have our being here,
Refreshed by his love,
And guarded by his care;
Thro' him behold the Father's face,
And taste the precious fruits of grace.

5.

All glory is thy due,
And everlasting praise;
For holy, just, and true,
Art thou in all thy ways!
The best we can, we do adore,
Yet help us, and we will do more.

HYMN 18.

"No man can *come* unto me, except the
Father, who hath sent me, *draw him*,"
John vi. 44.

1.

NO wit or will of man,
　　Or learning he may boast,
No pow'r of reason can
Draw finners unto Chrift;
So fall'n is nature, such her flaw,
None come,-except the Father draw.

2.

His Spirit muſt diſcloſe*
The deadly plague within,†
Uncover all our woes,
And ſhew the man of ſin;
And feeling thus our ruin'd ſtate,
We humbly fall at Jeſu's feet.

3.

The Comforter muſt teach
The Saviour's toil and ſmart,
And with conviction preach
Atonement to the heart;
Then ſinners gaze with raviſh'd eyes,
And feaſt upon the ſacrifice.

4.

The Spirit too muſt ſhew
The pow'r of Jeſu's arm
To vanquiſh every foe,
And guard the ſoul from harm,
Believers then grow ſtrong in faith,
And triumph over ſin and death.

5.

So let my heart be drawn
To Jeſus Chriſt my Lord,
And learn to feaſt upon
His perſon and his word,
Feel ſweet redemption thro' his blood,
And give the glory all to God.

* John xvi. 8.   † 1 Kings viii 38.
D 3

HYMN 19.

"My fheep hear my voice," John x. 27.
"He will fpeak peace unto his people,"
Pfal. lxxxv. 8.

1.

THE word of God is read
  Too feldom out of choice,
And few fee any need
To hear the Shepherd's voice;
A voice the fheep delight to hear,
And Jefus gives the hearing ear. *

2.

They hear his mild command,
  And like it mighty well;
His rods they underftand,
  And can their meaning tell;
His promifes they hear, each one,
And liften to their mellow tone.

3.

Yet on a choicer thing
The fheep do much attend,
The voice, not of a king,
But of a dying friend,
A whifper given to the heart,
Which bids their forrows all depart.

* Prov. xx. 12.

4.

O thou fweet voice of peace,
For pilgrim hearts defign'd,
The pledge of heav'nly blifs,
The Day-fpring in the mind!
Thy heav'nly joy no heart can feel,
Till Jefus brings the Spirit's feal.

5.

My dear and dying friend,
Be near my heart each day,
And fome kind whifper fend
To chear me on my way:
Thy voice, like mufic foft and fweet,
Makes dancing hearts and dancing feet.

HYMN 20.

" How can ye believe, who receive honour
one of another, and feek not the honour
which cometh from God only?" John
v. 44.

1.

MEN follow after fame,
'Tis nature's fond delight,
And court the world's good name,
And think it mighty right;
But how can fuch in Chrift believe,
Who court this honour and receive?

2.

A gracious man can feel
He has no room to boaſt;
Tho' gracious, empty ſtill,
And fed at Jeſu's coſt;
Preſerv'd alive at mercy's bow'r,
A begging life he lives each hour.

3.

When guilt and death appears
Engraven on a creſt;
How wildly honour ſtares,
If perch'd on ſuch a breaſt!
All muſt drop honour in the duſt,
Who in another's merit truſt.

4.

But if a gracious man
This worldly pride rejects,
The fluttering world again
This humble man neglects,
Deſpiſe him as a wretch forlorn,
And load his ſhoulders well with ſcorn.

5.

O Lord, I would be poor
And loathſome in mine eyes;
And lay at mercy's door,
Where no ambition lies;
Abaſe myſelf before the Lord,
And muſe and feed upon his word.

6.

So will my God beftow
A gracious look on me;
And heav'nly honour fhew,
The higheft that can be;
For fure he dwells in broken hearts,
And there his peace and love imparts.

HYMN 21.

" Jefus faid, Some body hath touched me,
for I perceive that virtue is gone out of
me," Luke viii. 46.

1.

A Female, much diftreft,
For help to Jefus came,
And thro' the croud fhe preft,
And touch'd his garment-hem;
Gave, as fhe thought, a touch conceal'd,
But gave in faith, and fhe was heal'd.

2.

This female holds a glafs
To fhew the ufe of faith;
Recorded is her cafe,
And much inftruction hath;
No virtue comes, no cure is made,
Till hands of faith on Chrift are laid.

3.

The promifes are fweet,
And meant to kindle hope;
Yet promife brings no meat,
Till faith can take it up;

As yet it proves a barren breaſt,
And yields a weary ſoul no reſt.

4.

Oh, let my Lord inſtruct
Me in this needful thing;
My hand aright conduct
All boſom-plagues to bring,
And feel the virtue ſtreaming forth,
To cruſh my vipers in their birth.

5.

Two goſpel-eyes I have,
And couched by thy ſkill;
A goſpel-hand I crave,
Or I am helpleſs ſtill;
My cure I ſee, yet ſickly ſtand,
Till thou doſt heal my wither'd hand.

HYMN 22.

" Then Jeſus *opened* their underſtanding,
  that they might underſtand the ſcrip-
  tures," Luke xxiv. 45.

1.

SOME of their reaſon boaſt,
  And haughty is it's ſway;
And ſome in learning truſt
  To find the goſpel-way;
I would not pertly theſe deſpiſe,
Yet want to ſee with better eyes.

2.

Thy reason may judge right
Of worldly things and men,
But spiritual truth and light
Are far beyond thy ken;
Here reason takes her proper road,
When she cries out for help to God.

3.

All seem to understand
The gospel mighty well;
And think in gospel-land
No darkness sure can dwell:
Yet gospel-truth no man can find,
Till Jesus opens his dark mind.

4.

Light of the world he is, *
And light springs at his word;
Yet men regard not this,
Nor call upon the Lord;
What need to ask for light? they say,
Cannot our eyes direct our way?

5.

May Jesus Christ reveal
His truth unto my heart;
And all his gracious will,
As I can bear, impart,
The mists of unbelief remove,
And bring the light of faith and love.

* John viii. 12.

6.

The Sun of righteousnefs
Muft guide a pilgrim's feet;
His rays alone can blefs
The foul with light and heat:
Then rife, thou heav'nly fun, and fhine,
And chear my heart with light divine.

HYMN 23.

"When I cry, and fhout, he fhutteth out
my prayer," Lam. iii. 8.

1.

I Hear a righteous man,
A prophet good and great,
In deep diftrefs complain,
And thus his grief relate;
I call on God, and cry and fhout,
But all my pray'r he fhutteth out.

2.

Ye drooping fouls give ear,
Who knock at Jefu's gate,
And no kind word can hear,
'Tho' knocking loud and late;
Such was the weeping prophet's cafe,
A man of God, a child of grace

3.

He cries, and cries again,
And yet no anfwers come;
He fhouts aloud thro' pain,
And ftill the Lord is dumb;

3   Like

Like some abardon'd wretch he moans,
And Jesus seems to mock his groans.

4.

Let every drooping saint
Keep waiting evermore;
And tho' exceeding faint
Knock on at mercy's door;
Still cry and shout till night is past,
And day-light will spring up at last.

5.

If Christ do not appear,
When his disciples cry,
He marketh every tear,
And counteth ev'ry sigh,
In all their sorrows bears a part,
Beholds their grief, and feels their smart.

6.

He lends an unseen hand,
And gives a secret prop,
Which makes them waiting stand,
Till he complete their hope:
So let me wait upon this Friend,
And trust him till my troubles end.

HYMN 24.

" Satan provoked David to numher Ifrael,"
1 Chron. xxi. 1.

1.

ONCE David fent to hear
    How many men of might
In Ifrael's tribes appear
Full grown, and fit for fight;
The tale is brought, and brings him pain,
It coft him feventy thoufand men.

2.

Right harmlefs was the thing,
Nor feems our cenfure worth;
Yet God rebukes the king,
And fends his judgments forth;
A pride he view'd in David's heart,
And pride will make a monarch fmart.

3.

Some caution we fhall need
In things that harmlefs are;
For mifchief thefe may breed,
And prove a woful fnare;
Wherever bufy pride creeps in,
It furely proves a fcourging fin.

4.

Here Satan fhews his art,
And here his foot will hide;
To harmlefs things impart
A puff of hellifh pride;
Thus David he provok'd before,
And will provoke thee lefs or more.

5.

Whatever God may give,
In providence or grace;
The gift with thanks receive,
And use it in it's place,
But trust not in the given store,
Nor count thy treasures o'er and o'er.

6.

Raw pilgrims oft relate
Their gifts and gracious walk,
Nor see how Satan's bait
Is laid in such fine talk;
Oh, let my soul be Jesu's guest,
And only on *his* fullness feast.

H Y M N 25.

" Jesus wept."   John xi. 35.

1.

THE heart of Jesus glows
With love divinely fair;
And Jesus only knows
What pity lodgeth there;
Yet babes will prattle of this thing,
And lisp the praises of their King.

2.

He wept to see the spoil
Which sin and Satan made,
Yet weeping gives a smile,
And offers man his aid:

E 2

Sweet mercy fings, and angels gaze
To fee the Lord with human face.

3.

A mourner he became,
A man of forrows made,
Wept o'er the blind and lame,
And o'er the dumb and dead;
A tear he dropt at every grief,
But wept the moft at unbelief.

4.

Still yearning o'er the earth,
He fees the loft fheep ftray,
And fends his fhepherds forth
To guide them in the way ;
Allures them with a tender cry,
" O Ifrael's houfe, why will ye die?"

5.

Poor drooping foul attend,
And caft away thy fears ;
Call on this weeping Friend,
And he will dry thy tears;
A weeping Saviour well fuits thee,
And weeping fouls he loves to fee.

HYMN 26.

" Let a man become a fool, that he may be wife," 1 Cor. iii. 18. " Except ye be-come as *little children, ye shall not* enter into the kingdom of heaven." Matt. xviii. 3.

1.

MOST of the learned eyes
Grow dim in Jefu's fchool,
Where none becometh wife,
Till he becomes a fool;
A doctrine ftrange enough and new,
Yet chriftian fcholars find it true.

2.

The wifdom of the brain,
Tho' fhallow at the beft,
Creates a chriftian pain,
And keeps him from his reft;
To Jefus none are reconcil'd,
Till they become a little child.

3.

Our wifdom findeth caufe
To quarrel with the Lord,
To fet afide his laws,
Or cavil at his word,
To murmur at his judgments juft,
And think his promife worth no truft.

E 3

4.

This wifdom is the gall
Of Adam's tainted loin,
True bloffom of the fall,
And bitter fruit of fin,
It fcorneth Jefus, hates control,
And fighteth hard againft his rule.

5.

To fweet fubmiffion bred,
And ignorant of pride,
A child or fool is led,
And love to have a guide,
Believe your word, come at your call,
Weep if they're chid, and run for all.

6.

Oh ! let me be this child,
Or be the gofpel-fool ,
For Jefus ever fmil'd
Upon a fimple foul,
He folds the children in his arms,
And lets the wife ones take their harms.

H Y M N 27.

" It is God, who *worketh* in you both to
will and to *do*, of his *good pleafure*," Philip.
ii. 13.

1.

HOW finners vaunt of pow'r
A ruin'd foul to fave,
And count the fulfome ftore
Of worth they feem to have,

And by such visionary props
Build up and bolster sandy hopes!

2.

But God must work the *will*
And *pow'r* to run the race;
And both thro' mercy still,
A work of freest grace;
His own *good pleasure*, not our *worth*,
Brings all the will and power forth.

3.

Disciples, who are taught
Their helplessness to feel,
Have no desponding thought,
But work with care and skill;
Work with the means, and for this end,
That God the will and pow'r may send.

4.

They feel a daily need
Of Jesu's gracious store,
And on his bounty feed,
And yet are always poor;
No manna can they make or keep,
The Lord finds pasture for his sheep.

5.

Renew, O Lord, my strength
And vigour ev'ry day,
Or I shall tire at length,
And faint upon the way;
No stock will keep upon my ground,
My all is in thy storehouse found.

HYMN 28.

" The Lord is nigh unto them that are of a
broken heart, and faveth fuch as be of
a contrite fpirit," Pfal. xxxiv. 18.

1.

SAY, is thy heart well broke,
 And feels the plague of fin;
And hateth Satan's yoke,
 It fweetly once drew in?
Give Chrift the piaife, he broke thy heart,
And taught thee how to feel the fmart.

2.

What if mount Sinai's fmoke
Should darken all the fkies,
And thy week ftomach choke,
And bring on weeping eyes,
It points the road to Sion's hill,
Where grace and peace for ever dwell.

3.

Thick glooms lay in the way
To Jefu's heavenly light;
Before a gofpel-day,
He fends a legal night;
And while the legal nights abide,
No Chrift is feen, altho' the guide.

4.

The Lord is furely near,
When drooping finners pray;
And lends a gracious ear,
But fteals himfelf away;

Regards their moan with pitying eye,
And brings at length salvation nigh.

5.

Oh, let my Lord bestow
That broken heart on me,
Which feeleth well it's woe,
And blushing looks to thee,
Amaz'd to see myself so vile,
And Jesus smiling all the while.

HYMN 29.

" He is altogether lovely," Canti. v. 16.

1.

JESUS, thou pleasant art,
And excellently fair,
And for a loving heart
None can with thee compare,
Majestic on a throne, yet mild;
A King, yet lowly as a child.

2.

The Saviour bows his ear,
When sinners humbly cry,
And true heart-broken pray'r
Is sure to bring supply;
He turns no beggars from his gate,
Come when they will, or soon or late.

3.

His hands a scepter hold,
Which none can grasp but he,
Inlaid with pearls and gold,
A shaft from grace's tree;

With this he rules his subjects well,
And all their inbred foes can quell.

4.

His head the fountain is,
Whence heav'nly wisdom flows;
And all things done amiss
Throughout his realm he knows;
If storms are gathering on his friends,
He marks it well, and succour sends.

5.

His face is fair and bright,
With blushes here and there,
As mild and soft as light,
And sweet as roses are;
A single smile from Jesus giv'n
Can lift a drooping soul to heav'n.

6.

This is the sinner's Friend,
Divinely fair and good;
Whose love can have no end,
When sealed with his blood!
His grace I sing, his name adore,
His person love, and would love more.

HYMN 30.

" All men fhould honour the Son, even as
they honour the Father," John v. 23.

1.

SOME will no worfhip pay
   To Jefus prince of life,
Reject his god-like fway,
   And rail with bitter ftrife;
And fome are fearful to beftow
The honours which are well his due.

2.

As God, our Jefus can
   Demand eternal praife,
And as our dear God-Man,
   He claims it various ways,
By his two natures clofe combin'd,
And by the Father's ftrict command.

3.

So well his natures blend,
   So clofe the union fram'd,
Blood of the *human* Friend
   The blood of *God* is nam'd!
And from this clofe compacted frame,
The human part will worfhip claim.

4.

Man's carcafe, weak and vile,
   Whilft to a fpirit ty'd,
Expects a courtly fmile,
   And high refpect befide,

Becoming rev'rence it will crave,
And crave it, till it takes a grave.

5.

Soon as the child is giv'n,
And breathes in Judah's air,
All angels haste from heav'n*
To pay him worship there,
The fame his own difciples do,
And Jefus takes the homage too.

6

So Thomas glorify'd
The God-man in the Son,
When firft he fairly fpy'd
Both natures link'd in one,
And fixing his adoring eyes,†
My *Lord*, my *God*, with tranfport cries

7.

May God the Father have
The worfhip which we owe,
And Jefus Chrift receive
Like worfhip here below ;
And where this honour men reftrain,
The Father's worfhip'd all in vain ‡

* Heb. 1. 6.   † John xx. 28.
‡ John v. 28.

3

HYMN 31.

"By the grace of God I am what I am,"
1 Cor. xv. 10.

1.

I Hear much lofty talk
Of man's amazing wit
To mend his naughty walk,
And scale the skies outright;
But Paul will tell this lofty race,
Whate'er I am, I am by grace.

2.

Converted unto Christ,
A brave apostle too;
Tho' last among the list,
He did them all outdo;
Yet every labour undergone,
By grace was wrought, and grace alone.

3.

Whate'er is mean and vile,
Or high and overgrown,
Whatever can defile;
The crop is all our own;
No real good dwells in the heart,
Till grace a savoury cast impart;

4.

If thou canst watch and pray,
And dearly love the Lord,
And bless him day by day,
And hang upon his word;

F

Oh, lay the thanks at mercy's door,
And see thyself exceeding poor.

5.

Thou canst not think aright
One single godly thought,
Nor keep thy heart upright,
Unless by Jesus taught;
This teaching thou wilt hourly need,
So helpless thou, so poor indeed!

6.

Keep Jesu's grace in sight,
And feed upon it well;
Be strong in Jesu's might,
And thy own weakness feel;
Then sing and boast along with Paul,
I nothing am, and Christ is all.

HYMN 32.

" Shew me a penny: whose image and superscription hath it? They answered and
said, Cesar's," Luke xx. 24.

1.

IF thou art Jesu's coin,
Cast in the gospel-mould,
And wrought with faith divine,
More precious far than gold;
A superscription thou wilt bring,
And some sweet likeness of the King.

2.

His name thou wilt revere,
And set his titles forth,
And openly declare
His riches and his worth,
Confessing with undaunted face
That all thy trust is in his grace.

3.

Such superscription does
To Jesu's coin belong;
And ev'ry penny shews
His likeness, faint or strong;
A likeness stampt in his own mint,
Where Christ is view'd in human print.

4.

Now, friend, thy penny shew
With Jesu's image fair,
For sure no coin will go,
Unless his stamp appear;
Some Judas thou or Demas art,
Unless the stamp is on thy heart.

5.

O Lord, do thou impress
Thine image fair on me,
My penny then will pass,
And sterling coin shall be;
My coin will spread thy fame abroad,
And shew that I am born of God.

F 2

HYMN 33.

"Help, Lord, for the godly man ceaseth,
for the faithful fail from among the children of men," Psal. xii. 1.

1.

SEND help, O Lord, we pray,
    And thy own gospel bless,
For godly men decay,
    And faithful pastors cease,
The righteous are removed home,
And scorners rise up in their room.

2.

While Satan's troops are bold,
    And thrive in number too,
The flocks in Jesu's fold
    Are growing lank and few,
Old sheep are moving off each year,
And few lambs in the folds appear.

3.

Old shepherds too retire,
    Who gather'd flocks below,
And young ones catch no fire,
    Or worldly-prudent grow;
Few run with trumpets in their hand,
To sound alarms by sea and land.

4.

O Lord, stir up thy pow'r
    To make the gospel spread;
And thrust out preachers more
    With voice to raise the dead,

With feet to run where thou dost call,
With faith to fight and conquer all.

5.

The flocks that long have dwelt
Around fair Sion's hill,
And thy sweet grace have felt,
Uphold and feed 'em still;
But fresh folds build up ev'ry where,
And plenteously thy truth declare.

6.

As one Elijah dies,
True prophet of the Lord,
Let some Elisha rise
To blaze the gospel-word;
And fast as sheep to Jesus go,
May lambs recruit his folds below.

*** This Hymn was occasioned by the death of Mr. Whitefield.

H Y M N. 34.

The following Ode is designed to vindicate
the ways of God in making use of most
unlikely means to compass his ends; and
chiefly with a view to his sending out
unlettered men to preach.

1.

WAYS seeming base and weak,
A God of might will try,
Such ways his presence speak,
And tell his arm is nigh;

His finger in the work is shewn,
And glory springs to God alone.

2.

But witlings of a span
Will think the Lord a fool;
They judge of God from man,
And measure by that rule;
The likely means a man will use,
And such they think a God will chuse.

3.

When sons of earth surround
An hostile city strong,
The cannons tear the ground,
And trenches creep along:
But when the Lord attacks a town,
With foolish horns * he blows it down.

4.

All preparations great
A feebleness bespeak,
If ten must lift a weight,
It proves each arm is weak;
Yet weaklings love this vast parade,
Nor view the weakness there display'd.

5.

From steeples tall I've seen
An human monster fly;
But, oh! what toil has been,
Before the flight drew nigh!

* Joshua vi. 5, 6.

What fweating up the fteeple-ftair,
To rear a fcaffold high in air!

6.

What pains to fix aright
The rope, above, below!
What crouds to fee the fight
With gaping wonder go!
At length a fky-lark fees him drop,
And, laughing, bids him now fly up.

7.

The greater is the mean
That brings about an end,
The more is weaknefs feen
With drudgery to blend;
The fteeple flight a moral brings,
Such pains to fly fhews want of wings.

8.

Means likely or unlike
With God are juft the fame;
All wait upon his beck,
Alert to fpread his fame;
Yet when he would difplay the God,
He muft forfake the common road.

9.

If water he will draw,
Or raife a purling brook,
The fpring-head is a jaw,*
The rivulet is a rock:†

* Judges xv. 19.　† Numb. xx, 11.

An angel or an afs's mouth *
Shall preach or carry tidings forth. †

10.

But boys will look to ears,
To voice, and coat, and pile,
And what a coarfe look wears
With them is counted vile;
Yet nothing vile was ever feen
Around God's works, excepting fin.

11.

To us an angel feems
A peerlefs prince of light,
Yet Jefus fuch efteems
Grafshoppers in his fight,
Will bid 'em fly and fly apace,
And fend 'em as he fends his afs.

12.

Where fundry fervants wait
In fome capacious hall,
On various matters meet
The mafter ufeth all,
Sometimes the chaplain will employ,
But oft'ner calls the ftable-boy.

13.

Why may not Jefus too
Send fervants at his will?
And fervants high or low,
His pleafure beft fulfil;

* Luke ii. 10.   † Numb. xxii. 28.

An angel's wing or afs's tongue
Alarm the giddy flirting throng.

14.

When ferpents bit the croud,
And Ifrael murmuring dy'd,
Had Mofes fpoke aloud,
" Let unguents be apply'd ;"
The cure with falves had failed not,
But God in med'cine lain forgot.

15.

Now when they fee a fnake
Fix'd on a fimple pole,
And no rich balfam take,
Nor drug to make them whole,
When with a look the wound is cur'd,
They muft confefs, it is the Lord.

16.

If thunders fhake the ground,
Who wonders at the fhock ?
A weighty caufe is found,
And we no further look ;
But if a feather fhook the earth,
That feather fets Jehovah forth.

17.

The afs's jaw,* and tongue,†
The falt,‡ and fnake‖ to heal,

* Judges xv. 19. † Numb. xxii. 28.
‡ 2. Kings ii. 21. ‖ Numb. xxi. 8.

The ram's-horn * sounding long,
The pitcher,† stick,‡ and meal ||
With one harmonious voice declare,
The God of all the earth is near.

HYMN 35.

" Wine, which cheareth God and man,"
Judges ix. 13.

1.

A Wondrous wine there is
None can with it compare,
Creating most exalted blifs,
Which God and man will chear.

2.

This most enchanting wine
To mortals is convey'd
From noble grapes of one true vine
At humble Nazareth bred.

3.

It is the wine of love,
That precious love divine,
Which knits and chears all hearts above,
And makes their faces shine.

4.

Believers know it's taste,
And can it's virtues tell,
Oft when their hearts are sinking fast,
One sip has made them well.

* Josh. vi. 5.   † Judges vii. 16.
‡ 2 Kings vi. 6. || 2 Kings iv. 41.

5.

A single taste on earth
Much heav'nly vigour brings;
The faint in rapture speaks it's wo
And claps his hand and sings.

6.

It is the cordial true;
Lord, chear me with it still,
'Till at thy feat I drink it new,
And take my hearty fill.

HYMN 36.

" Arise, my love, and come away,"
Cant. ii. 13.

1.

IF Jesus kindly say,
And with a whisp'ring word,
" Arise, my love, and come away;"
I run to meet my Lord.

2.

My soul is in mine ear,
My heart is all on flame,
My eyes are sweetly drown'd in tear,
And melted is my frame.

3.

My raptur'd soul will rise,
And give a chearful spring,
And dart thro' all the lofty skies,
To visit Sion's King.

4.

He meets me with a kifs,
  And with a fmiling face!
I tafte the dear enchanting blifs,
  And wonder at his grace!

5.

The world now drops it's charms,
  My idols all depart;
Soon as I reach the Saviour's arms,
  I give him all my heart.

6.

A foft and tender figh
  Now heaves my hallow'd breaft;
I long to lay me down and die,
  And find eternal reft.

HYMN 37.

" No man can tame the tongue; it is an
unruly evil, full of deadly poifon," James
iii. 8.

1.

O Thou unruly tongue,
  The finner's pride and fhame!
A member fmall, yet far too ftrong,
  For mortal man to tame!

2.

The ferpent marr'd thy worth,
  His venom on thee fell;
Thy flaming fparks, that iffue forth,
  Are lighted up from hell!

2   3. With

3.

With mifchief thou art fraught,
  And with a fierce defire
To caft thy burning brands about,
  And fet the world on fire.

4.

Who fhall deliver me
From all it's deadly woe?
No man has might to fet me free,
  None, but the Lord, I know.

5.

Lord Jefu, fhew thy pow'r,
  And make this tyger calm;
Bar up his paffage, bolt the door,
  And fcreen the mouth from harm.

6.

My tongue is apt to ftart,
  And hafty words let flip;
Oh, bid thy love command my heart,
  And that will guard my lip.

HYMN 38.

" Saw ye him, whom my foul loveth?"
Cant. iii. 3.

1.

AND have ye feen the Lord,
  The lovely Prince of peace?
With open'd eye beheld his word,
  And tafted of his grace?

G

2.

Then you can hear and feel
What I ſhall now relate;
Our kindred hearts, like flint and ſteel,
Some ſparks of fire may get.

3.

From Jeſus I did rove,
Nor ought of Jeſus knew,
Until he taught me how to love;
I wiſh all lov'd him too.

4.

The darling of my heart!
The balm for all my woe!
I would not with my Jeſus part
For thouſand worlds below!

5.

Nor health nor friends afford
My heart ſubſtantial reſt,
Nor plenty on my table ſtor'd,
If Chriſt is not my gueſt.

6.

Yet oft my Lord I grieve,
And ſeem without concern;
But when he takes an haſty leave,
I ſigh for his return.

7.

For thee my heart will pine,
Tho' much from thee it roam;
And ſure I would be only thine,
And keep with thee at home.

HYMN 39.

"If thine eye be single, thy whole body shall be full of light," Matt. vi. 22.

1.

TO Canaan art thou bound?
Walk on in Jefu's might;
But mark, the way is holy ground,
And needs an heart upright.

2.

Make Jefus all thy peace,
And make him all thine arm,
Rely *alone* upon his grace
To guard from *ev'ry* harm.

3.

To Jefus fome will pray,
Yet not with *single* eye,
They fquint and peep another way,
Some creature-help to fpy.

4.

In darknefs fuch are held,
And bound in legal fear;
A *double* eye is in the child,
The heart is not fincere.

5.

Such find no gofpel-reft,
But into bondage fall;
The Lord will not uphold thy breaft,
Till he is *all* in *all*.

G 2

6.

Lord, give me single sight,
And make it strong and clear,
So will my soul be full of light,
And feel the Saviour near.

H Y M N 40.

" Ye pharisees make the outside of the cup
clean, but your inward part is full of ra-
vening and wickedness," Luke xi. 39.

1.

THE man, that trusts his heart,
  Trusts in a slippery guide;
It bids him wash the outer part,
  And leave a foul inside.

2.

Be sober, just, and fair,
  And somewhat bounteous too,
And unto Sunday-church repair,
  And then the man will do.

3.

But sure his heart is foul,
  And feeds upon the earth;
And tempers fierce enflame his soul,
  And shew their hellish birth.

4.

The breast is all unclean,
  Where wanton fancies lay,
And brood and hatch up secret sin,
  And revel night and day.

5.

O Lord, thine holy eye
Infpects my heart throughout,
And will not pafs an evil by,
Tho' lurking in my thought.

6.

Send down thy holy fire
To confecrate my breaft,
A temple fill'd with pure defire,
And with thy prefence bleft.

HYMN 41.

" Fools make a mock at fin," Prov. xiv. 9.

1.

FOOLS make a mock at fin,
And with deftruction fport;
But death will ftop their fimple grin,
And cut their laughter fhort.

2.

Bethink, O thoughtlefs man,
What mis'ry fin brings forth;
All forrow, ficknefs, want, and pain,
From fin receives it's birth.

3.

On angels fin has caft
Deftruction without end;
Thro' fin the heavenly form they loft,
And funk into a fiend!

G 3

4.

The fin thou loveft well,
At laft will make thee mourn;
It has blown up a fire in hell,
Which will for ever burn.

5.

Sin bringeth ghaftly woe,
Yet comes with leering face!
Regard it as thy deadly foe,
And fly it's foul embrace.

6.

Lord, give me godly fear,
And *keep* me watchful too,
Elfe I may fit in fcorner's chair,
And mock as fcorners do.

H Y M N 42.

" To be fpiritually minded, is life and
peace," Rom. viii. 6.

1.

MUCH longs a fpiritual mind,
On fpiritual things to dwell;
It pants for joys which are refin'd,
And keep their relifh well.

2.

Accefs it feeks to God,
And is divinely taught
To foar along the heavenly road
With much delighted thought.

3.

In Jesus sweetly blest,
It tracks him to the skies,
And finds by faith his peaceful rest,
And life that never dies.

4.

It views with high disdain
The pomp of earthly things,
Looks on the vain parade with pain,
And pities courts and kings.

5.

Such mind I now implore,
A truly spiritual wing,
Which, like the lark, will upward soar,
And as it soars, will sing.

HYMN 43.

" We are (planted) in Jesus Christ; who
is the true God, and eternal life," 1 John
v. 20.

1.

AS branches from the vine
Their birth and growth receive,
And round the stem in friendship twine,
And by their *union* live.

2.

In Christ so christians dwell,
And life from him derive,
His root makes all the clusters swell,
And all the branches thrive.

3.

In fweeteft union join'd,
Emmanuel's name they know,*
And view the God with man combin'd,
And feel his virtue too.

4.

Eternal life is giv'n
To all his faints below;
A tafte he fends them of his heav'n,
While in the vale of woe.

5.

This makes them love their King,
And lift his name on high ;
And when with lufty praife they fing,
Amen, amen, fay I.

HYMN 44.

" He becometh poor, that dealeth with a
flack hand , but the hand of the diligent
maketh rich," Prov. x. 4.

1.

ALAS, what mean thofe fears,
That dry and wither'd look,
That head befprinkled with grey hairs,
And hands with palfy fhook?

* Matt. i. 2, 3.

2.

Thy heart once all a flame,
　Fed well on Jefu's ftore,
But ftarved now, and fick, and lame,
　Thou feemeft fadly poor.

3.

Befure, thou haft been flack,
　And fettling on thy lees,
The bible caft behind thy back,
　And feldom on thy knees.

4.

To Jefus thou art grown
　A ftranger once again;
No wonder he has made thee moan,
　And look like any Cain.

5.

Come, lift the feeble hand,
　And fhake the drowzy mind,
Gird up thy loins for Canaan's land,
　And faft thy fandals bind.

6.

To Jefus yet return,
　And Jefus will receive;
Awhile he makes the rambler mourn,
　And then his peace will give.

HYMN 45.

" He, that hath mercy on the poor, bleffed
is he," Prov. xiv. 21. Pfal. xli. 1, 2, 3.

1.

MUCH blessing he will find,
    Who much regards the poor,
And with fweet look and bowels kind
    Deals out his friendly ftore.

2.

So Jefus Chrift is bleft
    By all his chofen feed,
Becaufe he hears them, when diftreft,
    And helps at ev'ry need.

3.

Compaffion much he fhews
    To finners when they figh;
And loves to heal up heavy woes,
    And wipe a weeping eye!

4.

Such mercy melts the heart,
    And tunes the tongue for praife,
And whilft he acts the Saviour's part,
    An heavenly fong they raife.

5.

How fweet is Jefus then!
    Each bofom feels him dear,
Each face with fparkling love is feen,
    Each eye with gracious tear!

6.

On mercy, Lord, I live,
And mercy I would shew,
Free alms incline my heart to give,
And forgive ev'ry foe.

HYMN 46.

" In the light of the King's countenance is
life, and his favour is as a cloud of the
latter rain," Prov. xvi. 15.

1.

THE sick, with frequent sighs,
Pass many a tedious night;
But when the morning suns arise,
How chearing is the light!

2.

So when sad sinners pass
A legal night of fears,
And see the Sun of righteousness;
How sweet his light appears!

3.

It bids their guilt depart,
A heav'n in view it brings;
The peace of God revives the heart,
And life eternal springs.

4.

The seed, in sorrow sown,
Springs up and thrives apace;
New verdure on the field is grown,
And wears a smiling face.

5.

Yet grain, of kindly birth,
    Will sigh for help again,
Nor can be foster'd by the earth,
    Without a latter rain

6

The gospel-fields must call
    Upon the Gospel-king,
And when he bids his flowers fall,
    Oh, how they laugh and sing!

HYMN 47.

" As many as are led by the Spirit of God,
    they are the sons of God," Rom. viii. 14.

1.

AN earthly heart I have,
    And earthly made by sin!
No good, but sensual, it will crave,
    And sweetly drinks it in.

2.

No joy it finds in God;
    And when my tongue would pray,
My heart will take a different road,
    And start and prance away.

3.

No converse can we find
    With him, our God, we call,
No will or pow'r lodg'd in the mind
    To walk with God at all.

4. Such

4.

Such is man's nature now,
Sunk and bemir'd in earth!
And what can raife his fallen brow,
And give him heav'nly birth?

5.

Who can the fpirit turn,
And unto God unite,
And make the heart with fervour burn,
And in it's God delight?

6.

Thou, holy Spirit, muſt
The mighty work perform,
Awake the fleeper from his duſt,
And wing the growling worm.

7.

Oh, let thy breath infpire
All needful pow'r and will,
And make my foul to God afpire,
And with his prefence fill.

HYMN 48.

" I faid of laughter, it is mad, and of mirth,
what (good) does it?" Eccleſ. ii. 2.

1.

NO wonder worldly mirth
Should fuit a worldly mind,
No joy they tafte of heavenly birth,
So take the beft they find.

H

2.

Their laughter fure is mad,
Their mirth a crackling noife!
The giggling heart is left more fad
By all it's tittering joys.

3.

As fome poor blazing thorn
Will caft it's fparks about,
And in a moment ceafe to burn;
So is their mirth foon out.

4.

But, O thou man of God,
This empty mirth beware;
March off and quit the giggling road;
No food for pilgrims there.

5.

It checks the Spirit's aid,
And leaves the heart forlorn,
And makes thee look as Sampfon did,
When all his locks were fhorn.

6.

May Jefus be my peace,
And make up all my joy;
His love can yield me ferious blifs,
And blifs that will not cloy.

HYMN 49.

"Evil purfueth finners," Prov. xiii. 21.

1.

WHERE, finner, canft thou flee,
  Where God will not purfue?
Thy fecret fins the Lord can fee,
  And will repay them too.

2.

The evils, thou haft done,
  Will hunt thee ev'ry where,
And track thy footfteps, one by one,
  As hounds will track the hare.

3.

The fins, thou haft forgot,
  Or fain would overlook,
The Lord with careful hand has wrote
  Them in his dooms-day book.

4.

Tho' numerous years are paft,
  Thou furely wilt be caught,
Thy fin will find thee out at laft,
  And vengeance will be fought.

5.

Deftruction hafteth nigh,
  And hems thy feet around;
O lift up now a fervent cry,
  While mercy may be found.

H 2

6.

Delay not, left he fhut
And bar up mercy's door;
If once the thread of life is cut,
Sweet mercy pleads no more.

HYMN 50.

" The fons of God are born, not from blood,
(or defcent) nor from the *will* of the
flefh, nor from the *will* of man, but of
God," John i. 12, 13.

1.

A Child of God is made
Not from the parent's blood,
No worth the father has convey'd
To make his infant good.

2.

Nor may the *will* of man
Convert a finful heart,
Nor *fenfe* nor mighty *reafon* can
A fpark of help impart.

3.

No man has found the fkill
To make a child of God;
It foars above the human will,
And out of nature's road.

4.

Without the Spirit's aid,
An earthly worm I am;
Conceiv'd in fin, my foul is dead,
My worfhip blind and lame.

5.

O Lord, afford relief,
And quick'ning pow'r convey;
Or sure mine ear remaineth deaf,
And sure my feet will stray.

6.

Create my heart anew,
And breathe the life divine,
And fan it with fresh vigour too
Or soon it will decline.

HYMN 51.

"Ye have received the spirit of adoption,
whereby we cry, Abba, Father,' Rom.
viii 15. Gal iv 6.

1.

WELL, canst thou read thine heart,
And feel the plague of sin?
Does Sinai's thunder make thee start,
And conscience roar within?

2.

Expect to find no balm
On nature's barren ground,
All human medicines will do harm,
They only skin the wound.

3

To Jesus Christ repair,
And knock at mercy's gate,
His blood *alone* can wash thee fair,
And make thy conscience sweet.

H 3

4.

In season due he seals
A pardon on the breast;
The wounds of sin his Spirit heals,
And brings the gospel-rest.

5.

So comes the peace of God,
Which chears a conscience well;
And love shed in the heart abroad,
More sweet than we can tell.

6.

Adopted sons perceive
Their kindred to the sky;
The Father's pardoning love receive,
And, Abba, Father, cry.

HYMN 52.

" Jesus, thou Son of David, have mercy on
me," Mark x. 47.

1.

I Stand at mercy's door,
O Lord, look on me now,
A beggar knocks, exceeding poor,
And none can help but thou.

2.

Thro' sin born dark I was,
Nor cared for the light,
All knowledge of thy truth and grace
Was banish'd from my sight.

2

3.

Exceeding lame befide,
A cripple from my birth,
And need a crutch as well as guide
To help my ankles forth.

4.

A ragged foul I am,
My breaft and fhoulders bare,
And nothing left to hide my fhame
But fig-leaves here and there.

5.

With fore difeafe I fmart,
From pain am feldom free,
It is the *evil* in my heart,
My father gave it me.

6.

Lord, I have told my cafe,
Well known to thee before,
Let Jefus fhew his lovely face,
And heal up every fore.

7.

Mine eyes with falve anoint,
That I may fee thy light;
And ftrengthen every tottering joint,
That I may walk upright.

8.

My naked foul array
In thy own righteoufnefs;
And let thy precious blood convey
The pledge of heavenly peace.

9.

My *evil*, thou dost know,
Torments my bosom much,
But let the *King* of Israel shew,
He cures it with a *touch*,

10.

Some manna also bring
To feast my pilgrim days,
And thou shalt hear a beggar sing,
And shout forth Jesu's praise.

H Y M N 53.

" When I passed by thee, and saw thee
polluted in thine own blood, I said unto
thee, Live," Ezek. xvi. 8.

1.

POLLUTED in my blood,
  And filthy from my birth,
My froward heart, averse to good,
  All evil bringeth forth!

2.

Sunk in the mire of sin,
  And in my sin perverse!
Rebellious nature rul'd within,
  And well I lik'd it's course!

3.

But Jesus passing by,
  Beheld my woful case,
He call'd the wretched rambler nigh,
  And seiz'd me by his grace.

4.

He said unto me, Live,
And life his word convey'd;
The dead his quick'ning voice perceive,
And living souls are made.

5.

Henceforth my whole concern
Must be to shew his praise,
And in the school of grace to learn
Obedience all my days.

6.

But let my Lord renew
His quick'ning word each hour,
And bring my worthlessness in view,
To keep my spirit poor.

HYMN 54.

"O Lord, thou art my refuge," Psal. cxliii. 5.

1.

NO help in self I find,
  And yet have sought it well;
The native treasure of my mind
  Is sin and death and hell.

2.

To Christ for help I fly,
The friend of sinners lost,
A refuge sweet and sure and nigh,
And there is all my trust.

3.

All other refuge fails,
And leaves my heart diftreft;
But this eternally prevails
To give a finner reft.

4.

Lord, grant me free accefs
Unto thy pierced fide,
For there I feek my dwelling-place,
And there my guilt would hide.

5.

In ev'ry time of need
My helplefs foul defend,
And fave me from all evil deed,
And fave me to the end.

6.

And when the hour is near
That flefh and heart will fail,
Do thou in all thy grace appear,
And bid my faith prevail.

HYMN 55.

" Come up to me into the mount, and be
there," Exod. xxiv. 12.

1.

MY foolifh-heart would find
A portion here below;
Yet foon a rough and blafting wind
Nips every comfort through.

A

2.

Befool'd and vexed oft,
I would no longer rove,
But lift my weary eyes aloft
To Jesu's mount above.

3.

He kindly bids me come,
Nor linger longer here,
But make his happy mount my home,
And feast upon his cheer.

4.

I would mount up on high,
Above all earthly things;
Yet well thou know'st I cannot fly,
Unless thou lend me wings.

5.

Good wings of faith impart,
And I shall reach thy seat;
Good wings to cheer a drooping heart,
And brace up tardy feet.

6.

And tho' an earthly cell
My carcase still embrace,
My spirit on the mount shall dwell,
And feel thy perfect peace.

HYMN 56.

" It is the Lord; let him do what feemeth
good," 1 Sam. iii. 18.

1.

POOR angry bofom, hufh,
  Nor difcontented grow;
But at thy own fad folly blufh,
  Which breedeth all thy woe.

2.

If fick, or lame, or poor,
  Or by the world abhorr'd,
Whatever crofs lays at thy door,
  It cometh from the Lord.

3.

The lions will not tear,
  The billows cannot heave,
The furnace fhall not finge thy hair,
  Till Jefus give them leave.

4.

The Lord is juft and true,
  And upright in his way;
He loves, but will correct us too,
  Whene'er we run aftray.

5.

With caution we fhould tread;
  For as we fow we reap,
And oft bring mifchief on our head
  By fome unwary ftep.

6. Lord,

6.

Lord, plant a godly fear
Before my roving eyes,
Left some hid snake or wily snare
My heedless feet surprize.

7.

Or should I start aside,
And meet a scourging God,
Let not my heart grow stiff with pride,
But weep and kiss the rod.

HYMN 57.

" While one faith, I am of Paul; and another saith, I am of Apollos, are ye not
carnal?" 1 Cor. iii 4.

1.

SOON as the gospel-sound
Was publish'd all abroad,
The din of party echoes round,
And clogs the gospel-road.

2.

One cries, I am for Paul;
And one Apollos takes;
Each thinks his leader all in all,
And wild diffention makes.

3.

If carnal feuds appear,
Where gospel truth is taught,
Sweet love is quickly banish'd there,
And Jesus Christ forgot.

I

4.

The gospel suffers harm,
And infidels blaspheme,
When fierce disciples lift their arm,
And raise a party flame.

5.

Yet oft, full oft we see
Much unbecoming strife;
Nor sheep nor shepherds can agree
To lead a peaceful life.

6.

From thy disciples, Lord,
Such carnal strife remove,
Subdue them by thy gracious word,
And teach 'em how to love.

HYMN 58.

" Preach the unsearchable riches of Christ,"
Ephes. iii. 8.

1.

I Try and try again
To publish Jesu's worth,
And fain I would, but never can
Set half his riches forth.

2.

The love his bosom feels,
His tongue can only tell;
And till the Lord his love reveals,
No one admires it well.

3.

'Tis deep unfathom'd love,
And charms the hofts on high;
Yet will in man no wonder move,
Without an opened eye.

4.

His blood fo freely fpilt
Is loud proclaim'd to all;
Rich balm to heal the deepeft guilt!
Yet few regard the call.

5.

Sweet health his grace imparts,
And grace divinely free;
Rich grace to cleanfe the fouleft hearts!
Yet few fay, Give it me.

6.

Some footfteps of thy grace
My tutor'd heart can find;
And view fome beauties of thy face,
And yet at beft am blind.

7.

Our dear Redeemer is
An endlefs wealthy ftore;
And when we tafte his offer'd blifs,
We blefs, and afk for more.

HYMN 59.

*"Turn thee yet again, and thou shalt se-
greater abominations." Ezek. viii. 6, 13 15.*

1.

THAT image-chamber foul,
 Which met Ezekiel's eye,
Points out the breast of every soul
 Where lurking idols lie.

2.

When God the *vision* gives,
 A man his heart can read,
Abominations he perceives,
 And finds it bad indeed!

3.

Yet ask for further light,
 And turn to see thy woe,
And God will clear thy misty sight,
 And deeper visions shew.

4.

As we the light can bear
 To break upon our eyes,
Still deeper idols shall appear,
 And more will after rise.

5.

Thus pride is broken down
 And humbled in the dust,
We view our vileness, and in all
 The Lord is all our trust.

6.

May Jesus Christ disclose
The plagues within my heart,
And as my soul more humbled grows,
A brighter faith impart.

HYMN 60.

"Look unto me and be saved, all the ends
of the earth: for I am God, and none else."
Isa. xlv. 22.

1.

"O Christian, Jew, and Greek,"
The Prince of Israel faith
"All sinners, who salvation seek,
Look unto me by faith.

2.

Almighty pow'r I have,
Am God, and nothing less,
And surely none but God can save
So deep is your distress.

3.

How welcome is the light,
Which Jesus' word has giv'n!
Too much I fought with human might
To force my way to heav'n.

4.

My vapouring arm was weak,
Yet would be counted bold,
And in the fight my heart would break,
And could no weapon hold,

I 3

5.

Now, Lord, I look to thee,
To make the battle good,
To fight and give me victory,
And pardon thro' thy blood.

6.

My heart is naughty still,
And ugly things would do;
But he, who quells the winds at will,
Can quell my bosom too.

7.

Oh, bid my foot stand fast
Upon thy faithful word;
And sweetly teach me how to cast
All burdens on the Lord.

H Y M N 61.

" In the Lord shall all the seed of Israel be
justified, and shall glory," Isai. xlv. 25.

1.

THE sons of earth delight,
To spread their fame abroad,
To glory in their worth and might;
But such are not of God.

2.

The heavenly word declares,
And faithful is the word,
That Israel's seed, the royal heirs,
Shall glory in the Lord.

3.

In Jesus they shall trust,
From first to last, each one;
Thro' Jesus shall be counted just,
And boast in him *alone*.

4.

Amen, the word is good,
My trust is in his name;
I have redemption thro' his blood,
And I will shout his fame.

5.

He hears my sad complaints,
And heals old wounds and new;
Hosannah to the King of saints,
His ways are just and true!*

6.

His worth I love to tell,
And wish the world to know;
And where the Son is honour'd well,
The Father's honour'd too.†

HYMN 62.

"Lead me to the rock, that is higher than
I," Psal. lxi. 2. "And this rock is Christ,"
1 Cor. x. 4.

1.

A Rock salutes mine eye,
Which faith alone has trod;
It lifts a pilgrim near the sky,
And brings the heart to God!

* Rev. xv. 3.   † John v. 23.

2.

I held a flattering hope,
And thought, as some think yet,
This rock may sure be scrambled up,
By human hands and feet.

3.

But now amaz'd, I cry,
As David did before,
The rock is higher much than I,
And help I must implore.

4.

Upon it I would dwell,
But help is wanting here,
Except the Father draw me well,"
I never shall get there.

5.

Oh, lead me to this rock,
And keep me on it too;
For on this rock, thy favour'd flock
The promis'd land can view.

6.

Upon this happy hill
I would employ my days,
Till thou shalt call me higher still,
To sing eternal praise.

* John vi. 44.

HYMN 63.

" Jesus saith, I am the way; no man cometh unto the Father, but by me," John xiv. 6.

1.

A New and pleasant door,
  A friendly *way* to God,
Is open'd for the gospel-poor,
  Thro' Jesu's precious blood.

2.

Here mercy smiling sits
  The famish'd poor to feed,
Bestows a kiss on all she meets,
  And deals out heavenly bread.

3.

But sinners are so blind,
  From mercy they will stray;
Or lifted with a lofty mind,
  They will despise the *way*.

4.

I was a rover too,
  And roving found no rest;
But now at length the *way* I view,
  And here I build my nest.

5.

Of Christ I chirp and sing,
  And when he casts an eye,
I flutter up with brisker wing,
  And warble in the sky.

6.

Such is my pleasant tafk,
'To fing of this fweet load
And if the caufe a ftranger afk;
It is my way to God.

HYMN 64.

" Whofoever denieth the Son, the fame hath
not the Father," 1 John ii. 23.

1.

A Bafe and proud neglect
Of Jefus Chrift is fhewn;
His honours impious men reject,
And fcandalize the Son.

2.

But fcorners pert and wife
May from the Father know,
That all, who dare the Son defpife,
Reject the Father too.

3.

His Godhead who denies,
Or his atoning death,
Shall fall himfelf a facrifice,
And feel the Father's wrath.

4.

All, who in him believe,
And feek his offer'd grace,
A joyful pardon fhall receive,
And fee the Father's face.

5.

O my sweet Prince of peace,
Who bought me with thy blood.
Thy passion and thy love I bless,
And hail thee as my God.

HYMN 65.

" Jesus is ordained to be the Judge of quick
and dead," Acts x. 42.

1.

LET wanton men beware,
How Jesus they despise;
In awful pomp he will appear,
Descending from the skies!

2.

His trumpet will proclaim
" The Judge, the Judge is near!"
And earth will melt with fervent flame,
And seas dry up with fear!

3.

A shouting heav'nly host *
Around him will be rang'd!
The dead will hear and start up first,
And then the quick be chang'd!

4.

Ye wise and favour'd few,
Who lodge at mercy's gate,
Oh, keep the Saviour well in view,
And for his coming wait.

* 1 Theff. iv. 16.

2

5.

And hear, ye foolish men,
Who talk with impious breath,
And glory in a life unclean;
Such mirth will end in death.

6.

Your bitter sad remorse
No tongue can truly tell,
If Jesus once pronounce his curse,
And sink you down to hell.

7.

O thoughless men, be wise,
Before it be too late,
From sleep awake, from sin arise,
And knock at mercy's gate.

HYMN 66.

" Faith without works is dead," James ii. 20.

1.

FRIEND, if thy tree is good,
   And faith lay at the root,
It gathers life from Jesu's blood,
   And beareth goodly fruit.

2.

Assent is earthly weed,
And brings no profit forth;
But gospel-faith is noble seed,
And claims an heavenly birth.*

* Ephes. ii. 8.

3. It

3.

It surely works by love,
And acts a kindly part;
It draweth pardon from above,
And purifies the heart.

4.

Tho' baffled o'er and o'er,
Faith will prevail at length,
Because it fights in Jesu's pow'r,
And not in human strength.

5.

If faith work peace within,
And worketh merit out,
And beareth fruit, and conquer sin,
'Tis sterling faith, no doubt.

6.

Such faith, Lord, give to me,
As yields it's blossoms fair,
And sheweth fruit upon the tree,
And all it's fruit will rear.

HYMN 67.

" If the Son shall make you free, ye shall be
free indeed," John viii. 36.

1.

TO free myself I strove,
But feeble was my pow'r,
My galling guilt would not remove,
And sin prevailed more.

K

2.

At length I weary was,
And unto Jesus came,
And told him all my helpless case,
How weak I was and lame.

3.

A smile he cast on me,
And said, I know thy need;
But if the Son shall make you free,
You will be free indeed.

4.

Salvation would you have?
Upon me cast your cares;
None but the Saviour sure can save,
As well his name declares.

5.

Lord, let me know thy name,
That I may rescu'd be
From sin's dominion, guilt and shame,
And thy salvation see.

6.

I would have free access,
When unto God I cry;
And nourish'd with the word of grace,
Thy free-man live and die.

HYMN 68.

" Unto the *Son* he faith, Thy throne, *O God*,
is for ever and ever; a fceptre of righteoufnefs is the fceptre of thy kingdom,"
Heb. 1. 8.

1.

THO' fcorners thee defy,
   And proud blafphemers roar,
Thy throne, O Jefus, God moft high,
   Endureth evermore!

2.

Thine hands a fceptre hold,
   Which only God can grafp,
Which wifdom fway'd all times of old,
   And truth and mercy clafp.

3.

Thou loveft righteoufnefs,
   And wilt uphold it's feat,
And daring finners, great or lefs,
   Shall perifh at thy feet.

4.

Thy fubject I would be,
   And willing made by grace,
A fervant waiting here on thee,
   Till call'd to fee thy face.

HYMN 69.

To the Trinity.

1.

OUR Father who doſt lead
 The children of thy grace,
A new-born and believing ſeed,
 Throughout the wilderneſs!

2.

Thy providential care
 In dangers paſt we own,
And beg thine arm may ſtill be near,
 And ſtill thy love be ſhewn.

3.

Dear Jeſus, Lamb of God,
 Our lovely dying friend!
Reveal the virtue of thy blood,
 And truth and mercy ſend.

4.

Thou art a maſter kind,
 With voice and perſon ſweet,
Beſtow on us a loving mind,
 And keep us at thy feet.

5.

Thou, holy Spirit, art
 Of Goſpel-truth the ſeal,
Convincing pow'r thou doſt impart,
 And Jeſu's grace reveal.

6.

Oh, breathe thy quick'ning breath,
    And light and life afford;
Inftruct us how to live by faith,
    And glorify the Lord.

HYMN 70.

" Bleffed is the man, that watcheth daily
at my gates, and waiteth at the pofts of
my doors," Prov. VIII. 34.

1.

MY bus'nefs lays at Jefu's gate,
    Where many a Lazar comes,
And here I fue, and here I wait
    For mercy's falling crumbs.

2.

My rags and wounds my wants proclaim,
    And help from *him* implore;
The wounds do witnefs I am lame,
    The rags that I am poor.

3.

My Lord, I hear, the hungry feeds,
    And cheareth fouls diftreft,
He loves to bind up broken reeds,
    And heal a bleeding breaft.

4.

His name is Jefus, full of grace,
    Which draws me to his door;
And will not Jefus fhew his face,
    And bring his gofpel-ftore?

K 3

5.

Supplies of every grace I want,
  And each day want supply,
And if no grace the Lord will grant,
  I must lay down and die.

6.

But oh! my Lord, such news shall ne'er
  Be told in Sion's street,
That some poor soul fell in despair,
  And dy'd at Jesu's feet.

HYMN 71.

" Enter not into judgment with thy servant;
  for in *thy sight* shall *no man* living be justified," Psal. cxliii. 2.

1.

WHERE must a burden'd conscience go
  To find a sure relief?
Nor tears, nor alms a balm bestow
  To heal a sinner's grief?

2.

No help on nature's ground appears,
  Sin has such noisome breath,
A solemn voice from God declares,
  The wage of sin is death.

3.

With man thy conduct may be fair,
  Thy dealings all upright,
With God the best much faulty are,
  And guilty in his sight.

4.

Forbear to eafe thine aching heart
By merits of thine own,
Or God will mark thy ftrict defert,
And judgment weigh thee down.

5.

Thy finful debts to Jefus bring,
His payment makes thee juft;
And of thy furety think and fing,
And only in him truft.

6.

Yet afk him for a full receipt,
And lock it in thy breaft;
This makes obedience free and fweet,
And fets the heart at reft.

HYMN 72.

" The fruit of the Spirit is love, joy, peace,
long-fuffering, gentlenefs, goodnefs, faith,
meeknefs, and temperance," Galat. v.
22, 23.

1.

THAT man alone is truly bleft,
Who dwells in love divine,
Who finds the Saviour's joyful reft,
And keeps his peace within.

2.

He bears the wrongs that others bring,
Unmoved all the while;
His bounty bids the cripple fing,
And makes the widow fmile.

3.

By faith he acts a christian part,
   Much favoury in his talk,
Child like and lowly in his heart,
   And temperate in his walk.

4.

And can thefe plants of virtue grow
   In fuch a foil as mine?
Yes, if thy quick'ning Spirit blow,
   They fpring and open fine.

5.

A fallow ground if Jefus till,
   Tho' weeds were only there,
The fallows quickly own his fkill,
   And precious fruit will bear.

6.

Come then, my Lord. thy grace impart,
   Thy Spirit breathe on me,
Plant all it's fruit within my heart,
   And make me all like thee.

HYMN 73.

" He fhall let go my captives, not for price
    nor reward," Ifai. xlv. 13.

1.

ART thou by fin a captive led,
   And fin thy daily grief?
The man, who brake the ferpent's head,
   Can bring thee fweet relief.

2.

His name is Jefus, for he faves,
   And fetteth captives free;
His office is to purchafe flaves,
   And give them liberty.

3.

No money for thy ranfom take,
   But mercy much intreat;
Go with the chains about thy neck,
   And fall before his feet.

4.

Tell how thy bofom tyrants lafh,
   And rage without control;
Shew where the fetters gall thy flefh,
   And bruife thine inmoft foul.

5.

The fight will melt his piteous heart,
   Soon touch'd with human woe;
And healing up thy guilty fmart,
   His freed-man thou fhalt go.

HYMN 74.

" Carry them in thy bofom, as a nurfe
beareth the fucking child," Numb. xi. 12.

1.

O Lord, how lovely is thy name,
   How faithful is thine heart!
To-day and yefterday the fame,
   And always kind thou art!

2.

No change of mind our Jefus knows,
  A true and conftant friend!
Where once the Lord his love beftows,
  He loves unto the end!

3.

He well remembers we are flefh,
  At beft a bruifed reed,
And fainting fouls he will refrefh,
  And gently rear their head.

4.

Full breafts of milk, that cannot cloy,
  He, like a nurfe, will bring;
And when he draws the promife nigh,
  Oh, how we fuck and fing!

5.

No danger can thy foul await,
  While refting on this rock;
The winds may blow, and waves may beat,
  But he fuftains the fhock.

6.

Dear Jefus, let me lay and reft
  Within thy arms divine;
Thy daily care, to make me bleft;
  To love and praife thee, mine.

HYMN 75.

"I will clothe thee with change of raiment,"
Zach. iii. 4.

1.

DRESS uniform the foldiers wear,
  When duty calls abroad,
Not purchas'd at their coft or care,
  But by the prince beftow'd.

2.

Chrift's foldiers too, if Chrift-like bred,
  Have regimental drefs,
'Tis linen white and fac'd with red,
  'Tis Chrift's own righteoufnefs.

3.

A rich and fightly robe it is,
  And to the foldiers dear;
No rofe can learn to blufh like this,
  Nor lily look fo fair.

4.

No wit of man could weave this robe,
  'Tis of fuch texture fine;
Nor could the wealth of all the globe
  By purchafe make it mine.

5.

The robe was wrought by Jefu's hand,
  And dy'd in his own blood;
And all the cherubs gazing ftand
  To view this robe of God.

2

6.

Tho' worn, it never waxeth old,
    No spots upon it fall,
It makes a foldier brisk and bold,
    And dutiful withal.

7.

Array me in this robe complete,
    For this will hide my shame,
And make me sing, and make me fight,
    And bless my captain's name.

HYMN 76.

" Though he tarry, wait for him,"
Habak. ii. 3.

1.

IF guilt pursue thee with it's cry,
    And would to prison hale;
To Jesus Christ, the surety, fly,
    And he will offer bail.

2.

If hellish foes beset thee round,
    And grin and dodging stand;
On Jesus call, and keep thy ground,
    And he will help command.

3.

If hope, that us'd thy foul to chear,
    Now leaves thee dark as night,
And neither fun nor stars appear;
    Yet wait for morning-light.

4 Still

4.

Still look to Chrift with longing eyes,
　　Tho' both begin to fail,
Still follow with thy feeble cries,
　　And mercy will prevail.

5.

What, if he drop no gracious fmile,
　　Or bid thee leave his door;
Yet if thou knock, and wait awhile,
　　He muft relieve the poor.

6.

He tarries oft, till men are faint,
　　And comes at evening late;
He hears and will relieve complaint,
　　But we muft pray and wait.

H Y M N   77.

" So Daniel was taken up out of the den,
　　and no manner of hurt was found upon
　　him, becaufe he *believed* in his God,"
Dan. vi. 23.

1.

EACH human breaft is Daniel's den,
　　Where lufts, like lions, lay,
And yell and rend unfaithful men,
　　Who fall an eafy prey.

2.

But he, who in the Lord believes,
　　Has lions at his will;
The pow'r, which ftilled winds and waves,
　　A roaring luft can ftill.

L

3.

Yet if the monsters round thy head
    Lay harmless down, like sheep;
Ah, never once surmize them dead,
    They are but dropt asleep.

4.

While unbelief makes mid-night skies,
    For prey the lions roar;
But soon as faith bids morning rise,
    They lay them down and snore.*

5.

O Jesus, thou the tamer art,
    Faith rests upon thy pow'r,
Faith calls, and thou dost help impart
    In every needful hour.

6.

All dens to thee are just the same,
    Where thou art, there is rest;
Then give me Daniel's faith to tame
    The lions in my breast.

HYMN 78.

" My heart is smitten, and withered like
        grass," Psal. cii. 4.

1.

ALAS! poor soul, what ails thee now,
        So feeble and so faint?
Why hangs a cloud upon thy brow?
    Come, tell thy sad complaint.

* Psal. civ. 20, 22.

I

2.

" No wither'd ftick is half fo dry,
  " No flint fo hard is found,
" Like fome dead dog I lumpifh lie,
  " And putrify the ground."

3.

Well, Jefus fhews thee, what thou art,
  How naked, blind, and poor!
Difclofes all thy wretched heart,
  To make thee prize him more.

4.

Lay down fubmiffive at his feet,
  And meekly tell thy pain,
And with a figh his love intreat
  To fend a gracious rain.

5.

But when he brings a chearing gleam,
  And brooks gufh from the rock,
Boaft in your fountain, not the ftream,
  For human cifterns leak.

6.

The ftreams may take a various turn,
  Run ebb, or muddy flow,
Or dry up ere to-morrow's morn,
  But not the fountain fo.

7.

The fountain always full and clear
  Flows on ferenely ftill,
Is free and open all the year,
  For whofoever will.

8.

Oh, may this rock afford me reft,
 This brook ftill follow me;
To quench my thirft, and wafh my breaft,
 Till Canaan's land I fee.

H Y M N 79.

" In my profperity I faid, I fhall never be
 moved; my mountain ftandeth ftrong:
 but thou didft hide thy face, and I was
 troubled," Pfal. xxx. 6, 7.

1.

WHEN I can fit at Jefu's feet,
  And he anoints my head,
Such peace enfues, fo calm and fweet,
 I think my foes all dead.

2.

My fimple heart then fondly dreams,
 It fhall fee war no more;
Too firm to fhrink my mountain feems,
 And every ftorm blown o'er.

3.

While thus a queen in ftate I fit,
 Self hunts about for praife,
Talks much of frames and victories great;
 That you may hear and gaze.

4.

Then Jefus fends a trying hour,
 This lurking pride to quell;
My dead foes rife with dreadful pow'r,
 And drag me down to hell.

5.

Now faints my heart within me quite,
　My mountain difappears,
All grace is vanifh'd from my fight,
　And faith feems loft in fears.

6.

At length my Lord with fweet furprize
　Returns to loofe my bands,
Brings kind compaffions in his eyes,
　And pardons in his hands.

7.

I drop my vile head in the duft,
　And at my Lord's feet fall;
His grace is now my fong and boaft,
　And Chrift my all in all.

HYMN 80.

"I kill and I make alive; I wound and I
　heal," Deut. xxxii. 39.

1.

THE Saviour empties whom he fills,
　　And quickens whom he flays;
Our legal hope he kindly kills,
　To teach us gofpel-praife.

2.

He wraps in frowns, as well as fmiles,
　Some tokens of his love;
And if he wounds, or if he heals,
　In both his grace we prove.

L 3

3.

His simple flock are often slack,
   And make the Lord retire;
But when he frowns and turns his back,
   It is to draw them nigh'r.

4.

No sooner we begin to mourn,
   And feel a broken heart,
But Jesus cries, Return, return,
   And let me heal thy smart.

5.

The starv'd and wounded may receive
   Refreshments at his door,
Good bread and balms he loves to give
   To sinners sick and poor.

6.

My legal self may Jesus kill,
   And make my heart alive;
My guilty wounds may Jesus heal,
   And make my spirit thrive.

HYMN 81.

"Christ is precious unto you who believe,"
   1 Pet. ii. 7.

1.

EXCEEDING precious is my Lord,
   His love divinely free!
And sure his name does health afford
   To sickly souls, like me.

2.

It chears a debtor's gloomy face,
  And breaks his prison door;
It brings amazing stores of grace
  To feed the gospel-poor.

3.

And if with lively faith we view
  His dying toil and smart,
And hear him say, it was for you,
  This breaks the stony heart.

4.

An heavenly joy his words convey,
  The bowels strangely move,
We blush and melt, and faint away,
  O'erwhelmed with his love.

5.

In such sweet posture let me lie
  And wet thy feet with tears,
Till join'd with saints above the sky,
  I tune my harp with *theirs*.

HYMN 82.

" My soul thirsteth for thee in a dry and
  barren land, where no water is." Psal.
  lxiii. 1.

1.

WHERE must a weary sinner go,
  But to the sinner's friend?
He only can relieve my woe,
  And bid my sorrows end.

3.

His simple flock are often slack,
  And make the Lord retire,
But when he frowns and turns his back,
  It is to draw them nigh'r.

4.

No sooner we begin to mourn,
  And feel a broken heart,
But Jesus cries, Return, return,
  And let me heal thy smart,

5.

The starv'd and wounded may receive
  Refreshments at his door;
Good bread and balms he loves to give
  To sinners sick and poor.

6.

My legal self may Jesus kill,
  And make my heart alive;
My guilty wounds may Jesus heal,
  And make my spirit thrive.

HYMN 81.

" Christ is precious unto you who believe,"
  1 Pet. ii. 7.

1.

EXCEEDING precious is my Lord,
  His love divinely free!
And sure his name does health afford
  To sickly souls, like me.

2.

It chears a debtor's gloomy face,
　And breaks his prifon door;
It brings amazing ftores of grace
　To feed the gofpel-poor.

3.

And if with lively faith we view
　His dying toil and fmart,
And hear him fay, it was for you,
　This breaks the ftony heart.

4.

An heavenly joy his words convey,
　The bowels ftrangely move,
We blufh and melt, and faint away,
　O'erwhelmed with his love.

5.

In fuch fweet pofture let me lie,
　And wet thy feet with tears,
Till join'd with faints above the fky,
　I tune my harp with *their's*.

HYMN 82.

" My foul thirfteth for thee in a dry and
　barren land, where no water is," Pfal.
　lxiii. 1.

1.

WHERE muft a weary finner go,
　　But to the finner's friend?
He only can relieve my woe,
　And bid my forrows end.

2.

Thou art, O Lord, my refting-place;
 The promis'd land I fee,
And long to live upon thy grace,
 And lofe myfelf in thee.

3.

A glimpfe of thee, and thy fweet ftore
 Thou doft to me impart;
But kindly fhew me more and more,
 Till thou doft fill my heart.

4.

The wildernefs I cannot bear,
 So far from thee to ftand;
Nor yet from Pifgah's top to ftare
 Upon the promis'd land.

5.

I want to eat and drink my fill
 Of Canaan's milk and wine;
Let Mofes die upon the hill,
 And foon I fhall be thine.

6.

'Tis felf, that legal thing and bafe,
 Which keeps me from my reft,
Me from myfelf let Chrift releafe,
 And foon I fhall be bleft.

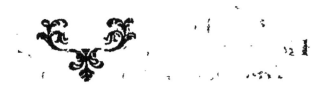

HYMN 83.

"I will raise up for them a plant of renown," Ezek. xxxiv. 29.

1.

THY glory, Jesus, fills the skies,
  Plant of renown thou art,
A tree desir'd to make one wise,
  And chear a drooping heart!

2.

Thou bearest ripe and goodly fruit,
  Fresh blooming all the year,
Which every famish'd soul will suit,
  And withering health repair.

3.

Upon this fruit whoever feeds,
  No want or care he knows,
None other food he seeks or needs,
  This healeth all his woes.

4.

No tree like this among the wood!
  It grows on Calvary,
And, water'd well with Jesu's blood,
  Bears choicest fruit for me.

5.

The fruit is righteousness divine,
  To cleanse and clothe my soul;
And all, who on the fruit can dine,
  Are made completely whole.

6.

Not like the tree of knowledge fair,
 Yet treacherous to the eye!
Whoever comes to banquet here,
 Shall eat and never die.

7.

Too long, O Lord, my soul has fed
 On graces, duties, frames,
Yet thefe are not my heavenly bread,
 Tho' lovely things and names.

8.

Thou art my gofpel-bread and food,
 Thou art my joyous feaft;
To eat thy flefh, and drink thy blood,
 Is gofpel-health and reft.

9.

Thy life and death are my repaft,
 The precious fruit of grace;
And when this dainty food I tafte,
 I live, and love, and blefs.

HYMN 84.

" The blood of Jefus Chrift cleanfeth us
from all fin," 1 John i. 7.

1.

DOES confcience lay a guilty charge,
 And Mofes much condemn,
And bring in bills exceeding large?
 Let Jefus anfwer them.

2.

He paid thy ranfom with his hand,
   And ev'ry fcore did quit,
And Mofes never can demand
   Two payments of one debt.

3.

Now juftice fmiles on mercy fweet,
   And looks well reconcil'd,
Join'd hand in hand they go to meet,
  And kifs a weeping child.

4.

But afk the Lord for his receipt,
   To fhew the payment good,
Deliver'd from the mercy-feat,
   And fprinkled with his blood.

5.

The law thy feet will not enlarge,
   Nor give thy confcience reft,
Till thou canft find a full difcharge
   Lock'd up within thy breaft.

6.

The fight of this will melt thine heart,
   And make thine eyes run o'er;
An happy pardon'd child thou art,
   And heav'n is at thy door.

HYMN 85.

" The wife man's eyes are in his head, but
the fool walketh in darkneſs," Ecclef. ii. 14.

1.

THE Lord proclaims that man a fool,
   Who does in darkneſs walk;
And tho' untaught in Jeſu's ſchool,
   Will of ſalvation talk.

2.

No peace he feels from Jeſu's blood,
   No work of grace begun,
Yet vainly hopes his path is good,
   And walks in darkneſs on.

3.

No goſpel way-poſt can he find,
   To prove his road is right;
Yet flattering hopes beguile his mind,
   And miſts deceive his ſight.

4.

A wife man's eyes are in his *head*,
   And Chriſt his head is found;
And while the head the members lead,
   They keep on goſpel-ground.

5.

Lord, let my light come down from thee,
   Thy head direct my feet;
For only in thy light I ſee
   The goſpel clear and ſweet.

HYMN 86.

HYMN 86.

"I am the good Shepherd, and know my
sheep, and am known of mine," John x. 14.

1.

WITH tender heart, and gentle hand,
　　And eyes that never sleep,
Our Shepherd leads to Canaan's land
　　His bleating helpless sheep.

2.

Of him they love to sing each day,
　　Of him they love to learn,
And when he talketh by the way,
　　Oh, how their bosoms burn!

3.

A word from Jesus fires their heart,
　　And sweetly tunes their tongue,
Bids every anxious care depart,
　　And helps their feet along.

4.

He knows his sheep, and tells their names,
　　And will not lose his own,*
The bleating ewes, and dancing lambs,
　　Are marked every one.

5.

And Jesu's sheep their shepherd know,
　　And follow out of choice;
They will not after strangers go,
　　Nor heed an hireling's voice.

* John xviii. 9.
M

HYMN 87.

"I determined to know nothing, save Jesus
Chrift, and him crucified," 1 Cor. 11. 2.

1.

SOME wife men of opinions boaft,
And fleep on doctrines found ;
But, Lord, let not my foul be loft
On fuch enchanted ground.

2.

Good doctrines can do me no good,
While floating in the brain ;
Unlefs they yield my heart fome food,
They bring no real gain.

3.

Oh, may my fingle aim be now
To live on him that dy'd,
And nought on earth defire to know
But Jefus crucify'd.

4.

Difputings only gender ftrife,
And gall a tender mind ;
But godlinefs in all it's life
At Jefu's crofs we find.

5.

Lord, let thy wondrous crofs employ
My mufings all day long,
Till in the realms of pureft joy
I make it all my fong.

HYMN 88.

" Ye are the temple of the living God, as
   God hath faid, I will dwell in them,"
2 Cor. vi. 16.

1.

GOD's living temple wouldft thou be,
   Devoted to his fear?
To Chrift thy bofom open free,
   And he will enter there.

2.

There he reveals his fecrets deep,
   And fheds his love abroad,
And there he teacheth us to keep
   Sweet fellowfhip with God.

3.

What if thy bofom is a den,
   Where gangs of robbers fleep,
Or fome foul cage of birds unclean,
   The ftable Chrift can fweep.

4.

If he but fhew his awful face,
   The wanton birds will fly,
And thievifh gangs march off apace,
   To fhun his piercing eye.

5.

Lord Jefus, confecrate my breaft,
   An houfe for God below;
And wafh it fweet, and keep it chafte,
   Thy blood can make it fo.

M 2

HYMN 89.

"Thou didst hide thy face, and I was troubled," Pfal. xxx. 7.

1.

IF but a single moment's fpace
    My Lord himfelf withdraws,
Dark clouds and ftorms come on apace,
    And debts and broken laws.

2.

My heart reveals it's drofs and dung,
    And loathfome is my breath,
My harp is on the willows hung,
    And Efau vows my death.

3.

Mine eyes refufe to lend a tear,
    My throat is hoarfe and dry,
I lifp and faulter in my prayer,
    And fick and faint am I.

4.

If Jefus loves the gofpel-poor,
    That broken-hearted be,
A mourner waiteth at thy door,
    Who wants a fight of thee.

5.

Look from the windows of thy grace,
    And chear a drooping heart;
A fingle fmile from thy fweet face
    Will bid my griefs depart.

6.

Thou art the life of all my joys,
 Thy prefence makes my heav'n;
Whatever elfe my Lord denies,
 Thy prefence, Lord, be giv'n.

HYMN 90.

"They, that wait upon the Lord, fhall renew their ftrength, and mount up with
wings as eagles," Ifai. xl. 31. "And I
will bring the blind by a way they knew
not," Ifai. xlii. 16.

1.

ART thou a weakling poor and faint,
 And forrowful each hour,
Exceeding full of fad complaint,
 Left Satan thee devour?

2.

Right welcome tidings Jefus brings
 To feeble hearts, like thine;
He will bear up the weak with wings,
 And chear the faint with wine.

3.

In darknefs doft thou penfive go,
 Nor any path canft find?
Thy Jefus ftill can bring thee thro',
 And loves to lead the blind.

4.

Tho' blind, ftep on and fear no ill,
 The Lord is near at hand,
And fafe thro' fire and water will
 Lead to the promis'd land.

5.

But afk for light, and patient look,
    Till Chrift himfelf reveals,
Till water iffuing from his rock
    Thy empty ciftern fills.

6.

Then walk with him, as loving friends,
    Nor from his fide depart,
And till your painful journey ends,
    Oh, keep him in your heart.

HYMN 91.

" Surely the land of Canaan floweth with
    milk and honey, and this clufter of grapes
    is the fruit of it," Numb. xiii. 27.

1.

TOO long, alas! I vainly fought
    For happinefs below,
But earthly comforts, dearly bought,
    No folid good beftow.

2.

If bleft with plenty, ftill my mind
    Sick and confumptive grew,
I fed on afhes, drank the wind; *
    And what can fuch food do?

3.

My carcafe may be fitly fed
    With what this earth fupplies;
My fpirit needs fome better bread,
    Or fick it grows and dies.

* Ifai. xliv. 20.   Hofea xii. 1

4.

At length thro' Jesu's grace I found
 The good and promis'd land,
Where milk and honey much abound,
 And grapes in clusters stand.

5.

My soul has tasted of the grapes,
 And now it longs to go,
Where my dear Lord his vineyard keeps,
 And all the clusters grow.

6.

Upon the true and living vine
 My famish'd soul would feast,
And banquet on the fruit divine,
 An everlasting guest.

7

And wouldst thou feed on Canaan's store,
 When all thy days are past?
Then taste it on this earthly shore,
 Or thou wilt never taste.

H Y M N 92.

" A *man* shall be an hiding-place from the
wind, and a covert from the tempest,"
Isai. xxxii. 2.

1.

A Man, with meek and lowly form,
 Can hide thee from the wind,
And from the rattling thunder storm,
 Which frights a guilty mind.

2.

His name is Jefus, mighty dear
   To them that know his name;
It charms away a finner's fear,
   And fets his heart on flame.

3.

This *man* of meeknefs doft thou know,
   And can his Godhead trace?
And fearlefs to him wouldft thou go?
   Look on his *human* face.

4.

The tender hufband, brother, friend,
   Meet in this lovely *man*,
And thefe are charms to recommend,
   Or furely nothing can.

5

Approach him, as they did of old,
   In Juda whilft he dwelt;
Thy griefs to this dear man unfold,
   And his kind heart will melt.

6.

A *man* of forrows much he was,
   Well vers'd in human woe,
And he can grieve at thy fad cafe,
   And needful help beftow.

7.

Upon the *man* thine eyes may gaze,
   And feel no guilty dread;
His excellence will not amaze,*
   When wrapt in human fhade.

* Job XIII. 11, 21.

8.

Behold *the man!* his wounds, his fmart! *
 See how he lov'd and dy'd!
The fight will melt thy ftony heart,
 And crucify thy pride.

H Y M N 93.

" Bring forth the blind people that have
eyes, and the deaf that have ears," Ifa.
xliii. 8.

1.

A Dark and empty fhade is man,
  Yet full of fancy'd light !
But all his penetration can
 Obtain no gofpel-fight.

2.

If heavenly truth is blaz'd abroad,
 His heart rejects the call ;
If gofpel newfmen fhew the road,
 He will grope for the wall.

3.

Perhaps he ftands to hear the found,
 But deaf his ears remain ;
No meaning in the word is found,
 It raifeth mirth or pain.

4.

O Lord, thine holy arm make bare,
 For thou the help muft find ;
Afford the deaf an hearing ear,
 And heal the brain-fick mind.

* John xix. 5.

5.

Behold, how unconcern'd they dwell,
 Tho' dark and deaf they be,
And think they hear and fee right well,
 And need no help from thee.

6.

Speak, and the deaf fhall hear thy voice,
 The blind their fight receive ;
And both fhall in thy name rejoice,
 And to thy glory live.

H Y M N 94.

" Whofoever will, let him take the water
 of life freely," Rev. xxii. 17.

1.

OF ciftern-waters art thou fick,
 And loathe the mire they bring ?
Then hither ftretch thy thirfty neck,
 And tafte a living fpring.

2.

A fpring, that iffues from a rock,
 Where pureft waters flow ;
And rocky hearts, by Mofes ftruck,*
 May to thefe waters go.

3.

No fpring will quench a thirft like this !
 It makes a confcience whole,
Infpires the heart with heav'nly blifs,
 And purifies the foul.

* Exod. xvii. 6.

4.

Whoe'er can truly say, I thirst,
  May come and take his fill,
'Tis free for good, and bad, and worst,
  For whofoever will.

5.

Come when thou wilt, or foon or late,
  It ftands inviting thee;
And will admit no market-rate,
  It is divinely free.

6.

It's owner is an heavenly king,
  And by his winning ways,
He draws the thirfty to his fpring,
  Who drink and fing his praife.

7.

Lord, draw me by thy fecret touch,
  Or backward I fhall ftart;
For fure I want intreating much,
  So fearful is my heart.

H Y M N 95.

" We glory in tribulations, knowing that
  tribulation worketh patience," Rom. v 3.

1.

HOW fimple are thy children, Lord,
  Unfkill'd in what they pray! *
Full oft they lift an hearty word,
  Yet know not what they fay.

* Mark x. 38.

2.

For patience when I rais'd a cry,
  Frefh burdens made me roar;
My foolifh heart would then reply,
  For patience pray no more.

3.

So much my Mafter feem'd to blame,
  I thought to leave his fchool;
But now I learn to blufh for fhame,
  And fee myfelf a fool.

4.

I fancy'd patience would be brought
  Before my troubles rofe ;
And by fuch granted help I thought
  To triumph o'er my woes.

5.

But Paul has clear'd my mifty fight,
  And taught by him I find,
That tribulations, working right,
  Produce a patient mind.

6.

When our dear Mafter would beftow
  Much patience on his friends,
He loads their fhoulders well with woe,
  And thus obtains his ends.

7.

I muft expect a daily crofs,
  Lord, fanctify the pain ;
Bid every furnace purge my drofs,
  And yield fome patient gain.

I   HYMN

HYMN 96.

" When thou makeft a feaft, call the poor,
the maimed, the lame, and the blind; and
thou fhalt be bleffed," Luke xiv. 13, 14.

1.

A Feaft of fat things Jefus makes,
　With ftore of choiceft wine,
And ftarved fouls he calls and takes
　To fit with him and dine.

2.

Come all ye poor, who cannot buy,
　Yet long for living bread;
The Saviour will your wants fupply,
　And make you rich indeed.

3.

Come every fick and bruifed foul,
　Who figh with guilty fmart;
This feaft will make the maimed whole,
　And heal a bleeding heart.

4.

Come all ye lame and crippled throng,
　Who limp in Jefu's ways;
His table-food will make you ftrong,
　And dance, and fing his praife.

5.

Come all ye blind, who inly pine
　For faith's reviving light;
A cup of Jefu's precious wine
　Will clear your cloudy fight.

N

6.

The poor and maimed, blind and lame,
    May come to Jefu's feaft;
And all that come will blefs his name,
    When of his cheer they tafte.

HYMN 97.

" Set me as a feal upon thine heart, as a feal
    upon thine arm," Solom. Song. viii. 6.

1.

I Afk my dying Saviour dear
    To fet me on his heart;
And if my Jefus fix me there,
    Nor life, nor death fhall part.

2.

As Aaron bore upon his breaft*
    The names of Jacob's fons,
So bear my name among the reft
    Of thy dear chofen ones.†

3.

Yea, fet me as a precious feal
    Of covenant grace divine,
Which may the covenant-love reveal,
    And mark me truly thine.

4.

And let the feal be ftamped clear,
    With holinefs in view,
That I may bear thine image fair,
    And others read it too.

* Exod. xxviii. 9, &c.   † John xv. 16.

5.

But feal me alfo on thine arm,
 Or yet I am not right,
I need thy love to ward off harm,
 And need thy fhoulder's might.

6.

This double feal makes all things fure,
 And keeps me fafe and well;
Thy heart and fhoulder will fecure
 From all the hoft of hell.

HYMN 98.

" Break up your fallow-ground, and fow
 not among thorns," Jerem. iv. 3.

1.

UNTILL'D by grace, the human heart
 Refembles fallow-ground,
Unbroken, churlifh, proud and pert,
 And weeds in plenty found.

2.

If gofpel-feed is fown thereon,
 It takes no kindly root,
Is quickly picked up and gone,
 Or choaked if it fhoot.

3.

Then let the Lord my fallows till,
 And plough them every year,
For fure my heart is churlifh ftill,
 And loathfome weeds are there.

4.

Root up the thorns of worldly grief,
  And fprigs of felf-conceit,
That monfter too of unbelief
  O'erturn, o'erturn him quite.

5.

If thus my heart is broken fmall
  With Jefu's gofpel-plough,
And harrow'd till the clumpers fall,
  The gofpel-feed will grow.

6.

But water too the fpringing-crop,
  Or yet it fprings in vain;
Refrefh my faith, and love, and hope,
  With gracious dew and rain.

7.

So will my foul become a child,
  And lean on Jefu's breaft,
Be fimple, loving, meek, and mild,
  And find his promis'd reft.

HYMN 99.

" Little children, abide in him,"
  1 John ii. 28.

1.

OH, let my Jefus teach me how
  I may in him abide;
From wand'ring fave my foolifh heart,
  And keep it near thy fide.

2.

Thy fide is all the tow'r I have
　To fcreen me from my foes,
And in that fide a fountain is,
　Which healeth human woes.

3.

When at this fountain-fide I keep,
　All things go wondrous well;
But if I take a wandering ftep,
　I meet with death and hell.

4.

Put round my heart thy cord of love,
　It hath a kindly fway,
But bind me faft, and draw me ftill,
　Still nearer every day.

5.

No more I would from thee depart,
　No more thy fpirit grieve,
But love and follow like a child,
　And like a child believe.

6.

United as the groom and bride,
　Or as the branch and vine,
Yet fo, that death fhould not divide,
　But make thee ever mine.

HYMN 100.

" Wait on the Lord, be of good courage,
and he will ftrengthen thine heart; wait, I
fay, on the Lord," Pfal. xxvii. 14.

1.

AND does thy heart for Jefus pine,
 And make it's penfive moan?
He underftands a figh divine,
 And marks a fecret groan.

2.

Thefe pinings prove a Chrift is near,
 And teftify his grace;
Call on him with unceafing pray'r,
 And he will fhew his face.

3.

Tho' much difmay'd, take courage ftill,
 And knock at mercy's door;
A loving Saviour furely will
 Relieve his praying poor.

4.

He knows how weak and faint thou art,
 And muft appear at length;
A look from him will chear thine heart,
 And bring renewed ftrength.

5.

Thefe holy hung'rings in thy breaft,
 Are not for mockery meant;
He has prepar'd a royal feaft
 To give thy foul content.

6.

Then wait, I say, upon the Lord,
  Believe and ask again;
Thou haft his kind and faithful word
  That none shall ask in vain.

H Y M N 101.

To the Trinity.

1.

ETERNAL Father, Lord of all,
  By heav'n and earth ador'd!
Regard a guilty creature's call,
  " Who much reveres thy word."*

2.

Thou askest for my worthless heart;†
  Be it thine earthly throne;
And there a father's love impart,
  And make thy mercy known.

3.

Lord Jesus, Son of God most high,
  Of all the rightful heir,
Ador'd by hosts above the sky,
  And by the faithful here!

4.

Thee, Saviour of the world we own,
  Incarnate Lord and God!
Refresh us now, and send us down
  The blessings of thy blood.

* Isa. lxvi. 2.   † Prov. xxiii. 26.

5.

Thou, Holy Ghoſt, who doſt reveal
　　The ſecret things of grace,
And knoweſt well the Father's will,
　　And his deep mind can trace :*

6.

Diſcloſe the heavenly myſteries,
　　And bring the goſpel-feaſt;
Give gracious hearts, and opened eyes,
　　That we may ſee and taſte.

H Y M N   102.
The hundredth Pſalm paraphras'd.

1.

LET all the nations of the earth
　　Be joyful in the Lord,
With pleaſant ſongs and godly mirth
　　The Saviour's name record.

2.

The *Lord* we know, is God indeed,
　　Emmanuel is his name;
A helping God loſt ſinners need,
　　And Jeſus helping came.

3.

His *word* brings every creature forth,
　　No help we could afford;
His *grace* gives ſinners heav'nly birth,
　　And be his grace ador'd.

* 1 Cor. 11. 10.

4.

To sin and Satan we were sold,
  And long in bondage were;
But Jesus call'd us to his fold,
  And keeps us by his care.

5.

Our Shepherd we have cause to bless,
  And bless we will his name,
Frequent his courts, and sing his grace,
  And loud his love proclaim.

6.

A gracious Lord! whose mercy still
  Remaineth ever sure;
Whose truth and faithful promise will
  From age to age endure.

HYMN 103.

" *Buy* and eat without money," Isa. lv. 1.

1.

GOLD or spices have I none,
  For a present to my King,
All my livelihood is gone,
Only rags and wounds I bring.

2.

But I'll traffic, Lord, with thee,
For thy market suits me well;
All my blessings must be free,
And I know thou wilt not sell.

5.

Thou, Holy Ghoſt, who doſt reveal
  The ſecret things of grace,
And knoweſt well the Father's will,
  And his deep mind can trace.*

6.

Diſcloſe the heavenly myſteries,
  And bring the goſpel-feaſt;
Give gracious hearts, and opened eyes,
  That we may ſee and taſte.

HYMN 102.
The hundredth Pſalm paraphras'd.

1.

LET all the nations of the earth
  Be joyful in the Lord,
With pleaſant ſongs and godly mirth
  The Saviour's name record.

2.

The *Lord* we know, is God indeed,
  Emmanuel is his name;
A helping God loſt ſinners need,
  And Jeſus helping came.

3.

His *word* brings every creature forth,
  No help we could afford;
His *grace* gives ſinners heav'nly birth,
  And be his grace ador'd.

* 1. Cor. ii. 10.

4.

To fin and Satan we were fold,
 And long in bondage were;
But Jefus call'd us to his fold,
 And keeps us by his care.

5.

Our Shepherd we have caufe to blefs,
 And blefs we will his name,
Frequent his courts, and fing his grace,
 And loud his love proclaim.

6.

A gracious Lord! whofe mercy ftill
 Remaineth ever fure;
Whofe truth and faithful promife will
 From age to age endure.

HYMN 103.

" *Buy* and eat without money," Ifa. lv. 1.

1.

GOLD or fpices have I none,
 For a prefent to my King,
All my livelihood is gone,
Only rags and wounds I bring.

2.

But I'll traffic, Lord, with thee,
For thy market fuits me well;
All my bleffings muft be free,
And I know thou wilt not fell.

3.
Yet my Jefus bids me *buy*,
Something fure he would receive;
Well, to pleafe him I will try,
And my fomething I will give.

4.
Take my burdens for thy reft,
Take my death for thy life giv'n,
Take my rags for thy rich veft,
Take my hell for thy fweet heav'n.

5.
Now the fale I underftand,
Know what Jefu's market is;
Much he afketh of my hand,
All my woe to *buy* his blifs.

HYMN 104.

" My foul is even as a weaned child,"
Pfal. cxxxi. 2.

1.
JESUS, caft a look on me,
  Give me fweet fimplicity,
Make me poor, and keep me low,
Seeking only thee to know.

2.
Weaned from my lordly felf,
Weaned from the mifer's pelf,
Weaned from the fcorner's ways,
Weaned from the luft of praife.

3.

All that feeds my bufy pride,
Caft it evermore afide,
Bid my will to thine fubmit,
Lay me humbly at thy feet.

4.

Make me like a little child,
Of my ftrength and wifdom fpoil'd,
Seeing only in thy light,
Walking only in thy might.

5.

Leaning on thy loving breaft,
Where a weary foul may reft;
Feeling well the peace of God
Flowing from thy precious blood.

6.

In this pofture let me live,
And hofannas daily give;
In this temper let me die,
And hofannas ever cry.

H Y M N 105.

" I Jefus am the bright and morning ftar,"
Rev. xxii. 16.

1.

"MORNING Star," I wait for thee,
Let thy welcome light appear,
Thou my guide in trav'ling be,
And no danger need I fear.

1

2.

" Star of good old Jacob's loin,"*
Who the God of Israel art!
On thy drooping pilgrims shine,
Chearing each benighted heart.

3.

Guard me, " day-spring," from all ill,†
Guard my heart, and mend my pace,
Till I come to Sion's hill,
And adore thee face to face.

4.

Thou the wise men well didst lead ‡
By a star-light from the east;
Shew me also where to tread,
Else I rove, and miss my rest.

5.

Go before me in the way,
Shine upon me sweet and clear,
Sparkle brighter ev'ry day,
Till my star " a sun appear."§

* Num. xxiv. 17.   † Luke i. 78.
‡ Matt. ii. 1, 2.   § Malac. iv. 2.

HYMN 106.

H Y M N 106.

" He would fain have filled his belly with
the hufks that the fwine did eat, but no
man gave unto him. And when he came
to himfelf, he faid, I will arife and go to
my father," Luke xv. 16, 17, 18.

1.

PINCH'D with want, and full of fores,
  Craving hufks, and them deny'd,
Spent are all my living ftores,
Nothing left befides my pride!

2.

Dig I cannot, and to beg
Much my heart afhamed is,
Loth to ftoop and make my leg,
Loth to tell my grievances.

3.

But I am in woful cafe,
Perifh muft without relief,
And there is an houfe of grace,
Where one Jefus is the chief.

4.

Mighty kind he is, they fay,
Rich as any king, and more,
Liftens hard when beggars pray,
Pleas'd to fee 'em at his door.

O

5.

Others, bringing their complaints,
To this friend of strangers go;
I will tell him too my wants,
Who can tell what he may do?

6.

Jesus, on a stranger look,
Much afflicted have I been,
Poor and wretched here I knock,
Breadless, friendless am I seen.

7.

Lame I limp without a shoe;
Only rags around my breast,
These are sadly filthy too;
Canst thou harbour such a guest?

8.

" Yes," he cries, " I feel thy woe,
" And will wash thy filth away,
" Clothe thee well from top to toe,
" Feed thee well from day to day.

9.

" As a brother thee receive,
" Make thee mine adopted heir,
" Riches, honours freely give,
" Let thee in my kingdom share."

10.

" This is *grace* of Sion's King,
" Canst thou take it, and adore?"
Yes, my Lord, this is the thing,
Well it suits the gospel poor.

11.

Hallelujah to the Lamb!
Sinners, beggars hither come,
Sick or poor, and blind or lame,
Jesus Christ will find you room.

H Y M N 107.

" God is the rock of my salvation,"
Psal. lxxxix. 26.

1.

SELF-condemned and abhorr'd,
   How shall I approach the Lord?
Hard my heart, and cold, and faint,
Full of ev'ry sad complaint.

2.

What can soften hearts of stone?
Nothing but *the Rock* alone.
Thou *the Rock*, my Jesus, art;
Lay the Rock upon my heart.

3.

This would bruise my bosom well,
Press my fulsome pride to hell,
Squeeze my idols from my breast,
Bring the blessed gospel-rest.

4.

Oh, the rock, which Moses struck,
Soon would make my heart a brook!
Only this can make me feel!
Bring it with thy burial-seal.

5.

With it's oil my limbs amoint,*
That will supple ev'ry joint;
Of it's honey let me eat,
That will make my temper sweet.

H Y M N 108.

" My beloved is the chiefest among ten
thousand," Solom. Song v. 10.

1.

SOON as faith the Lord can see
  Bleeding on a cross for me,
Quick my idols all depart,
Jesus gets and fills my heart.

2.

None among the sons of men,
None among the heav'nly train,
Can with Jesus then compare,
None so sweet, and none so fair!

3.

Then my tongue would fain express
All his love and loveliness,
But I lisp and faulter forth
Broken words, not half his worth.

4.

Vex'd, I try and try again;
Still my efforts all are vain:
Living tongues are dumb at best,
We must die to speak of Christ.

* Deut. xxxii. 13.

5.

Bleſſed is the upper ſaint,
Who can praiſe and never faint,
Gazing on thee evermore,
And with flaming heart adore.

6.

Let the Lord a ſmile beſtow
On his liſping babes below;
That will keep their infant-tongue
Prattling of him all day long.

H Y M N 109.

" Why gaddeſt thou about ſo much ?"
Jer. ii. 36.

1.

LIGHT and fickle is my mind,
Veers about with every wind!
Jeſus, mighty to ſubdue,
Take my heart, and keep it too.

2.

Sure it would be thine alone,
Yet it leaves the corner-ſtone,
Rambles from it's reſting-place,
Not cemented well with grace,

3.

Like the dove from Noah ſent,
Wand'ring, but without content;
Thus I rove, and would be bleſt,
Rove and find no ſettled reſt.

O 3

4.

Let me covet nothing here,
Only reckon Jesus dear;
Leaving all the world behind;
Only to my Jesus join'd.

5.

Dearly love him evermore,
And his dying love adore;
Taste and see that he is good,
Live upon him as my food.

6.

Let the King a look bestow,
That will fix my eyes, I know;
Let the King his love impart,
That will stay my gadding heart.

HYMN 110.

" Why have I found grace in thine eyes, that
thou shouldst take knowledge of *me*, seeing I am a stranger?" Ruth ii. 10.

1.

LONG, O Lord, I went astray,
Wand'ring from the gospel-way,
Down a steep destructive road,
Far from peace, and far from God.

2.

Earthly good was all my aim,
Worldly pastime, wealth, and fame :
In the paths of death I trod
With the giddy multitude.

I

3.

But my Jesus pitying saw,
Check'd me with an holy awe,
Dropt his collar on my neck,
Turn'd me round and drew me back.

4.

Now I stand amaz'd to see,
Why the Lord should look on me,
Since I was a stranger poor,
And had slighted him before?

5.

Well; to him be all the praise,
What I am, I am by grace!
Might I live as Enoch long,
Mercy shall be all my song.

6.

Thou hast fetch'd me back from hell;
Let me love and praise thee well;
Lead me safe to Canaan's shore,
There to love and praise thee more.

HYMN III.

" I will satisfy her poor with bread,"
Psalm cxxxii. 15.

1.

MOST are fair in their own eyes,
Beautiful, and strong, and wise,
Prattling of their virtuous store:
Lord, I am, and would be poor.

2.

Poor in fpirit, meek and fmall,
Of my brethren leaft of all,
Faft abiding at thy gate,
Knocking early, knocking late.

3.

Finding no fupplies at home,
Poor and deftitute I come,
Seeking to the church's head ;
Give me, Lord, the church's bread.

4.

Gofpel-bread the poor may eat,
And I want no better meat ;
This my foul will fatisfy,
Give it, Lord, or I muft die.

5.

Should I perifh at thy door,
How the Philiftines would roar !
Shall this tale be told of thee ?
No, my Lord, it cannot be.

6.

Sure I muft believe thee kind,
And may look fome help to find ;
Let me, Lord, not afk in vain,
Feed me, and I'll come again.

H Y M N 112.

" I dwell with him that is of a broken and
humble fpirit," Ifai. lvii. 15.

1.

WELL; at length I plainly fee,
  Ev'ry man is vanity,*
In his beft and brighteft form,
But a fhadow or a worm.

2.

Such a fhade I am in view,
Empty, dark, and fleeting too;
Such a worm, of nothing worth,
Crawling out and in the earth.

3.

Very foolifh, very bafe,
Notwithftanding Jefu's grace!
Murm'ring oft for gofpel-bread,
Growing wanton, when full fed!

4.

Brifk and dull in half an hour,
Hot and cold, and fweet and four!
Sometimes grave at Jefu's fchool,
Sometimes light, and play the fool!

5.

What a motly wretch am I,
Full of inconfiftency?
Sure the plague is in my heart,†
Elfe I could not act this part.

  * Pfalm xxxix. 5.   † 1 Kings viii. 38.

6.

Let me come unto my Lord,
Self-condemned and abhorr'd,
Take the finner's fafe retreat,
Lay and blufh at Jefu's feet.

7.

If my heart is broken well,
God will furely with me dwell;
Yet amazed I would be,
How the Lord fhould dwell with me!

HYMN 113.

To the Trinity.

1.

HOLY Father, fovereign Lord,
    Always meet to be ador'd!
At thy gracious throne I bow,
Univerfal Parent thou!

2.

Fall'n I am, and yet I cry,
Dwell with me, O thou Moft High!
Blefs a poor returning child,
Shew the Father reconcil'd.

3.

Son of God, the Father's love,
Worfhipped by all above,
Worfhipped by faints below,
Trufted and beloved too!

4.

Bare thine arm, and shew thy face,
Spread the gospel of thy grace,
Teach the earth thy praise to sing,
Yielding honours to it's king.

5.

Holy Ghost, who didst inspire
Mortals with prophetic fire,
Thee divine we own and bless,
" Spirit of glory, truth and grace !" *

6.

Breathe upon my languid soul,
" Stir the waters in the pool," †
Life, and love, and peace impart,
Bringing Jesus to my heart.

H Y M N 114.

" Go ye and *learn* what that meaneth, I
will have mercy and not sacrifice,"
Matt. ix. 13.

1.

ALL, that seek the Lord, beware
How ye come to Jesu's door,
Bring no sacrifices there,
None of your own gracious store.

* 1 Pet. iv. 14. John xiv. 17. Heb. x. 29.
† John v. 3, 4.

2.

Kind acceptance would ye find?
Only bring your prefent woe;
Leave your righteous felf behind,
Chrift will only mercy fhew.

3.

If the guilty bofom fmart,
And a thoufand fears arife,
Go to Jefus, as thou art,
" Mercy I will have," he cries.

4.

Seems thy prayer mighty flat,
And thy heart like any ftone?
What of this, or what of that?
Afk, and mercy will be fhewn.

5.

Mercy doft thou no more need,
Seeming in thyfelf complete?
Jefus loathes thy pride indeed,
And will fpurn thee from his feet.

6.

I would love and well obey,
Yet be found in fpirit poor,
All my truft on Jefus lay,
Seeking mercy evermore.

7.

As commanded by the Lord,
Well to know his will I crave,
Learn the meaning of that word,
" Mercy, mercy I will have."

HYMN

H Y M N 115.

" Abraham faid of Sarah his wife, She is
my fifter: and Abimelech, king of Gerar,
fent and took Sarah," Gen. xx. 2.

1.

MAN at beft is only man,
Floating up and down thro' life!
Who would think that Abra'm can
Thro' a fright deny his wife?

2.

See how craftily he treads,
Tells his artful ftory well,
Falls into the pit he dreads!
Oh! remark how Abra'm fell.

3.

Had he fought to God *alone*,
Refting on his mighty arm,
Sarah ftill had been his own,
He had felt no fin or harm.

4.

Twice diffembling he was caught,*
Yet of faithful fouls the firft!
Thus the beft of men are taught,
Strength and fafety lay in Chrift.

5.

Know thy weaknefs, O my foul,
Take the Saviour for thy guard;
If the wifeft play the fool,
What is human watch and ward?

P

* Gen. xii. 13.

6

Jesus, make my heart upright,
Full of sweet simplicity,
Trusting only in thy might,
Casting all my care on thee

HYMN 116.

" Abimelech said, In the integrity of my
heart, and the innocence of my hands,
I have done this. And God said unto
him, I know thou didst this in *the integrity* of thy heart, for *I with-held* thee
from sinning against me," Gen. xx.
4, 5, 6.

1.

LORD, how wonderful thou art,
Working with a gentle hand,
Acting on the human heart,
Drawing it to thy command.

2.

While we fancy reason's aid
Turns our feet aside from ill,
And no thanks to grace are paid,
'Tis the Lord directs us still.

3.

Secretly his pow'r is shew'r,
Over-rules without constraint,
And we think the deed our own,
And we make ourselves the saint.

4.

Thus Abimelech replies,
Sure my hands and heart are clean
True, the God of spirits cries,
For I kept thee back from sin

5.

Know, it was my secret sin
Curbed in thy rampant neck,
And the woman sav'd from harm,
For my servant Abram' sake

6

Here my Master teacheth me,
What restrains my giddy feet
Lord, the thanks are due to thee,
Take them as thy tribute meet

7.

When my will is well inclin'd,
It obeys the call of grace,
Tho' no curb no force can bind,
Nor my heart thy finger trace

8.

Not my wisdom, or my might,
Makes a gracious walk, I know;
God creates the heart upright,*
Working both to *will* and *do.*†

* Pfal. li. 10   † Philip. ii 13.

HYMN 117.

" The Lord faid unto Jofhua—Ifrael hath
finned—therefore they could not ftand
before their enemies — An accurfed
thing is in the midft of thee," Jofh. vii.
10, 11, 12, 13.

1.

IS the chriftian foldier beat,
  Can he feel no Saviour nigh,
Does he pray, and yet retreat,
Turn his back, and wounded fly?

2.

Surely fome accurfed foe
Lodgeth lurking in his breaft,
Makes him weak, and brings him low,
Fearful keeps him, and diftreft.

3.

In the battle we are foil'd,
If we cherifh idols bafe,
Either Achan's wedge of gold,
Or fome Babylonifh drefs.

4.

Till the bofom is fincere,
Till the camp is purged well,
That no favour'd luft be there,
We fhall fight, but not excel.

5.

Jesus, take my roving heart,
Make it willing to be thine,
Freely with it's idols part,
All the world for thee resign.

6.

If a traitor lodge within,
Lust, or pride, or mammon's hoard,
And the serpent lurk unseen,
Shew it, and expel it, Lord.

H Y M N. 118.

" A troop shall overcome him, but he shall
overcome at last," Gen. xlix. 19.

1.

TROOPS a feeble saint engage,
Armed with relentless rage,
Troops within and troops without
Hard beset him round about.

2.

Satan is the leader chief,
Bringing pride and unbelief,
Stubborn wills and tempers vile,
Wanton lusts that will defile.

3.

Troops assault him from the earth,
Mammon base and gaudy mirth;
Troops beside of Esau's race,
Taught to make a mock of grace.

4.

While a pilgrim yet is weak,
Mighty apt he is to sneak,
Then the troopers thrust him home,
Wound him oft, and oft o'ercome.

5.

But the promise standeth sure,
Will from age to age endure,
Tho' the pilgrim oft is cast,
He shall overcome at last.

6.

Keep the promise well in sight,
Trust in Jesu's word and might,
Pray and fight, and pray again,
Faith will overcome and reign

HYMN 119.

"He, that hath a bountiful eye, shall be
blessed, for he giveth of his bread to the
poor," Prov. xxii. 9.

1.

JESUS hath a bounteous eye,
  Calls the sick and needy nigh,
Seeks the friendless as they roam,
Brings the wretched outcast home.

2.

Gathers crouds around his door,
Looks and smiles upon the poor,
Gives the bread for which they cry,
Bread, which princes cannot buy!

3.

Pleas'd to help 'em in their need,
Pleas'd, if hungry they can feed,
Pleas'd to hear 'em tell their case,
Pleas'd to chear 'em with his grace.

4.

All that hunger for his bread
May and will be kindly fed;
He will pass no beggar by,
You may eat, and so may I.

5.

Hallelujah to the Lamb,
Let the poor exalt his name,
Raise your voice, as angels raise,
Sing, and give him lusty praise.

6.

Jesus, with thy bread, impart
Something of thy bounteous heart;
I would learn to copy thee,
Feed the poor, as thou dost *me*.

H Y M N 120.

" Foolishness is bound in the heart of a child,
but the rod of correction shall drive it
far from him," Prov. xxii. 15.

1.

FOLLY in a child is found,
  Round about his heart is bound,
Bred and born with it, no doubt,
But a rod shall drive it out.

2.

Mark the promife made to you,
God is wife, and God is true;
Rods apply'd with faith and pray'r,
Make the folly difappear.

3.

Much indulgence fpoils a child,
Makes him mafterful and wild,
But correction makes him wife,
Silencing his froward cries.

4.

And art thou a child of God?
Then expect to feel his rod;
Adam dwelleth in thee ftill,
And has got a faucy will.

5.

Yet the plague is in thy heart,
And with folly loth to part!
This a gracious Father knows,
And his loving ftripes beftows.

6.

Oft he brings an heavy crofs,-
Biting pain or nipping lofs;
Thus the children fteady grow,
Meek and rulable by woe.

7.

Father, fanctify the rod,
Dip it in the Saviour's blood,
Let the ftripes my folly heal,
And a father's love reveal.

H Y M N 121.

" Praife is comely for the upright,"
Pfal. xxxiii. 1.

1.

NEIGHBOUR, is thy heart upright,
Doft thou walk in Jefu's light?
If thy faith his glory fee,
Come and fing along with me.

2.

Praife is comely fure for fuch;
We fhould love and blefs him much,
Chearful fing his works and ways,
Give him everlafting praife.

3.

Loft we were, and roam'd about,
Till his pity fought us out,
And reveal'd his lovely face;
Oh! the riches of his grace!

4.

We were wholly dead in fin,
Hateful, wretched, and unclean,
Till he brought us home to God;
Oh, the virtue of his blood!

5.

We were open rebels quite,
Acting treafon in his fight;
Yet he drew us from above,
Oh, the fweetnefs of his love!

6.

We are fometimes flack and cold,
Sometimes mighty pert, and bold,
But he chides and loves his friends,
Oh, his mercy never ends!

7.

Sweet and gentle is the Lamb!
Let us love and blefs his name,
Live and feed upon his ftore,
Feed and blefs him evermoie.

H Y M N 122.

" Let not thine heart be glad when thine
enemy ftumbleth or falleth; left the Lord
fee it, and it difpleafe him, and he turn
away his wrath from him (to thee),"
Prov. xxiv. 17, 18.

1.

LORD, how evil is my heart,
 Much corrupt in ev'ry part!
Moft unkindly it will ftray
From the friendly gofpel-way.

2.

If fome harm befel my foe;
How I danced at his woe!
If he ftumbled into fin;
How refresh'd my heart has been.

3.

Had he perish'd by a fall,
Sure I had not car'd at all;
Had he pin'd away in want,
Truly I had been content.

4.

What a sorry wretch am I!
Justice says, I ought to die:
Vengeance might have reach'd my head,
Spar'd the foe, and struck me dead.

5.

May the mercy I have found,
Ever in my bowels found;
Mercy yet I daily want,
Mercy let me freely grant.

6.

Jesus, teach me how to live,
Always ready to forgive;
Teach me also how to pray
For offenders night and day.

7.

Holy skill I now desire,
How to cast sweet mercy's fire
On a spiteful neighbour's crown,
Not to burn, but melt him down.

HYMN 123.

"He that tilleth his land, shall have plenty
of bread," Prov. xxviii. 19.

1.

PINEST thou for Jesu's bread,
  And with plenty wouldst be fed?
Learn to work with godly skill,
And the ground unweary'd till.

2.

Ground I mean of thy own heart,
Churlish sure in ev'ry part,
Most unhealthy, barren ground,
Such as no where else is found.

3.

Get it broken up by grace,
Else it weareth legal face,
Sow it well with Bible-seed,
Else it bringeth only weed.

4.

Dung the ground with many pray'rs,
Mellow it with gracious tears,
Drench it too with Jesu's blood,
Then the ground is sweet and good.

5.

Watch the swine, a filthy train,
Swinish lusts will eat the grain;
Hoe up all the ragged thorn,
Worldly cares will choak the corn.

I   6. Muse

6.

Muſe upon the goſpel-word,
Seek direction from the Lord,
Truſt the Lord to give it thee,
And a bleſſing thou ſhalt ſee.

7.

He will cram the barn with ſtore,
Make the wine-preſs trickle o'er,
Bleſs thee now, and bleſs thee ſtill,
Thou ſhalt eat, and have thy fill.

H Y M N 124.

" He, that truſteth in his own heart, is a
　　fool," Prov. xxviii. 26.

1.

HE, that truſteth in his heart,
　　Acts a raw and fooliſh part,
Baſe it is, and full of guile,
Brooding miſchief in a ſmile.

2.

Does it boaſt of love within?
So it may, and yet may ſin:
Peter lov'd his Maſter well,
Yet a loving Peter fell.

3.

Does it feel a melting flame?
David alſo felt the ſame;
Yet he made a woful trip,
And perceiv'd his mountain ſlip.

Q

4.

Does it talk of faith and boaſt ?
Abram had as much as moſt ;
Yet beguil'd by unbelief,
Twice he durſt deny his wife.*

5.

Truſt in no received ſtore,
Elſe thou wilt be quickly poor ;
Manna kept, as Moſes tells,
Breedeth worms, and quickly ſmells.

6.

I will thank my loving Lord
For the grace he does afford,
Yet on nothing I receive
Would I reſt, or can I live.

7.

Every prop will firſt or laſt,
Sink and fail, but Jeſus Chriſt :
On this ſure foundation-ſtone
Let me build and reſt *alone*.

H Y M N 125.

' Chriſt is all and in all, or all in every thing,'
Coloſſ. iii. 11.

1.

LOFTY ſinners love to talk
  Of their wiſdom and their walk,
Of their merit and their might,
Till they weary patience quite.

* Gen. xii. 13. and xx. 2.

2.

From the word of God I know,
Man is weak and worthlefs too,
Man is obftinately blind,
Till the light of Chrift he find.

3.

Something once I feem'd to have,
And to Jefus fomething gave;
Now I tell to great and fmall,
Jefus Chrift is all in all.

4.

All my wifdom to direct,
All my power to protect,
All the merit I can claim,
All my hope is in his name.

5.

Bountiful is Sion's King,
All he is in every thing,
Giveth eyes to fee my way,
Will and pow'r to watch and pray.

6.

Will and pow'r to love the Lord,
Will and pow'r to truft his word,
Will and pow'r to run the race;
Glory be unto his grace.

HYMN 126.

"David departed to the cave, Adullam,
and every one in diſtreſs, or in debt, or
diſcontented, gathered themſelves unto
David, and he became a captain over
them," 1 Sam. xxii. 1, 2.

1.

ALL in debt or in diſtreſs,
  Diſcontented much or leſs,
All that would protection have,
Poſt away to David's cave.

2.

What a baſe and motly crew
In this royal band I view!
Yet the Son of David takes
Scoundrels ſuch, and ſuch like rakes.

3.

All, who find their ſinful debt,
Deep and deeper growing yet,
All who have been Satan's tool;
Much his madman or his fool.

4.

All who diſcontented are,
Full of guilt and full of fear;
Ev'ry ſoul, who would not die,
Unto Jeſu's *cave* muſt fly.

5.

Jefus all your debts will **pay,**
Chace your legal duns away,
Ev'ry foe he will fubdue,
World and flefh, and devil too.

6.

Hafte and feek the Saviour's face,
Rife and blefs him for his grace,
To his fcorned *cave* repair,
He will wafh and feaft you there.

H Y M N 127.

"Who am I? and what is my life? or what
my father's family? that I fhould be fon-
in-law to the king," 1 Sam. xviii. 18, 23.

1.

WHO *am I*, that I fhould be
Rais'd to royal dignity!
Made a child of heaven's King,
Call him Father, as I fing!

2.

From the duft I had my birth,
And fhall foon return to earth;
Stript of all my comely form,
Sin has funk me to a worm!

3.

What has been my *former life?*
Full of vain or noify ftrife,
Making light of Jefu's blood,
Rambling in a way not good!

Q 3

4.

What has been my *father's house?*
Nothing in it good or choice,
Bafe and proud enough they were,
Juft as all the children are!

5.

O my Father, now I fee,
Why fuch love is fhewn to me,
Sinner of a finful race;
All is owing to thy grace!

6.

Mercy, mercy thou wilt have!
Freely, freely thou wilt fave!
Raife a beggar from his duft!
Love and blefs thee fure I muft!

7.

Make me thy obedient child,
Simple, tractable, and mild;
Acting now a thankful part,
Loving thee with all my heart.

HYMN 128.

"Adam, where art thou?" Gen. iii. 9.

1.

FATHER Adam, *where art thou?*
  Much afham'd I fee thee now;
All thy righteoufnefs is gone,
Holy raiment thou haft none.

2.

Why alarm'd with ghaſtly fear?
Sure ſome horrid guilt is there.
Why the leaves around thy waiſt?
Sorry ſcreen for filthy luſt.

3.

Why afraid of Jeſu's voice?
Chriſt is no more Adam's choice;
Sure I hear thy rebel-heart
Saying unto God, " Depart."

4.

Why ſo hid behind a tree?
What! has God no eyes to ſee?
Yes, but Adam waxeth blind,
Sin has darken'd all his mind.

5.

Why of Eve this idle tale,
As if made to work thy fall?
Adam muſt the trade begin,
Teach us how to cover ſin.

6.

Why amaz'd at Abel ſlain?
In thy likeneſs born was Cain!
Well he wears the father's face!
Thou haſt murder'd all thy race!

7.

Here I ſtand a guilty ſoul!
Adam, thou haſt made me foul,
Brought a curſe upon my name,
Fill'd my heart with ſin and ſhame.

8.

Second Adam, fpring of hope!
Help a fallen finner up;
O thou bleffed woman's feed,
Rife and bruife the ferpent's head.

HYMN 129.

" I will put thee in a cleft of the rock,
while my glory paffeth by," Exod.
xxxiii. 22.

1.

WOULD thy ravifh'd eyes behold
Glory better felt than told?
Wouldft thou hear the Lord proclaim
All the glory of his name?

2.

He muft lead thee to the rock,
Which his fervant Mofes ftruck;
Rock to build his mercy on,
While eternal ages run!

3.

In the rock is found a cleft,
Which in Herod's time was reft
By a wanton foldier's fpear;
And the Lord muft put thee there.

4.

There the Lord reveals his face,
Paffeth by in love and grace,
Bids the mountain-guilt depart,
And beftows a loving heart.

5.

Bleſſed Rock! for ever bleſt!
Bringing weary pilgrims reſt;
Here they ſing and joyful ſtand,
Gazing on the promis'd land.

6.

On the Rock I would abide,
In the cleft my head would hide;
Long a rambler I have been,
Reach thy hand, and put me in.

H Y M N 130.

" The ſpirit that dwelleth in us, luſteth to
envy," James iv. 5.

1.

ENVY, ſource of pining woes,
From a curſed parent roſe!
Satan firſt the child begat,
Then impos'd on Eve the brat.

2.

She with much unkindly care,
Made each riſing child her heir;
Now 'tis in each boſom pent,
Nurs'd by pride and diſcontent.

3.

Nature wallows in this mire,
Pining much with baſe deſire,
Sick'ning at a neighbour's health,
Famiſh'd by a neighbour's wealth!

4.

Gracious men the poison know,
And are often pining too
At a brother's gifts or grace,
And would foil a brother's face.

5.

Jesus, let me not repine
At a better lot than mine;
From my heart this hell remove,
Quench it by a flood of love.

6.

Take this envy from my breast,
Making up a devil's feast,
Give me love, which thinks no ill,
Bearing all a pure good-will.

7.

Pleased with their health and store,
Though I should be sick and poor;
Pleased with their honour'd name,
Though it darken all my fame.

HYMN 131.

" My soul is exceeding sorrowful, even
unto death," Matt. xxvi. 38.

1.

WHAT a doleful voice I hear!
What a garden-scene is there!
What a frightful ghastly flood!
Jesus welt'ring in his blood!

2.

Groaning on the ground he lies,
Seems a flaughter'd facrifice!
Tells me with a feeble breath,
" Sorrowful, yea unto death!"

3.

How his eyes aftonifh'd are;
Sure they witnefs huge defpair!
On his face what fadnefs dwells!
Sure he feels a thoufand hells!

4.

O my Jefus, let me know
What has brought this heavy woe?
Swords are piercing through thy heart;
Whence arofe the tort'ring fmart?

5.

" Sinner, thou haft done the deed,
" Thou haft made the Saviour bleed,
" Juftice drew it's fword on me,
" Pierc'd my heart, to pafs by thee.

6.

" Now I take thy deadly cup,
" All it's dregs am drinking up;
" Read my anguifh in my gore,
" Look and pierce my heart no more."

7.

O thou bleeding Love divine!
What are other loves to thine?
Their's a drop, and thine a fea,
Ever full, and ever free!

8.

If I lov'd my Lord before,
I would love him ten times more;
Drop into his sea outright,
Lose myself in Jesus quite.

HYMN 132.

" The wages of sin is death," Rom. vi. 23.

1.

AWFUL is thy threat'ning, Lord!
Let me mark the solemn word,
What the righteous Ruler saith,
" Wages due to sin is death."

2.

Then I stand condemn'd to die,
By the mouth of God most High!
Sins I have, a thousand too,
And a thousand deaths are due.

3.

Should I spend my life in pray'rs,
Water all my couch with tears,
Turn from every evil past,
Still I am condemn'd and cast.

4.

Could I run no more in debt?
Old arrears are standing yet;
Still the law remains in force,
Breathing out it's deadly curse.

5. Lord,

5.

Lord, I own the sentence just,
Drop my head into the dust,
If my soul is cast to hell,
'Thou, O Lord, art righteous still.

6.

In myself I have no hope,
Justice ev'ry plea will stop;
Yet for mercy I may plead,
Springing from the church's Head.

7.

Knock I may at Jesu's door,
Mercy for his sake implore,
Mercy, such as thou wilt give,
Shew it, Lord, and let me live.

H Y M N 133.

" Eternal life is the gift of God, through
  Jesus Christ our Lord," Rom. vi. 23.

1.

LIFE eternal is bestow'd
  Not for thy good service done,
'Tis a precious gift of God,
Freely granted thro' his Son.

2.

Gift alone from first to last;
God in Christ is all in all,
Seeking up the poor outcast,
Granting him a gracious call.

R

3.

Working forrow for his fin,
With a godly hatred too,
Bringing peace and love within,
With an heart created new,

4.

Salting well his table-talk,
Daily helping to believe,
Teaching how with God to walk,
And in fweet communion live.

5.

But the faint's a finner ftill,
Soil will cleave unto his feet,
All his beft works ever will
Want a bleeding Saviour yet.

6.

God will hold his mercy faft,
Give what finners cannot claim,
Grace at fir ft, and glory laft ;
Hallelujah for the fame !

H Y M N 134.

To the Trinity.

" Holy, holy, holy Lord God Almighty,
who was, and is, and art to come," Rev.
iv. 8. Ifai. vi. 3.

1.

HOLY Father, God moft high,
Thron'd in awful majefty!
Juft and true in all thy ways,
Worthy of eternal praife!

2.

Plant thy grace within my heart,
Peace and righteoufnefs impart,
Thy fair image on me feal,
And thy love in Chrift reveal.

3.

Holy Jefus, Lamb of God!
Send thy healing word abroad,
Shew how ftrong and kind thou art,
Lift thine arm, and bare thy heart.

4.

Tend the flocks in ev'ry fold,
Make them lufty grow and bold,
Sing thy praifes and adore,
Love and truft thee evermore.

5.

Holy Spirit, quick'ning breath!
Raifing finners dead from death,
Working faith, infpiring peace,
And creating holinefs!

6.

Breathe upon us from above,
Teach us truth, and give us love;
All that feel thy quick'ning flame
Will adore and blefs thy name.

7.

Holy, Holy, Holy Three!
Each in peerlefs might agree;
Each in one eternal home,
Was, and is, and is to come!

HYMN 135.

"A fountain open'd for sin," Zech. xiii. 1.

1.

A Fountain! cries the man of God,
  A fountain with a purple flood!
A fountain open'd for the poor,
Where sickly souls may find a cure!

2.

It softens well the heart of stone,
And kindly knits a broken bone,
Restoring hearing, speech, and sight,
And puts all guilty fears to flight.

3.

It heals the soul of feverish heat,
And helps a pulse with grace to beat;
The fretful look, the wanton eye,
And lordly self before it fly.

4.

No spring, like this, makes lepers whole;
Not that renown'd Bethesda's pool,*
Nor Siloam's† stream, nor Jordan's ‡ flood,
Were altogether half so good.

5.

Come hither souls, defil'd with sin,
And wash the heart, and make it clean;
Ah! do not pass it loathing by,
Or you must wash, or you must die.

* John v. 2.   † John ix. 7.
‡ 2 Kings v. 2.

6.

Faſt by this fountain let me ſtay,
And drink and waſh my ſores away;
If but a moment I depart,
Sick is my head, and faint my heart.

HYMN 136.

" Come unto Me," Matt. xi. 28.

1.

WHAT pleaſant voice is this I hear?
It whiſpers ſoftly in mine ear,
Come hither, ſtranger, and be bleſt,
Come unto Me, and take my reſt.

2.

I like the ſweet inviting word,
And ſure the voice is from the Lord;
But tell me, Jeſus, how to come,
And guide a wand'ring ſinner home.

3.

Come laden well with guilty woe,
And come in rags, as vagrants do;
No apron bring thy ſhame to hide,
But caſt thy fig-leaves all aſide.

4.

Come weary of the world's purſuit,
It's empty traſh, and griping fruit;
Come loathing of thyſelf and ſin,
And Jeſus Chriſt will take thee in.

5.

Caft all thy burdens on my back,
And put my collar round thy neck,
And lay thy foul at mercy's door,
The friendly gate for fick and poor.

6.

O Lord, I view the friendly gate,
But find a lamenefs in my feet;
They ftumble in this narrow path;
Inftruct me how to come in faith.

HYMN 137.

"Abide in Me," John xv. 4.

1.

REMARK, my foul, the gracious word,
A fecond meffage from the Lord;
"Come to Me," finner, firft he cry'd;
And now he fays, "In Me abide."

2.

Abide in *me*, thou roving heart,
Nor from my pierced fide depart;
Keep in the haven of my breaft,
And there enjoy the gofpel-reft.

3.

Nor canft thou walk, if left alone,
Nor fhew thy face before the throne;
Thy Aaron muft his mitre bring
To hallow every holy thing.*

* Exod. xxviii. 36, &c.

4.

Thy heart, if wand'ring far from me,
A dry and wither'd ftick will be,
No fruit or bloffom fair can bring,
No will to work, or pray, or ling.

5.

I keep my lepers mighty poor,
Allow no month or weekly ftore,
But feed them daily, foon and late,
And thus retain them at my gate.

6.

Enough, my Lord, I fee it meet
To lay, like Mary, at thy feet;
I would not leave thy pierced fide,
But in that pleafant cave abide.

HYMN 138.

" If any man will come after me, let him
take up his crofs daily, and follow me,"
Luke ix. 23.

1.

AFFLICTIONS are the lot of faints,
And Jefus fends a needful crop;
But naughty children make complaints,
Nor care to take the croffes up.

2.

If inward conflicts prefs me fore,
And pain me much, and bow me quite,
Still let me reft on Jefu's pow'r
To put thefe bofom foes to flight.

3.

In darknefs when I penfive go,
And fee no fun or ftar appear,
Inftruct me how to truft thee fo,
And wait till day-light draweth near.

4.

If houfe-hold friends againft me rife,,
Or taunting neighbours round me dwell,
Yet let me give no tart replies,
But bear the fad unkindnefs well.

5.

Should famine caft a meagre ftare,
And thruft his head within my door;,
Still let me truft in Jefu's care
To feed and clothe his helplefs poor.

6.

Should pain o'er my weak flefh prevail,
And fevers boil within my breaft,
And heart, and ftrength, and reafon fail,
Be yet my foul on Jéfus caft.

7.

In every trial let me be
Supply'd with all-fufficient grace,
My fpirit calmly ftay'd on thee,
And fweetly kept in perfect peace.

HYMN 139.

" Let not the water-flood overflow me,"
Pfal. lxix. 15.

1.

THE roaring waves and ruffling blasts,
 Like pirates, keep my foul in chace;
They break my anchor, fails, and masts,
And yield me no repofing place.

2.

Temptations come, like hasty floods,
And plunge me in the deep outright;
My heav'n is oft o'ercast with clouds,
And fheds an awful low'ring light.

3.

Storm after storm is black with ill,
And thunders rattling make me start;
Wave after wave come dashing still,
And burst their foam upon my heart.

4.

Oh! that my fhip was fafe on fhore,
Lodg'd in the port, where Jefus is;
Where neither winds nor waters roar,
And all the tides are tides of blifs.

5.

But while my fhip is doom'd to ride
And beat on life's tempeftuous fea,
My floating ark may Jefus guide,
And pilot and fheet-anchor be.

HYMN 140.

"Zaccheus, make hafte, and come down,"
Luke xix. 5.

1.

ZACCHEUS mounts himfelf on high
To feek, O Lord, a fight of thee,
And thus we hope to fcale the fky,
By perching on a legal tree.

2.

But lofty branches foonefl break,
And breaking, bring a fatal fhock,
Truft not a leafy arm fo weak,
Come down, and reft upon the Rock.

3.

Make hafte, and quit thine airy feat,
Thou art above the gofpel-terms ;
Relinquifh every high conceit,
And meekly fink into my arms.

4.

This day falvation Jefus brings,
And brings it freely to thy home,
A prefent from the King of kings !
Incline thine ear, and quickly come.

5.

To publicans the grace I give,
Which fcorners think below their care;
And all, that would my gifts receive,
May with Zaccheus take a fhare.

6.

Then Jesus, since thy gifts are free,
A share or two of them impart;
I come a publican to thee,
And ask a loving, lowly heart.

HYMN 141.

" Make thy face to shine upon thy servant,
and teach me thy statutes," Psal. cxix. 135.

1.

JESUS, thou dearest, sweetest friend,
    The Joy of all thy feeble train!
Some tokens of thy presence send,
Or we shall sing and pray in vain.

2.

Reveal thyself, and shew thy face,
And make thy tender mercies known;
Breathe on our souls a breath of grace,
And send the Holy Spirit down.

3.

Thy gracious coming here we wait,
And long to view thee, as thou art;
We bow as sinners at thy feet,
And bid thee welcome to our heart.

4.

Our broken walls and gates repair,
And water well thy Sion's hill;
The feeble hearts with kind words chear,
And famish'd souls with good things fill.

5.

Make darknefs vanifh by thy light,
And make our rugged tempers plain,
Lead on thy foldiers to the fight,
'Till unbelief and death are flain.

6.

Refrefh us in the wildernefs,
And when to Jordan's bank we come,
Bid thofe rough waves afunder pafs,
And bring the pilgrims dry-fhod home.

HYMN 142.

" Why will ye die, O houfe of Ifrael,"
Ezek. xviii. 31.

1.

THE fearful debt of endlefs woe,
Which finners unto juftice owe,
Was by the heav'nly furety paid,
And blood for blood the ranfom made.

2.

He freely took our deadly cup,
Beheld the dregs, and drank them up,
And having brought falvation nigh,
His heart complains, " Why will ye die?"

3.

O *Ifrael's houfe* to Chrift repair,
His blood will wafh the fouleft fair,
His arms, like rainbows, open ftand,
And pardons feal'd are in his hand.

I

4. Free

4.

Free love and mercy, truth and grace,
The sun-beams are of Jesu's face,
Sweet beams to thaw a frozen heart,
And make the gloom of hell depart.

5.

Ye mourning souls, lift up your eyes,
And view the Lord, your sacrifice;
His gaping side cries, " Here is room,
" Drop all your guilt within this tomb."

6.

Go, sinners go, approach him near;
When Christ invites, you need not fear;
He calls you to his bleeding breast,
The seat of love and gospel-rest.

HYMN 143.

" At thy right-hand are pleasures for evermore," Psalm xvi. 11.

1.

O Happy saints, who dwell in light,
And walk with Jesus, cloth'd in white,
Safe landed on that peaceful shore,
Where pilgrims meet to part no more.

2.

Releas'd from sin, and toil, and grief,
Death was their gate to endless life;
An open'd cage to let 'em fly,
And build their happy nest on high.

S

3.

And now they range the heav'nly plains,
And sing their hymns in melting strains;
And now their souls begin to prove
The heights and depths of Jesu's love.

4.

They gaze upon his beauteous face,
His lovely mind, and charming grace,
And gazing hard with ravish'd eyes,
His form they catch, and taste his joys.

5.

He chears them with eternal smile;
They sing hosannas all the while,
Or, overwhelm'd with rapture sweet,
Sink down adoring at his feet.

6.

Ah! Lord, with tardy steps I creep,
And sometimes sing, and sometimes weep;
Yet strip me of this house of clay,
And I will sing as loud as they.

HYMN 144.

" I will feed my flock, saith the Lord God;
I will seek the lost, and bring again the
scattered, and bind up the broken, and
strengthen the sick," Ezek. xxxiv. 15, 16.

1.

WITH watchful eye and wisdom deep,
Our gentle Shepherd tends his flock,
Leads on and guards the helpless sheep,
And grounds them on himself, the Rock.

2.

He seeks the lost with tender care,
And finds them in the wilderness,
Conducts them to his pastures fair,
And feeds them with his word of grace.

3.

Some from his fold are forc'd away
By howling wolves, a rav'nous train,
And these he follows when they stray,
And brings them to his fold again.

4.

He lends his shoulder to the we__,
And bears the lambkins in his a_ms,
And all the broken and the sick
Are healed by his Calvary balms.

5.

And while they walk in humble love,
His pleasant heritage are they,
And he defends them from above,
And guides them in the gospel-wa

6.

So guide and guard us, dearest
As children walking, hand in
And many a gracious look a
To chear us thro' this barre

HYMN 145.

"Come in, thou bleffed of the Lord; why
ftandeft thou without? And he came in,
and unladed his camels," Gen. xxiv. 31,32.

1.

COME in, come in, thou heav'nly gueft,
Why ftands my Lord without the door?
Thou feek'ft a lodging in my breaft,
And I would keep thee out no more.

2.

Thy camels bring embroidery
To garnifh out a homely bride,
And brides are waiting here for thee,
And wifh the marriage-knot was ty'd.

3.

Rebeccas, looking for the Lord,
With eager expectation ftand,
And only wait his afking word,
To give the chearful wedding-hand.

4.

Yet, Lord, we need a wedding-fuit,
A robe of righteoufnefs divine,
Of thy fweet love the coftly fruit,
A robe to make the virgins fine!

5.

oply us too with fervent pray'r,
raifes flaming up above,
h eye with gracious tear,
t with bridal love.

6.

And tho' be found no wealth or wit,
Nor merit in thy freckled maid,
Yet sure she looks and stands complete,
When in thy righteousness array'd.

HYMN 146.

"What is thy Beloved more than another
beloved? He is altogether lovely," Song
of Solom. v. 9, 16.

1.

IF gazing strangers want to know
What makes me sing of Jesus so;
I love his name, 'tis very dear,
And would his loveliness declare.

2.

His head abounds in wisdom deep,
No secret can his notice slip;
And sweet instruction he conveys,
To mend my heart, and guide my ways

3.

No sinful taint his bosom knows,
But with amazing kindness glows;
He wrought a righteousness divine,
And bids me take and call it mine.

4.

His eyes are full of melting love,
More soft and sparkling than the dove·
A single smile, from Jesus giv'n,
Will lift a drooping soul to heav'n.

S 3

5.

His open arms, like rainbows, ſtand,
And circle round a guilty land ;
And in his ſide is dug a cave,
Where all my guilt may find a grave.

6.

His mercies, like himſelf, endure,
And like his love, are ever ſure ;
And when your eye his worth can view,
Your heart, like mine, will love him too.

H Y M N 147.

" And Moſes made a ſerpent of braſs, and
    put it on a pole, and it came to paſs,
    if a ſerpent had bitten any man, when
    he beheld the ſerpent of braſs, he lived,"
Numb. xxi. 9.

1.

WHEN Jacob's tribes, with travel faint,
    Had utter'd raſh and pert complaint,
Some fiery ſerpents nip their pride,
And much were ſtung, and many dy'd.

2.

Right humbly now they raiſe a cry,
And ſee a ſerpent rear'd on high,
A ſnake of braſs upon a pole,
And all, who give a look, are whole.

3.

A moft myfterious cure is wrought,
Like what the crofs of Chrift has brought,
A look of faith in both we find,
One heals the flefh, and one the mind.

4.

While fcorners turn the face afide,
And fuch myfterious cure deride,
Revile it as an hope forlorn,
And laugh and perifh in their fcorn.

5.

Here would I fix adoring eyes,
And look and gaze with fweet furprize;
For fure each look of faith imparts
Renewed health to contrite hearts.

6.

Oh, let me blefs the Saviour's name,
And glory in the crofs's fhame!
My life is bound up in his death,
And comes convey'd by looks of faith.

HYMN 148.

"My fon, give me thine heart," Prov.
xxiii. 26.

1.

AND will the Lord accept my heart?
Moft freely with it I would part;
Much daily plague it gives me, fure,
And nought on earth can find it cure.

I

2.

It proves a churlifh piece of ftuff,
Rebellious, wafpifh, proud enough;
A ftubborn foe to gofpel-light,
And full of guile, and full of fpite!

3.

Here Jefus once fet up his throne,
And lov'd and call'd the houfe his own;
But foon it turn'd Apollyon's inn,*
A peft-houfe for the man of fin.

4.

This vile polluted heart I bring,
And yield up to it's ancient King;
Re-enter, Jefus, with thy grace,
And hallow this unholy place.

5.

Thy gentle arm beneath it keep,
Or when I wake, or when I fleep;
And near thy bofom let it dwell,
And it will love thee dearly well.

6.

It is exceeding prone to ftray,
And wilder than a beaft of prey;
No human fetter can it bind,
But thou canft tame and make it kind.

* Rev. ix. 11.

HYMN 149.

" A great multitude ſtood before the throne
clothed in white robes," Rev. vii. 9.

1.

WHite robes the goſpel-warehouſe brings
 For Jeſu's choſen prieſts and kings;
White robes of righteouſneſs divine,
The wedding-robes of linen fine!

2.

Faith eyes the rich embroider'd ſuit,
Of Jeſu's glorious toil the fruit;
And finds the royal robe will hide
All rags, and warm the breaſt beſide.

3.

It brings the wearer tempers ſweet,
A loving heart, and nimble feet;
And now to court he may repair,
And ſee no angel look ſo fair.

4.

Some of the robe can lightly talk,
But ſhew they want it by their walk;
The world a welcome gueſt within,
The robe a goodly cloak for ſin!

5.

Yet let me not the coat deſpiſe,
Nor caſt it off with loathing eyes;
It ſurely claims a ſeat above,
And fills the heart with humble love.

6.

When Jacob unto Isaac goes,
Equipp'd in Esau's Sunday-cloaths;
The father pores upon the vest,
He felt and smelt, then kist and blest.*

HYMN 150.

" The law is not of (the same nature with)
faith," Gal. iii. 12.

1.

THE law demands a weighty debt,
    And not a single mite will bate;
But gospel sings of Jesu's blood,
And says it made the payment good.

2.

The law provokes men oft to ill,
And churlish hearts makes harder still;
But gospel acts a kindly part,
And melts a most obdurate heart.

3.

Run, John, and work, the law commands,
Yet finds me neither feet nor hands;
But sweeter news the gospel brings,
It bids me fly, and lends me wings.

4.

Such needful wings, O Lord, impart,
To brace my feet, and brace my heart:
Good wings of faith. and wings of love,
Will make a cripple sprightly move.

* Gen. xxvii. 27.

5.

With thefe a lumpifh foul may fly,
And foar aloft, and reach the fky;
Nor faint nor faulter in the race,
But chearly work, and fing of grace.

HYMN 151.

" In Chrift dwelleth all the fulnefs of the
Godhead bodily," Col. ii. 9.

1.

HOW glorious is thy human frame,
Divine Redeemer, true God-Man!
No feraph's tongue can reach thy fame,
Yet babes will prattle, as they can.

2.

A temple is thine earthly cafe,
Where true fubftantial Godhead dwells;
And wifdom, goodnefs, pow'r and grace,
The man with all their fulnefs fills.

3.

Tho' vail'd on earth thy glory was,
The *God* fhone out to human view;
And all who could difcern thy face,
Beheld the Father's image too.*

4.

All human gifts and heav'nly ftores
In Jefu's wondrous perfon meet;
The Godhead fills him with it's pow'rs,
And forms the Saviour all-complete!

* John xiv. 9.

5.

His perſon ſoareth out of ſight,
A myſt'ry, magnify'd by Paul !*
A child, and yet the God of might,†
A worm, and yet the Lord of all !‡

6.

The *man*, believers worſhip now,
As eaſtern ſages did the *child*; §
And all before the *man* muſt bow; ‖
Saints, ſeraphs, fiends, and ſcorners wild.

HYMN 152.

" Lord, thou wilt ordain peace for us, becaufe thou haſt wrought all our works in
us," Iſa. xxvi. 12.

1.

VAIN are the hopes that ſinners build
On works which their own hands have
wrought ;
The ciſtern is no ſooner fill'd,
But leaks it's miry waters out.

2.

Our aim no ſpiritual ſtore can bring,
No joy in God, or heavenly peace,
No loyal heart to Chriſt our king,
No faith that works and ſings of grace.

* 1 Tim. iii. 16. † Iſa. ix. 6. ‡ Pſ. xxii. 6.
§ Matt. ii. 11. ‖ Philip. ii. 10.

3. Unleſs

3.

Unless the Lord work on my heart,
Whate'er I seem, I nothing am,
Defiled still in ev'ry part,
And foul as from the womb I came.

4.

Then, O my God, thy help bestow,
And send the holy Spirit-down ;
Work in me both to *will* and *do,*
And let almighty grace be shewn.

5.

A nature give me, new and kind,
A broken spirit, meek and poor,
A lovely, child-like, waiting mind,
Which taps and calls at Jesu's door.

6.

The work of faith in me fulfil,
And daily send some gracious rain;
Conduct my soul to Calvary's hill,
And peace for me thou wilt ordain.

HYMN 153.

" Blessed are the poor in spirit, for their's is
the kingdom of heaven," Matt. v. 3.

1.

IN darkness born, I went astray,
And wander'd from the gospel-way;
And since the Saviour gave me sight,
I cannot see without his light.

T

2.

My limping feet are apt to trip,
And need a prop at every step;
If Jesus once let go his arm,
I fall and get some woful harm.

3.

I cannot walk without his might;
I cannot see without his light;
I can have no access to God
But thro' the merit of his blood.

4.

So poor, and blind, and lame I am,
My all is bound up in the Lamb;
And blessed am I, when I see
My spirit's inmost poverty.

5.

It makes me feel my ruin'd state,
It lays my soul at mercy's gate;
And Jesus smiles at such a guest,
And chears him with an heav'nly feast.

HYMN 154.

" Acquaint thyself with God, and be at
peace," Job xxii. 21.

1.

AND does my Maker condescend
To ask a worm to be his friend?
Will God forgive a rebel wild,
And make the hateful wretch his child?

2.

O height of grace, and depth of love!
Sure angels stand amaz'd above!
Amaz'd, that God with man should dwell,
A slave of sin, a child of hell!

3.

Oh, take this worthless heart, my God,
And rinse it in the Saviour's blood,
From earthly idols set it free,
And keep my breast intire for thee.

4.

In holy silence let me wait,
A daily watchman at thy gate,
And feel thy gracious presence near,
And all thy loving counsels hear.

5.

Much heart-acquaintance carry on,
'Till life it's hourly sands has run;
Then call me up to see thy face,
And sing eternal songs of grace.

HYMN 155.

" While the king sitteth at his table, my
spikenard sendeth forth the smell thereof,"
Song of Solomon i. 12.

1.

THE King of saints a table spreads
    For servants in his courts below,
And while with them he sits and feeds,
Not one distressing thought they know.

T 2

2.

His look enlivens every gueft,
Makes budding grace in bloffom rife,
Re-kindles love in every breaft,
And lifts the heart above the fkies.

3.

As morning funs refrefh the earth,
And make the bloffoms open fair,
And draw the balmy fragrance forth,
And fcatter odours thro' the air.

4.

So when the Sun of righteoufnefs
Arifeth on the plants of grace,
They fpring up into beauteous drefs,
And with their fongs perfume the place.

5.

O deareft, fweeteft, heavenly Friend,
The fpring of life and heav'nly joys,
Some look afford, or meffage fend,
Or all devotion quickly dies.

6.

No fragrance rifeth with our pray'r,
No fpices in our praifes found,
Unlefs the King himfelf appear,
And then the harp in tune is found.

HYMN 156.

"When pride cometh, then cometh shame,"
Prov. xi. 2.

1.

IN heav'n no hateful pride appears,
It cannot breathe on holy ground,
But covets damp unwholesome airs,
And in polluted breasts is found.

2.

The plague on angels first began,
And thrust 'em quickly down to hell.
Then stole upon aspiring man,
And pierc'd his soul, and down he fell.

3.

Let Jesu's simple flock beware,
Nor once surmize the danger o'er;
This deadly fruit is dazzling fair,
And hides it's canker in it's core.

4.

If once thy bosom catcheth fire,
Delighted with it's gifts or grace,
The Saviour drops thee in the mire,
And fastens shame upon thy face.

5.

O Jesus, save me from this foe,
A fiend with most enchanting smile,
Who stabs my bosom thro' and thro',
Yet can delight me all the while.

T 3

HYMN 157.

" Thy name is as ointment poured forth,
therefore do the virgins love thee,"
Song of Solomon i. 3.

1.

JESUS, how lovely is thy name,
  To virgin-hearts betroth'd to thee,
To all the poor, and sick, and lame,
Who thy salvation taste and see.

2.

Like precious ointment poured forth,
Thy name perfumes a faithful soul;
And by it's rich and fragrant worth
Revives and makes a sinner whole.

3.

It brings the hungry soul a feast,
Where all delightful dainties meet;
And when the royal chear we taste,
Oh! then thy name is charming sweet!

4.

No harmony so heals the heart,
No music so delights the ear,
No concert can such joy impart,
As thy melodious name to hear!

5.

It proves our daily joy and boast,
Our rock of hope and bulwark strong,
Our anchor when the ship is tost,
And will be our eternal song.

6.

Thy name, like vernal mornings, will
Seem always pleafant, always new,
And groweth dear and dearer ftill,
As we can take a clofer view.

HYMN 158.

" The hand of the diligent fhall bear rule,
    but the flothful fhall be under tribute,"
    Prov. xii. 24.

1.

YE followers of the Lamb give ear,
    And keep this counfel in your heart,
A diligent hand the rule fhall bear,
And flothful under tribute fmart.

2.

The man, who walks with jealous care,
And fix'd on Jefus keeps his eye,
And watcheth daily unto pray'r,
Shall find the Lord's help ever nigh.

3.

His inbred foes with rage may rife,
And kindle war within his breaft,
But Jefus Chrift will fend fupplies,
And make him rule and give him reft.

4.

But lazy fouls that live at large,
And lounge along with pray'rlefs pace,
Unmindful of the Saviour's charge,
Will find no help from Jefu's grace.

5.

Much gofpel-truth may croud the head,
No gofpel-grace their hearts controul,
But under tribute they are laid,
And tyrant-lufts oppress the foul.

6.

O Lord, aroufe my dronifh heart,
And make me fight and make me rule;
Elfe I fhall act a fluggard's part,
And prove at laft a gofpel-fool.

HYMN 159.

" Woe unto you, when all men fhall fpeak
well of you," Luke vi. 26.

1.

AN awful truth the Lord declares,
And meant to ftartle worldly ears,
A woe on fuch good people lays,
Whom all the world agree to praife.

2.

An earthly man feeks earthly fame,
Ambitious of the world's good name,
And much prefumeth on his caufe,
If it procures the world's applaufe.

3.

Yet if thy heart is right with God,
And finds it's peace from Jefu's blood,
If dead to pleafure thou fhalt be,
The world will take offence at thee.

4.

They love the men that decent are,
The tombs that shew a whitewash fair,
With such they walk and kindly prate,
But hearts renew'd by grace they hate.

5.

Lord, make me dead to all below,
Content to have the world my foe,
Content to hear 'em blaft my name,
Nor turn my head afide from shame.

6.

Keep worldly prudence from mine eyes,
And let me only Jesus prize,
Tread in the track by Jesus giv'n,
Purfu'd by scorn quite up to heav'n.

HYMN 160.

" Being ignorant of God's righteoufnefs,
and going about to eftablifh their own
righteoufnefs, they have not fubmitted
themfelves to the righteoufnefs of God,"
Rom. x. 3. " Even the righteoufnefs of
God which is (received) by faith in Jefus
Chrift, (imputed) unto all that believe,"
Rom. iii. 22. " Even as David de-
fcribeth the bleffednefs of the man, unto
whom God imputed righteoufnefs without works," Rom iv. 6. " And as Abraham is the father of all them that believe,
though they be not circumcifed, that

righteousness might be imputed to them also," Rom iv. 11. "So by the obedience of *one* shall many be made righteous," Rom. v. 19. "And that *one* is Jesus, whose name is, the Lord our righteousness," Jerem. xxiii. 6. "Wherefore believers sing this song, In the Lord have I righteousness: and in the Lord shall all the seed of Israel be justified and shall glory," Isa. xlv. 24, 25. "And David leads up the chorus with his harp, saying, I will make mention of thy righteousness, and of thine *only* (to justify me)" Psal. lxxi. 16.

1.

IMPUTED righteousness is strange,
Nor will with human fancies range;
We guess the lurking motive well,
And Paul the hateful truth shall tell.

2.

The lofty heart cannot *submit**
To cast itself at Jesu's feet;
It scorns in borrow'd robes to shine,
Tho' weav'd with righteousness divine.

3.

Proud nature cries, with loathing eyes,
This imputation I despise;
And from it she will pertly start,
Till grace has broken down her heart.

* Rom x 3.

4.

Oh, give me, Lord, thy righteousness
To be my peace and wedding-dress;
My sores it heals, my rags it hides,
And makes me dutiful besides.

HYMN 161.

"Without holiness no man shall see the
Lord," Heb. xii. 14.

1.

A Sinner's claim to heavenly bliss,
Rests on the Lord's own righteousness;
Our legal debts he came to clear,
And make a *title* full and fair.

2.

Yet holiness the heart must grace,
A *meetness* for his dwelling-place;
No filthy souls in heav'n appear,
They cannot breathe in holy air.

3.

The faith that feels the Saviour's blood,
And finds in Christ a title good,
Rebellious lusts will conquer too,*
And build the soul divinely new.

4.

And where no work of grace is wrought,
Nor holiness with hunger sought,
Such barren souls, with all their boast,
Are sinners dead, and sinners lost.

* 1 John v. 4.

5.

May Jefu's grace to me convey
Much pow'r to watch, and will to pray,
Much feeking of the things above,
Much ftore of faith, and fruits of love.

6.

More-broken hearted let me be,
And more devoted unto thee;
More fweet communion with thee find,
And more of all thy heavenly mind.

HYMN 162.

"Left we fhould *offend* them, go thou to the
fea and caft an hook, and take up the fifh
that firft cometh up, and when thou haft
opened his mouth, thou fhall find a piece
of money; that take, and give unto them
for me and thee," Matt. xvii. 27.

1.

NO tax on Jefus might be laid,
  Who was the Lord of earth and fkies;
Yet needlefs tribute Jefus paid,
And paid left fome *offence* fhould rife.

2.

Here, chriftian brother, paufe a while,
And on thy lovely pattern look;
Good foldiers march in rank and file,
And take the ftep their captain took.

3   Be

3.

Be guided by the Saviour's light,
And act with grace and gospel-sense;
Insist not on a meagre right,
For fear thou give the world offence.

4.

Where self prevails, and nature reigns,
The hand will grasp it's own till death;
But gracious men forego some gains,
To shew and recommend their faith.

5.

In Jesu's footsteps let me tread,
And not depend on gospel-talk;
But by his loving Spirit led,
Adorn the gospel by my walk.

6.

May heav'nly truth enlarge my mind,
And heav'nly love inspire my heart,
To make me gentle, meek and kind,
And with a small right freely part.

HYMN 163.

" *All things* are delivered unto me by my
Father — (therefore) come unto me,"
Matt. xi. 27, 28.

1.

ALL *things* a sinner wants below,
    All things the saints above receive;
All things the Father can bestow,
Are lodg'd in Jesu's hand to give.

U

2.

Supreme in heav'n the Man appears,
And rules with univerfal fway,
Guides all events thro' circling years,
And holds up all without decay.

3.

He calls and wakes the dead in fin,*
And gives repentance unto life; †
He brings the peace of God within, ‡
And trains the bride-maid for his wife.

4.

The Saviour calls, Come unto Me,
And reft your fouls upon the Lord;
All things are ready now for thee;
Eternal life is in my word.

5.

I come, O Lord, or perifh muft,
And thank thee for thy loving call;
My foul rejects all other truft,
And takes thee as my God, my all.

6.

Of thee I love to mufe and fing,
And thou wilt hear me when I pray;
My heart fays, Jefus is it's King,
And feeks and loves his gentle fway.

* John v. 25.   † Acts v. 35.
‡ John xiv. 27.

7.

Lord, guide the stewards how to speak
Of thy sweet person, and thy grace;
And draw the people, wise or weak,
To trust in thee, and seek thy face.

HYMN 164.

" What things soever ye desire, when ye
pray, believe that ye receive them, and
ye shall have them," Mark xi. 24.

1.

YE poor afflicted souls give ear,
  Who seek the Lord, but fear his
    frown;
What things ye ask in fervent pray'r,
Believe, and Christ will send 'em down,

2.

If sin is loathsome to thine heart,
And shews a most ill-favour'd face;
If guilt affords thee fearful smart,
It flows from Jesu's love and grace.

3.

A feast is now prepar'd for thee;
Reject it not by unbelief;
A feast of mercy, sweetly free
For sinners, and the sinners' chief.

4.

No guilt contracted by long years,
His tender mercies shall confine;
No bar but unbelief appears;
The pray'r of faith makes all things thine.

U 2

5.

Take courage then, afk and believe,
Expecting mercy from the Lord ;
The promife runs, Afk and receive,
And Chrift is faithful to his word.

6.

O Lord, increafe my feeble faith,
And give my ftraiten'd bofom room
To credit what thy promife faith,
And wait till thy falvation come.

HYMN 165.

" Bleffed be the Lord my ftrength, who
teacheth my hands to war — Thou art
my fhield, in whom I truft," Pfalm
clxiv. 1, 2.

1.

BESET I am with crafty foes;
  Which ftir up war againft my foul,
And hourly break my fweet repofe,
Nor can mine arm their rage control.

2.

My feeblenefs I clearly fee,
And fee my help on Jefus laid ;
And much I long to truft in thee,
But feel my heart is oft afraid.

3.

I reft not wholly on thine arm,
But heave my fhoulder to the fight ;
And then I furely meet fome harm,
My foes fall on, and flay me quite.

4.

Thine armour teach me how to wield,
To brandiſh well the Spirit's ſword,*
To lift up faith's victorious ſhield,
And caſt my burdens on the Lord.

5.

On thee be fix'd my aſking eye,
On thee be ſtay'd my helpleſs heart;
And let the Lord attend my cry,
And help, in time of need, impart.

H Y M N 166.

" Whoſo eateth my fleſh, and drinketh my
blood, hath eternal life," John vi. 54.

1.

TOO long, O Lord, my ſoul has fed
   On earthly traſh, on froth and air,
And farniſh'd by this huſky bread,
My heart cries out for better cheer.

2.

No more the world allures my ſight,
I bid it's ſtarving feaſt adieu;
No more my beſt works give delight,
I quit their fluttering merit too.

3.

Nor on the earth, nor in myſelf,
I find a ſingle meal of good;
Then reach my Bible from the ſhelf,
For there I find ſubſtantial food.

* Eph. vi. 17.

U 3

4.

The Saviour is a sumptuous mess;
His flesh, or living work, supplies
A naked soul with legal dress,
And gives him title to the skies.

5.

The garden-sweat, and stripes he bore,
The cross's wounds, and groans, and blood,
Revive the gospel sick and poor,
And feast 'em with the peace of God,

6.

Upon this banquet let me feed,
And find eternal life is mine;
For sure thy flesh is meat indeed,
And sure thy blood is heav'nly wine.

HYMN 167.

" Unite my heart, to fear thy name,"
Psalm lxxxvi. 11.

1.

HOW long, my Saviour, must I find
　A gadding heart, and roving eye?
Hast thou no charms my heart to bind,
To draw it near, and keep it nigh?

2.

E'er while I muse upon thy love,
And find it excellently sweet;
Yet soon my thoughts begin to rove
On some gay object that I meet.

3.

Of all I meet I weary grow,
Each roving step creates me pain;
Then turning unto thee I go,
But quickly start aside again.

4.

O Lord, unite my soul to thee,
A grafted branch in thy true Vine,
Nor let the branch a straggler be,
But round thy lovely person twine.

5.

With faithful claspers arm my heart,
And every lofty shoot retrench,
And to my clasping soul impart
Thy heav'nly sap to feed my branch.

6.

Thus nourish'd from thy kindly root,
And cleaving closely to thy stem,
My branch will bend with clust'ring fruit,
And glorify *thy gracious* name.

HYMN 168.

To the Trinity.

1.

FATHER, to thee we lift our voice,
Supremely wife, and just, and good,
Whose mercy makes our hearts rejoice,
Whose bounty fills our mouths with food.]

2.

When rebel man was doom'd to die,
Thy love reliev'd his ruin'd race,
And sent a Saviour from the sky,
To build a glorious throne of grace.

3.

Our Jesus is that heav'nly *word*,
Which all things form'd, and richly dreft,
The life in him did life afford
To angels, insects, man, and beaft.

4.

He tends us with a shepherd's care,
And paid our ranfom with his blood;
In him we live, and move, and are,
Hofanna to the Son of God!

5.

Spirit of wifdom, grace and pow'r!
Our comforter, and quick'ning fpring!
With Father, Son, thee faints adore,
And holy, holy, holy fing!

6.

Breathe on our fouls the breath of grace,
And feed the lamp of love within,
Reveal the Father's fmiling face,
And quicken finners dead in fin.

HYMN 169.

" Mark the upright man, for the end of
that man is peace," Pfalm xxxvii. 37.

1.

HOW finners pafs their life away!
A fhort and mirthful time it feems,
In riot fpent, or childifh play;
But death will end their pleafant dreams!
And late, too late they learn to mourn,
When bound in bundles up to burn.

2.

But upright men the Lord obey,
And walk diftinguifh'd from the croud;
And if a ftorm perplex the day,
Their fun fhall fet without a cloud;
Behold they die in Jefu's peace!
Sweet earneft of eternal blifs!

3.

Then give me, Lord, this *upright* heart,
Well nurtur'd with a godly fear,
Which from thy precepts will not ftart,
When clouds and threat'ning ftorms appear,
But march along with even pace,
Refrefh'd and fortify'd by grace.

4.

Let active faith infpire my breaft,
And love conftrain me by it's pow'r,
And, Jefus, let me find thy reft
In every fharp afflicting hour,

And sing thy love with fervent breath,
When passing thro' the vale of death.

HYMN 170.

"In chains they shall come after thee (Jesus),
and shall fall down, and make supplica-
tion unto thee, saying, *Surely God is in
thee*," Isaiah xlv. 14.

1.

WHILE sinners wander far from peace,
    And feel no deadly harm in sin,
Deaf ears they turn to calls of grace,
And wallow on in works unclean,
To Jesus Christ they make no moan,
And his true Godhead oft disown.

2.

But if the Lord give heav'nly light,
A sinner learns to fear and feel;
He sees in sin a loathsome sight,
And knows it's damning nature well;
And finds himself so fast a slave,
That nothing less than God can save.

3.

He comes a captive bound in chains,
And humbly falls at Jesu's feet,
And of his heart and guilt complains,
And peeps upon the mercy-seat,
Beholds the Lord with open'd eye,
And in the man his God can spy.

4.

At length the sprinkled blood appears,
Which in the heart sheds love abroad,
And sweetly bringing gracious tears,
He cries, it is the *blood* of *God!**
I feel it's virtue, and I know
That *God is surely in thee* now.

HYMN 171.

" O house of Jacob, come ye, and let us
walk in the light of the Lord," Isa. ii. 5.

1.

VAIN mortals seek no better sight
Than what their own dim eyes afford;
They blow up sparks to give them light,
Regardless of the *written word* ;
But such in sorrow shall lay down,†
And find their sparks extinguish'd soon.

2.

But, *O ye House of Jacob, come,*
And in the light of Jesus walk;
His heav'nly sun must guide you home,
And you of him should think and talk;
His word, with pray'r devoutly read,
Will plant new eyes within your head.

3.

Come, let us seek more light of faith,
To chear the heart, and guide the feet,

* Acts xx. 28.   † Isai. l. 11.

To keep us from the shades of death,
And open wide the mercy-seat:
Each act of faith will faith increase,
And kindle up a brighter peace.

4.

Lord, warm us well with holy fire,
And sweetly thaw the frozen breast;
Bid every heart approach thee nigh'r,
And daily seek and find thy rest;
Walk in the light of Jefu's face,
And sweetly feast upon his grace.

HYMN 172.

" When he (the Spirit of truth) *is come*, he
will convince the world of sin, because
they *believe not* on Me," John xvi. 8, 9.

1.

NO awful fense we find of sin,
    The sinful *life* and sinful *heart*;
No loathing of the plague within,
Until the Lord that feel impart;
But when the Spirit of truth *is come*,
A sinner trembles at his doom.

2.

Convinc'd and pierced thro' and thro',
He thinks himself the sinner chief;
And confcious of his mighty woe,
Perceives at length his *unbelief*;
Good creeds may stock his head around,
But in his heart no faith is found.

I   3. No

3.

No pow'r his nature can afford
To change his heart, or purge his guilt;
No help is found but in the Lord,
No balm but in the blood he spilt;
A ruin'd soul, condemn'd he stands,
And unto Jesus lifts his hands.

4.

So lift I up my hands and eyes,
And all my help in Jesus seek;
Lord, bring thy purging sacrifice
To wash me white, and make me meek;
And give me more enlarged faith,
To view the wonders of thy death.

HYMN 173.

" When the Spirit of Truth is come, he
will convince the world of (my) righteousness, because I go to the Father,
and ye *see me no more*," John xvi. 8, 10.

1.

A Righteous garment much we want,
To clothe and beautify the soul;
Not rent and patch'd, or light and scant,
But one full piece, and fair and whole;
The *perfect law* such coat demands,
And on the coat our *title* stands.

2.

Such coat our Jesus wove for us,
To hide a naked sinner's shame,

W

Up from the cradle to the crofs
He toiled only in our name ;
And wrought the garment rich and good,
And dying dipt it in his blood.

3.

No more on earth the Lord comes down,
A proof the robe was made complete ;
And we muft have the Lord's coat on,
Or much afham'd the Lord fhall meet :
Yet till the Spirit fhews our cafe,
We loathe *imputed* righteoufnefs.

4.

Put on me, Lord, thy goodly robe
To hide my rags and naked breaft ;
Not all the worth of all the globe,
Can make me fair without thy veft :
In Jefu's righteoufnefs I truft,
And *his obedience* makes me *juft.**

HYMN 174.

" When the Spirit of Truth is come, He
will convince the world of judgment,
becaufe the prince of this world is
judged," John xvi. 8, 11.

1.

NO man with all his wit can know
How poor and wretched is his cafe ;
He neither feels his inbred woe,
Nor fees a need of Jefu's grace :

* Rom. v. 19.

The Holy Spirit must impart
Such truth, and seal it on his heart.

2.

In Sunday church, and outward deeds
The most of man's religion lays;
He will not seek, or think he needs
A bosom fill'd with love and praise:
A tyrant foul his heart obeys,
And much approves the tyrant's ways.

3.

But when the Spirit of Truth is come,
And shews the serpent in his breast;
The lawless lusts that wanton roam,
And tempers fierce that break his rest;
With lifted hands and earnest eyes,
Create my heart anew, he cries.

4.

So prays my heart to thee, O God;
The serpent's wicked seat pull down,
And sprinkle it with Jefu's blood,
And there erect thy gracious throne:
An holy heart for heav'n is meet,
Thro' Christ my title is complete.

HYMN 175.

" The mixt multitude fell a lusting, and
the children of Israel also wept, and said,
Who shall give us flesh to eat ? Our soul
is now dried away, and there is nothing
at all besides this manna before our eyes,"
Numb. xi. 4, 6.

1.

WHEN tidings new of gospel-grace
    First strike upon a list'ning cloud,
With tears and sighs the guilty race
Cry out aloud for Jesu's blood ;
They hunger much for heav'nly bread,
And sweet the manna seems indeed !

2.

But if the gospel-seed is sown
In stony or in thorny ground,
The heavenly cry is quickly gone,
When storms begin to gather round ;
The bread is dry, they now complain,
And pine for Egypt's leeks again.

3.

Such lustings oft the children taint,
And make them fretful, sick, and weak ;
A softer preaching now they want,
And ramble far to find a leek ,
Or trench themselves in doctrines deep,
Lay down their arms, and fall asleep.

4.

From all such lusting save me, Lord,
And wholesome appetite create;
Thy manna in much love afford,
And make me find it dainty meat;
No more for Egypt's garlick pine,
But sweetly on thy manna dine.

HYMN 176.

"A rod for a fool's back," Prov. xxvi. 3.

1.

I Wonder not, if giddy men
Run roving all the world about,
Pursuing folly with much pain,
And weary'd oft, yet give not out;
The world must be their fluttering aim,
Who see no charm in Jesu's name.

2.

Yet none so foolish are and base,
As they who felt the legal lash,
And having tasted gospel-grace,
Good manna leave for earthly trash:
When such from wisdom's teaching start,
A rod shall make their shoulders smart.

3.

In vain they seek the world's relief,
The Lord will weary them with woe,
And lash them well with grief on grief,
With rods and stinging scorpions too:

W 3

They drink of ev'ry bitter cup,
Till sick, they cast their idols up.

4.

My heart too after idols sought,
And roved from the gospel-track;
And by such rovings I have brought
A thousand stripes upon my back;
Lord, take my foolish heart at last,
And guide it right, and hold it fast.

HYMN 177.

" Turn away thine eyes from me, for they
    have overcome me," Cant. vi. 5.

1.

THOU poor, afflicted, tempted soul,
   With fears and doubts, and tempests tost,
What if the billows rise and roll,
And dash thy ship, it is not lost:
The winds and waves, and fiends may roar,
But Christ will bring thee safe on shore.

2.

What ail those eyes bedew'd with tears,
Those labouring sighs that heave thy breast,
Those oft repeated broken pray'rs?
Dost thou not long for Jesu's rest?
And can the Lord pass heedless by,
And see a mourning sinner die?

3.

Alas, thou art a stranger yet
To Jesu's sympathizing heart;

When finners mourn and clafp his feet,
In all their grief he bears a part;
His bowels melt at ev'ry cry,
And while they groan, he gives a figh.

4.

If once the wound is ripe to heal,
A balm fhall make thy heart-rejoice,
The Saviour will thy pardon feal,
And whifper with enchanting voice,
" Oh, turn away thofe weeping eyes,
" Thou haft o'ercome me with thy cries."

HYMN 178.

" Ye cannot ferve God and Mammon,"
Matt. vi. 24.

1.

THE heart by nature earthly is,
And from the earth it's comfort draws,
No tafte it has for heav'nly blifs,
No love for Jefus and his caufe;
To church the man may faunt'ring come,
But leaves his carnal heart at home.

2.

As well may heat with coldnefs dwell,
And light with darknefs come abroad,
As foon may heav'n unite with hell,
As man may ferve the world and God:
Until the heart's created new,
It fhrinks from God, and hates him too.

3.

And where the falt of grace appears,
To feafon all the inward part,
If wanton mirth, or thorny cares,
Or idols bafe beguile the heart,
A lumpifh frame the pilgrim feels,
And drives without his chariot-wheels.

4.

From fordid Mammon, fave me, Lord,
It's pining cares, and gaudy mirth,
From all the traps it can afford,
And all the bafenefs it brings forth;
From all it's idols fet me free,
And make my heart intire for thee.

HYMN 179.

" The companions hearken to thy voice;
caufe me to hear it," Cant. viii. 13.

1.

MY heart would quickly weary be
Of him, who fhould no anfwer make,
Nor caft a chearful look on me;
Such filence muft communion break:
Nor could my heart in Chrift rejoice,
Unlefs it heard his chearing voice.

2.

No wonder finners weary grow
Of praying to an *unknown* God,
Such heartlefs pray'r is all dumb fhow,
And makes them liftlefs, yawn, and nod;

The voice of God they cannot hear,
Till Jesus gives the *waken'd* ear.*

3.

Such waken'd ear the sheep receive,
Despised flock of Jesu's fold,
His voice they hear and well perceive,†
And sweet communion with him hold;
Yet all *communion* is absurd,
If God is neither felt nor heard.

4.

This voice the scorners much deride,
And pass it off as godly cant;
Yet let me hear no voice beside,
'Tis all I wish, and all I want;
It sure creates my present peace,
And brings a pledge of future bliss.

HYMN 180.

" The carnal mind is enmity against God,"
Rom. viii. 7.

1.

THE natural man with carnal mind
    Seeks only from the world his food;
What earthly joy, his heart can find,
He takes, and makes his sov'reign good;
Delights in pleasure, wealth, and fame,
And wonders all do not the same.

* Isai. l. 4, 5.   † John x. 27.

2.

Poffeft with fuch felf-feeking view,
The carnal mind abhors reftraint,
Will tread on law and gofpel too,
And loathe the very found of faint;
Yet oft he fears a fcourging rod,
Which makes him hate the holy God.

3.

Devotion puts their heart in pain;
How can they pray to one they hate?
Yet think, oh think, ye foolifh men,
An hated God how can ye meet?
No carnal heart with God can dwell,
It makes a finner ripe for hell.

4.

O Lord, a fpiritual mind impart,
To lift my thoughts to things above,
To give new relifh to my heart,
And light the lamp of heav'nly love,
To make my foul with thee unite,
And in thy holy law delight.

HYMN 181.

" Awake, O fword, againft my Shepherd,
againft the man that is my *fellow* (my
equal) faith the Lord of Hofts," Zech.
xiii. 7.

1.

A Wake, O fword, with vengeance wake,
Againft the man, my *fellow* found;

Ruſh on him, make his bowels quake,
And gaſh him well with ghaſtly wound;
Aſſault his hands, his feet, and head,
Then pierce his heart, and ſtrike him dead.

2.

My fellow is that wondrous man,
In whom is found my awful name,*
Eternal with a mortal ſpan,
Almighty with a feeble frame ! †
The man can bleed, the God atone,
And both ſhall build my gracious throne.

3.

O Lord of Hoſts, and God of love !
We bleſs thee for this act of grace :
Amazing mercy ſure we prove
Tewards a loſt rebellious race,
Which bid the ſword awake and ſmite
Thine only Son, thy heart's delight !

4.

And, O thou bleeding Love divine !
What tender pity fill'd thy breaſt,
To take my hell and make it thine,
And toil thro' death to bring me reſt !
Eternal praiſe to thee be giv'n
By all on earth, and all in heav'n.

* Exod. xxiii. 21. † Iſa. ix. 6.

HYMN 182.

" My son, be ftrong in the grace that is in
Chrift Jefus," 2 Tim. ii. 1.

1.

A Child of earth, untaught of God,
 Would fain be ftrong in nature's might,
And learn to walk the heav'nly road
By human ftrength and human light,
And vainly thinks a wither'd arm
May well defend his breaft from harm.

2.

A new born child to God will cry,
Of all his earthly props bereav'd,
And feeks from heav'n a rich fupply,
Yet lives at firft on grace *receiv'd*,
Is happy when his comforts dawn,
But faints when fun-fhine is withdrawn.

3.

At length the child is better taught,
And lives not on it's gracious hoard,
But, with more heav'nly wifdom fraught,
Lives on the grace in Jefus ftor'd;
Looks up to Jefus every hour,
And refts upon his love and pow'r.

4.

So let my foul on Jefus reft,
And with his comforts be fupply'd ;

1   And

And while his love conftrains my breaft,
Lean on the man that lov'd and dy'd;
Not refting on a comfort-prop,
But on the Lord my ftrength and hope.

HYMN 183.

" If a man ftrive for the maftery, yet is he
not crowned, except he ftrive *lawfully*."
2 Tim. ii. 5.

1.

MUCH haplefs pains fome mortals take
To build their houfe upon the fand;
With fruitlefs ftruggling ftrive to make
The heart fubmit to God's command;
And by fome faucy merit find
A balm to heal the troubled mind!

2.

If man may wafh the black Moor white,
Or make the leopard change his fpots,
Then he may plant his heart upright,
And cleanfe the confcience from it's blots:
Such buildings make Apollyon fmile,
And mock the foolifh builder's toil.

3.

In *lawful* way the foul muft build,
And Chrift the *lawful way* is found;
His precious blood on Calvary fpill'd,
Alone can heal a guilty wound;
His Spirit turns the tempers right,
And makes the heart in God delight.

X

4.

The lawful way I learn to prize,
And well I may, 'tis rich with gain:
Here let me walk with stedfast eyes,
And gather ease from Jesu's pain;
Still look to him to mend my heart,
And feel he acts a Saviour's part.

HYMN 184.

" God hath exalted this (man) Jesus, to be
a Prince and a Saviour, for to *give re-*
pentance to Israel, and *remission* of sins,"
Acts v. 31. Luke xxiv. 47.

1.

HOW oft we hear vain sinners talk
   Of mighty things their hands can do,
To change the heart, and guide the walk,
And give themselves repentance too;
And by such works of human might
Atonement make for sin outright.

2.

A lean repentance sinners find,
Which their own will and wisdom breed;
It cannot break the sturdy mind,
And will a fresh repentance need;
This humbling grace we must *receive,*
And Jesus must repentance *give.*

3.

A gift it is, which none can earn!
A gift, which Jesus must bestow!

I

And Jefus makes a mourner learn
That all things from his bounty flow,
Then *grants forgivene/s* thro' his blood,
And makes falvation underftood.

4.

What human ftrength cannot procure,
Of Jefus Chrift I muft entreat,
An heart well broken, meek and poor,
Which lays and fawns upon his feet;
But let my Lord his peace impart,
To warm and chear the broken heart.

HYMN 185.

" Thus faith the Lord thy *Redeemer*, I am
the Lord *thy God*, who teacheth thee to
profit," Ifai. xlviii. 17.

1.

AN able teacher much I need,
Who fweetly can allure my heart,
And in the path of duty lead,
Or fetch me back, if I fhould ftart:
Much human teachers I have try'd,
And find I want an abler guide.

2.

Rough ftorms arife within my breaft,
And beat all human counfel down;
And only he can give me reft,
Who ftills them with a word or frown;
Then fure to Jefus I muft look,
For ftorms are ftill, at his rebuke.

3.

His voice divine can rouse the dead,
And such a voice would suit me well;
For oft I drop my drowsy head,
And not a spark of life can feel;
And when the spiritual feel is gone,
My earthly heart can give me none.

4.

His voice will help the blind to see,
The lame to leap, the deaf to hear!
Then only Jesus Christ for me;
None other can with him compare!
His teaching will revive my heart,
And eyes, and ears, and feet impart.

HYMN 186.

" If the prophets had caused my people to
hear *my words*, then they should have
turned the people from their *evil way*,"
Jer. xxiii. 21, 22.

1.

HEAR, O ye priests of Aaron's house,
This message sure is meant for you;
To Jesu's word be true and close,
Or you shall toil and nothing do,
Shall much exhort, rebuke, and pray,
Yet none forsakes his evil way.

2.

The strictest morals you may teach,
And wet your sermon-case with tear,

Yet nothing will the confcience reach,
And no good fruit will yet appear;
The liftlefs flocks will doze around,
Unlefs they hear a gofpel-found.

3.

If much your heart has been perplext
To find the Sunday-teaching vain;
And at the flock's fupinenefs vext,
Have felt a tender Shepherd's pain;
Then take good counfel from the Lord,
" Your fermon fuits not with *his word.*"

4.

Lift up your voice and cry aloud,
And fhew to Jacob's houfe their fin;
Proclaim to all the yawning croud,
Your hearts and lives are all unclean;
And tell with ftouteft look and breath,
The wages due to fin is death.

5.

When fin and guilt are underftood,
To Jefus Chrift direct their eye;
And preach a pardon thro' his blood,
And bid them on his grace rely,
And bid them afk in earneft pray'r
For peace, and love, and godly fear.

6.

So will the Lord your labours own,
And dig and dung the fallow-ground;
From gofpel-feed, when truly fown,
Some heavenly crop will fure be found;

Good morals will fpring up and fhoot,
When grafted on a gofpel-root.

HYMN 187.

"Our Father, who art in heaven!"
Matt. vi. 9.

1.

THOU great and good, and wife and true,
 The firft and laft, and Lord of all,
A God majeftic we can view,
Yet him a tender parent call ;
With kind affection taught to fay,
"Our Father," when we kneel to pray.

2.

Our Father's throne is on the fky,
And heavenly hofts around him dwell,
And he beholds with piercing eye,
All things on earth, and things in hell,
Beholds with fharp and awful ken
The workings in the hearts of men !

3.

O *Father*, give me love to thee,
And love to all thy children dear,
And thy free love reveal to me,
Attefted by thy Spirit clear,
Thro' Jefus take me for thy child,
And make me lowly, meek, and mild.

4.

Our *Father*, who in heaven art !
Direct my eyes up to thy throne,

And bless me with a praying heart,
And lively faith in thy dear Son.
A stranger make me here on earth,
To shew the world my heavenly birth.

HYMN 188.

"Hallowed be thy name," Matt. vi. 9.

1.

O Father, tell the world thy fame,
And shew them what Jehovah is,
A God, unchangeably the same,
Of perfect truth and righteousness,
Who built up all things at his will,
And reigneth on his heavenly hill!

2.

Behold! the heathen still adore.
A carved god of wood and stone!
Arise, Jehovah, and restore
The worship due to thee alone;
Be jealous for thy own renown,
And cast the breathless idols down.

3.

But Christians act a baser part,
Who much a carved god disdain,
Yet rear up idols in their heart,
And take thine awful name in vain!
Plant in their breast a godly fear,
And make thy name be honour'd there.

4.

Jehovah, send thy Spirit forth,
And light and saving health impart,
That all the ends of all the earth
May know how great and good thou art,
Thy lofty name with reverence treat,
And learn to worship at thy feet.

HYMN 189.

" Thy kingdom come," Matt. vi. 10.

1.

O Father, let thy kingdom come,
    Thy kingdom built on love and grace,
In every province give it room,
In every heart afford it place;
The earth is thine, set up thy throne,
And claim the kingdoms as thine own.

2.

Still nature's horrid darkness reigns,
And sinners scorn the check of fear;
Still Satan holds the heart in chains,
Where Jesu's messengers appear!
We pray that Christ may rise and bless
The world with truth and righteousness.

3.

Bid war and wild ambition cease,
And man no more a monster prove;
Fill up his breast with heavenly peace,
And warm it well with heavenly love,

To Jesus bid the people go,
And Satan's kingdom overthrow.

4.

More labourers in the vineyard send,
And pour thine unction on them all;
Give them a voice to shake and bend
The mountains high, and cedars tall,
That flocks of sinners, young and old,
May shelter seek in Jesu's fold.

HYMN 190.

" Thy will be done on earth, as it is in
heaven," Matt. vi. 10.

1.

O Father, where thy truth is spread,
And brings the light of gospel-day,
Thy holy Spirit richly shed,
And sweet transforming grace convey;
New cast the heart in gospel-mould,
And stamp thine image fair and bold.

2.

Root out the carnal selfish mind,
Averse to thee and thy command,
And plant a will and temper kind,
A ready foot and liberal hand,
With mind alert, and waiting still
To hear and do thy holy will.

3.

As angels in thy courts above
Pay suit and service to their King,

And all thy pleasure hear and love,
And execute with rapid wing;
So may we move, so may we feel,
Pick up their wing, and catch their zeal.

4.

When burdens sore of pain or loss
Are on the feeble shoulder thrown,
Instruct us how to bear the cross
Without a peevish look or groan;
And in the furnace while we lay,
Let all our dross be purg'd away.

HYMN 191.

" *Give* us this day our daily bread,"
Matt. vi. 11.

1.

OUR Father, unto thee we cry,
  Give us this day our daily bread,
And with a gracious hand supply.
Whate'er thy helpless children need ;
With daily wants beset we are,
And need thy providential care.

2.

If hungry ravens, when they croak,
And ravenous lions, when they roar,
Do find their food by thee bespoke,
And are replenish'd from thy store!
He, who for birds and beasts will carve,
Can never let his children starve.

3.

We only afk for *this* day's food ;
And afk for bread, not dainty meat ;
But fare that homely is and good,
Such as the hungry child may eat ;
Nor dare we afk it thro' defert,
But as a *gift*, the bread impart.

4.

And if the carcafe has it's meal,
The lamp within of heavenly fire,
Some daily feeding needeth ftill,
Or quickly muft the lamp expire ;
Refrefh the lamp, to make it fhine,
And feed the foul with bread divine.

H Y M N 192.

" Forgive us our debts, as we forgive our
debtors," Matt. vi. 12.

1.

O Father, much we are in debt,
Much failing in obedience due,
And daily running deeper yet ;
Paft follies multiply'd by new !
Nor compenfation can we bring,
For all we have, we owe the King.

2.

The wages due to fin is death ;
A deep and ghaftly debt to pay !
And yet we fin with daily breath ;
O Lord, our God, what fhall we fay ?

Forgive the vaſt and deadly ſum,
Nor let the threaten'd vengeance come.

3.

If awful juſtice draw the ſword,
And aim it at my guilty breaſt,
Let ſmiling mercy help afford,
And interpoſe to make me bleſt;
And mercy wins, if ſhe intreat,
For Jeſus is my mercy-ſeat.

4.

With gracious heart I would forgive,
When debtors have no mite to pay,
Nor drag them in a gaol to live,
But ſend the bankrupts clear away;
So let my Father deal with me,
And ſtrike my debts off full and free.

H Y M N 193.

" And *lead* us not into temptation, but deliver us from *evil*," Matt, vi. 13.

1.

O Father, ſave me from the ſnares
Which would to ſure temptation *lead*,
From wealthy pride, or hungry cares,
And with the food convenient feed;
Leſt I be rich, and thee blaſpheme,
Or needy, and diſtruſt thy name.

2.

I find a much rebellious will,
And ſelfiſh tempers moſt unkind;

A load

A load of unbelief I feel,
And pride before me and behind;
Much evil in my heart I fee,
Lord, from it's plague deliver me.

3.

Allurements in the world are found,
To court me from the gofpel-road;
And evil men, in pleafure drown'd,
Would draw or drive my heart from God;
With fubtil baits the world is ftrown,
Lord, fave me from it's fmile and frown.

4.

A wicked tempter too unfeen
Will craftily befiege mine ear,
And with a gay or frightful mein
Would breed prefumption or defpair;
All human mifchief he has done;
Lord, fave me from this evil one.

HYMN 194.

" For thine is the kingdom, and the power,
and the glory, for ever. Amen." Matt. vi. 13.

1.

O Father, caft a gracious eye
    Upon thy children, as they pray;
In mercy all our wants fupply,
And all our fins put far away:
Our fins and wants are not a few;
Yet what will not a Father do?

Y

2.

We have been Satan's subjects true,
His tempers shewn and ugly face,
But now we seek a kingdom new,
Of mercy, peace, and righteousness;
Thine is the kingdom, which we crave,
And what is thine a child may have.

3.

But not the hand of human might
Can rear this kingdom in my heart,
Nor can the head of human wit
A single gem or pearl impart;
Thine is the pow'r to set it up,
Nor can it fail with such a prop.

4.

The kingdom is thy work and care;
Thine is the glory, thine alone!
Which raiseth hope in every pray'r,
That God will see the work is done:
The glory thine! we shout again,
And will be *ever* thine; *Amen.*

HYMN 195.

" The loftiness of man shall be bowed down,
and the Lord *alone* shall be exalted in
that day," Isai. ii. 17.

1.

IN that sweet day of dawning grace,
When Jesus gives a sinner light,
He first perceives his ugly face,
And stands amazed at the sight!

His sins, a frightful number too,
And quite forgot, start up in view.

2.

His former lofty looks are gone,
His fancy'd merit all is lost,
His haughty heart is bowed down,
The Lord *alone* is all his trust;
On Jesus Christ he turns his eyes,
And hungers for the sacrifice.

3.

And now he loathes his filthy heart,
It's sore and sickness taught to feel;
And now he owns his sin's desert,
Convinc'd it's proper wage is hell;
And now for mercy sweetly cries,
The mercy he could once despise.

4.

And now the Saviour precious is,
The chief among ten thousand fairs;
And when he feels the cross's peace,
His eyes are wet with gracious tears,
And loud he sings in lovely tone,
Hosanna to *the Lord alone*.

HYMN 196.

"My foul cleaveth unto the duft, quicken
thou me," Pfalm cxix. 25.

1.

HOW damp and earthly is my heart!
How apt thro' floth to gather ruft!
From Jefus Chrift it loves to ftart,
And like a child, roll in the duft!
This hour, perhaps, is heav'n-ward bound,
The next, is burrowing under ground.

2.

I cannot hold my heart, I feel,
All tricks I try, but all in vain;
It flips my hand, much like an eel,
And flides into the mud again;
And there would lay and famifh too,
In fpite of all that I can do.

3.

But, O my Lord, thy check it fears,
And pays obedience to thy word;
Thy foft commanding voice it hears,
And hearing fprings up to the Lord,
Shakes off it's duft, and claps it's wings;
And foars aloft, and fweetly fings.

4.

If thou wilt take my heart in hand,
And lodge it near thy bleeding breaft,
It muft and will adoring ftand,
And cling and clafp the Saviour faft;

Forget it's kindred to the earth,
And triumph in it's heavenly birth.

HYMN 197.

" Where the carcafe is, there will the
eagles be gathered together," Matt.
XXIV. 28.

1.

MY Jefus crucify'd and flain,
A noifome carcafe is to moft;
A loathed food and flighted gain,
By men in mirth and pleafure loft;
Who bafely fpurn the holy feaft,
Or pafs it heedlefs by at leaft.

2.

But where the Saviour brings his light,
And gives the foul an eagle-eye,
The carcafe is a pleafing fight,
And draws the hovering eagles nigh;
They ken the banquet of his death,
And on the carcafe feed by faith.

3.

This banquet only fuits the poor,
Who feed, and full contentment find;
Borne up with eagles-wing they foar,
And leave all earthly thought behind;
Forget their woe, and drop their care,
And fing and breathe in heavenly air.

Y 3

4.

Upon thy carcafe let me feed,
And richly prize the feaft divine;
For fure thy flefh is meat indeed,
And fure thy blood is choiceft wine;
And all, who learn to banquet here,
No fting in death fhall feel or fear.

H Y M N 198.

" And Noah went into the ark, and his
wife, and his fons, and his fon's wives,
and fome of beafts clean, and unclean,
and of fowls, and of every creeping
thing," Gen. vii. 7, 8.

1.

JESUS, my heavenly ark thou art,
    My Noah too, my gofpel reft;
Thou calleft fome of every fort,
Of cleanly and of unclean beaft;
And beafts, tho' furious fierce before,
Come at thy call, and feek the door.

2.

The door is fixed in thy *fide*,*
And *fafely* thou doft fhut them in,†
Subdue their rage, and quell their pride,
And make them kind, and wafh them clean:
At length on Mount Ararat's top,‡
They land and view their heavenly hope.

* Gen. vi. 16. † Gen. vii. 16. ‡ Gen. vii. 4.

3.

Some gentle call I feel of grace,
And foftly to thine ark repair;
But fuch a monfter rough and bafe,
As never yet came waddling there;
Of wanton heart, and growling throat,
A mefs of lion, bear, and goat!

4.

If in thine ark I may be hid,
Transform the lion to a lamb,
The bear into a kindly kid,
And bid the goat a fheep become;
Then land me on the heavenly mount,
And loud I will thy love recount.

HYMN 199.

"Thou art weighed in the ballance, and
found wanting," Dan. v. 27.

1.

HEAR, O my foul, what God has faid,
And let thine ear retain the found,
"In fcales of juftice thou art weigh'd,
"And in the ballance wanting found!"
Stern juftice cries, thou art undone,
And where canft thou for fafety run?

2.

To Jefus, Father, I will fly,
And in his full atonement truft,
Confefs myfelf condemn'd to die,
And own the awful fentence juft,

Cry out againſt my guilty head,
And Jeſu's mighty merit plead.

3.

Convinc'd I am that warmeſt pray'rs,
And kindeſt ſervice I can pay,
And floods of penitential tears,
Will never waſh my guilt away;
My every action is too light,
And death is due for want of weight.

4.

But if no merit I can claim,
The blood of Jeſus will prevail,
Alone prevail to ſave from blame,
And in my favour turn the ſcale;
Thro' faith in him I ſtand complete,
Who undertook and paid my debt.

H Y M N 200.

" Wait ye upon me, ſaith the Lord, until the
  day that I riſe up to the prey," Zeph. iii. 8.

1.

O Thou with battering tempeſt toſt,
    Perplex'd and ſhatter'd here and there,
Bewilder'd on a *legal* coaſt,
And finding no deliverance near,
On Jeſus calling with ſad thought,
But Jeſus ſeems to mind thee not!

2.

To furious beaſts thou art a prey,
Which yell, and make an hideous din,

And rend thy bofom night and day,
And leave no room for peace within;
Difcover'd is thy beaftly heart,
And guilty terrors make thee ftart!

3.

Soon as thy heart can moaning cry,
What muft a wretched finner do?
To Jefus lift thy weary eye,
For whither elfe can finners go?
And Jefus will not fail thy hope,
But *on him wait*, till he rife up.

4.

He will rife up the prey to take,
His mighty arm he will make bare,
He will, for his own mercy-fake,
Bereave thee of thy guilty fear,
And tame the beafts within thy breaft,
But *on him wait*, till he give reft.

HYMN 201.

"He (Jefus) fhall build my city, not for
price nor reward, faith the Lord of hofts,"
Ifai. xlv. 13.

1.

A Ruin'd fabric man is found,
Where once Jehovah fix'd his throne,
But fin profan'd the holy ground,
It's great inhabitant is gone,
The heart a tyrant now receives,
Who makes the breaft a den of thieves!

2.

A thousand men with subtil wit
A thousand simple tricks have try'd,
To mend the house, and furnish it,
But Satan all their wit defy'd;
He laugh'd to see such weakness shewn,
And puff'd the paper-building down

3.

No one but Jesus Christ can build,
The work divine is all his own;
His arm with matchless strength is fill'd
To lay the ground and crowning stone;
A workman by the Lord *prepar'd*,
Who builds the house *without reward*.

4.

Thou, O my Jesus, build for me
An house to stand the rudest shock,
Completely furnished by thee,
And grounded on thyself, the Rock;
But build the house, an house of pray'r,
And let me feel my Father there.

H Y M N 202.

" He (Jesus) shall let go my captives, not
for price nor reward, *saith the Lord of
hosts,*" Isai. xlv. 13.

1.

SAY, wast thou not a captive born,
And art thou not a captive led,

With fetters loaded every morn,
And chained down each night in bed?
Do not thy lusts befet thee ftill,
And take thee captive at their will!

2.

Do not rough tempers, proud and bafe,
Infult and rend thy helplefs foul?
And what can tame the lufts, but grace,
Or what the tempers will control?
No man has wit or might enough,
To file a fingle fetter off.

3.

We hear indeed of wondrous men,
Who boaft of fkill and valour brave,
To fnap at will the ftouteft chain,
Who yet fhall live and die a flave;
The work for Jefus is prepar'd,
Who does the work without reward.

4.

His blood muft purge the confcience clean,
And fhew a reconciled God;
His Spirit write the law within,
And guide us on the gofpel-road;
And all, that feek to him, fhall know
That Jefus *lets the captives go.*

HYMN 203.

" O God, my God, early will I seek *thee*,"
Psalm lxiii. 1.

1.

A Godliness which feeds on form,
    And lip-devotion, barren cheer,
Will satisfy an earthly worm,
Who learns to think and call it pray'r;
Contented with the husky part,
A moving lip, and silent heart.

2.

All such of praying weary grow,
Where God with no desire is sought,
It proves a scene of dreary woe,
Without a single chearing thought!
No presence of the Lord they find,
But all is dull, and dead, and blind.

3.

O Lord, thy Spirit's aid impart,
And fill me with devotion's fire;
Create anew my earthly heart,
And heavenly breathings there inspire;
Bid heart and flesh cry out for thee,
And thou my joyful portion be!

4.

Let incense smoking from my breast
In praise and pray'r ascend thy hill;

And

And where I rove, or where I reft,
Do thou, my God, furround me ftill;
My heavenly intercourfe increafe,
Till as a river, flows my peace.

HYMN 204.

" The grace of the Lord Jefus Chrift, and
the love of God, and the communion of
the Holy Spirit, be with you all. Amen."
2 Cor. xiii. 14.

1.

WE blefs the lovely, bleeding Lamb,
The Saviour of a finful race;
A man, and yet the great *I am*,*
Procuring caufe of gofpel-grace;
The church's peace and glorious head,
Who rofe triumphant from the dead.

2.

And, Father, we adore that love,
Which moft divinely fills thy breaft,
And fent us Jefus from above,
To make a ruin'd finner bleft;
Love, flowing from thy gracious heart,
And not from rebel-man's defert.

3.

Moft Holy Spirit, all divine,
Whofe office is to teach and feal,

* John viii. 58.

Z

And bring the heart to God, and join,
And make it sweet communion feel;
Breathe on us now, and shed abroad
The grace of Christ, and love of God.

4.

In name * and nature link'd we know,
The holy, holy, holy *Three*;
To each eternal thanks we owe,
To each eternal honours be;
And let the earth with heav'nly host
Bless Father, Son, and Holy Ghost.

HYMN 205.

" My soul is even as a weaned child,"
Psalm cxxxi. 2.

1.

DEAR Jesus, cast a look on me,
   I come with simplest pray'r to thee,
    And ask to be a child;
Weary of what belongs to man,
I long to be as I began,
    Infantly meek and mild.

2.

No wild ambition I would have,
No worldly grandeur I would crave,
    But sit me down content;

* All the Three Persons are in scripture
distinctly called by *one* name, *Jehovah*, or
God.

Content with what I do receive,
And chearful praifes learn to give
   For all things freely fent.

3.

'Well weaned from the world below,
It's pining care, and gewgaw fhow,
   It's joy and hope forlorn;
My foul would ftep a ftranger forth,
And, fmit with Jefu's grace and worth,
   Repofe on him alone.

4.

I would love him with all my heart,
And all my fecret thought impart,
   My grief, and joy, and fear;
And while the pilgrim life fhall laft,
My foul would on the Lord be caft
   In fweet believing pray'r.

5

His prefence I would have each day,
And hear him talking by the way
   Of love, and truth, and grace;
And when he fpeaks and gives a fmile,
My foul fhall liften all the while,
   And every accent blefs.

HYMN 206.

"Sir, we would fee Jefus," John xii. 21.

1.

ON wings of love the Saviour flies,
　And freely left his native fkies,
　　To take an human birth;
The wife and righteous men go near,
His wonders fee, his fermons hear,
　　And think him nothing worth.

2.

A remnant fmall of humble fouls
His grace myfterioufly controls
　　By fweet alluring call;
They hear it, and his perfon view,
They learn to love and follow too,
　　And take him for their all.

3.

One of this remnant I would be,
A foul devoted unto thee,
　　Allured by thy voice;
No more on gaudy idols gaze,
No longer tinfel grandeur praife,
　　But fix on thee my choice.

4.

Thou knoweft well my fecret fmart,
And readeft all my aching heart,
　　And heareft every figh;

Can any creature give me reft,
Or any bleffing make me bleft,
   Unlefs my Lord is nigh?

5.

While walking on the gofpel-way,
" *I would fee Jefus*" every day,
   And fee in all his grace;
See him my prophet, prieft, and king,
See him by faith, and praifes fing,
   Then fee him face to face.

HYMN 207.

" If any man thirft, let him come unto
   me and drink," John vii. 37.

1.

LET him who thirfts for heavenly joys,
   Come unto Me, the Saviour cries,
     And drink at my fpring-head;
Leave all your boafting felf behind,
And from the Saviour you fhall find
     A glorious life indeed.

2.

I come, O Lord, and thirft for thee,
Some living water give to me,
   Or I fhall faint and die;
All other means my heart has try'd,
All other ftreams are vain, befide
   What flows from Calvary.

3.

I long to taste the purple flood,
And feel the virtue of thy blood,
  And gaze and tarry here;
So shall I sweetly sing and pray,
And serve thee kindly ev'ry day
  Without a guilty fear.

HYMN 208.

" My house is the house of prayer, but ye
  have made it a den of thieves," Luke
  xix. 46.

1.

MY bosom was design'd to be
  An house of pray'r, O Lord, for thee,
  A temple undefil'd;
But vile outrageous thieves broke in,
And turn'd the house into a den,
  And all it's glory spoil'd.

2.

There anger lays, and lust and pride,
And envy base it's head will hide,
  And malice brooding ill;
There unbelief the Lord denies,
And falshood whispers out it's lies,
  And avarice gripeth still.

3.

O Lord of Hosts, lift up thine eyes,
Behold, thine house a nuisance lies,
  And riot reigns within;

No worſhip of the Lord is there,
The thieves have ſtol'n away all pray'r,
   And made the houſe unclean.

4.

Thy help, Almighty Lord, impart,
And drag the tyrants from my heart,
   And chaſe the thieves away;
Within my boſom fix thy throne,
And there be lov'd and ſerv'd alone,
   And teach me how to pray.

5.

The work is thine to cleanſe the place,
I can but look up for thy grace,
   Nor this without thine aid;
Then let thine indignation burn,
And all thy foes o'erturn, o'erturn,
   And rear again my head.

HYMN 209.

" The very hairs of your head are all num-
   bered. Fear ye not therefore," Matt. x.
   30, 31.

1.

HOW watchful is the loving Lord,
   How ſweet his providential word
    To children that believe!
Your very hairs are number'd all,
Not one by force or chance can fall
    Without your Father's leave.

I

2.

Why fhould I fear, when guarded fo;
Or fhrink to meet a deadly foe!
 His mouth is held with bit:
I need not dread his utmoft fpite,
Nor can he bark, nor can he bite,
 Unlefs the Lord permit.

3.

No crofs or blifs, no lofs or gain,
No health or ficknefs, eafe or pain,
 Can give themfelves a birth;
The Lord fo rules by his command,
Nor good nor ill can ftir a hand,
 Unlefs he fends 'em forth.

4.

Since thou fo kind and watchful art,
To guard my head, and guard my heart,
 And guard my very hair,
Teach me with childlike mind to fit
And fing at my dear Saviour's feet
 Without diftruft or fear.

5.

So, like a pilgrim let me wait,
Contented well in every ftate,
 Till all my warfare ends;
Keep in a calm and chearful mood,
And find that all things work for good,
 Which Jefus kindly fends.

HYMN 210.

"Our fufficiency is of God," 2 Cor. iii. 5.

1.

O Lord, with fhame I do confefs
My univerfal emptinefs,
  My poverty and pride;
I cannot keep thee in my fight,
Nor can I think one thought aright,
  Unlefs thy Spirit guide.

2.

I cannot from my idols part,
Nor love the Lord with all my heart,
  Nor can myfelf deny;
I cannot pray, and feel thee near,
Nor can I fing with heavenly cheer,
  Unlefs the Lord is nigh.

3.

Since life divine in Adam fell,
On fpiritual things we cannot dwell,
  The heart is turn'd afide;
And none can raife to life the dead
But he, who rais'd himfelf indeed,
  And for dead finners dy'd.

4.

On him almighty help is laid,
An all-fufficient Saviour made,
  And ftands within my call;

Tho' nothing in myself I am,
But deaf and dumb, and blind and lame,
   Thro' him I may do all.

5.

Then let this mighty Jesus be
An all-sufficient help for me,
   Creating pow'r and will;
Thy grace sufficed saints of old,
It made 'em strong, and made 'em bold,
   And it sufficeth still.

HYMN 211.

" They should seek the Lord, if haply they
   might feel after him and find him," Acts
   xvii. 27.

1.

MEN seek the Lord with careless thought,
   And say their pray'rs like children
      taught,
   With no sweet love or fear;
They tramp along the beaten road,
And pray, but feel not after God,
   Nor find his presence near.

2.

They lift their eyes, and lift the hand,
And decently devout they stand,
   But no communion find;
Well pleased when the pray'r is done,
And weary of it when begun,
   They loathe it in their mind.

3.

With mind fo dark, and temper fuch,
Men evermore hate praying much,
 And hate all them that do;
Yet vainly think the Lord will hear
Such moft offenfive tinkling pray'r,
 And pay them for it too.

4.

I cannot like fuch heathen faint;
Communion with my God I want,
 Or when I fit or kneel:
Of pray'r and praife I weary grow,
The work is dry, the heart is low,
 Unlefs my God I feel.

5.

As Enoch walked, fo would I,
Beholding God with ftedfaft eye,
 And never from him rove;
Enjoy his prefence every hour,
Surrounded with his mighty pow'r,
 And nourifh'd by his love.

HYMN 212.

" I will take away the ftony heart out of
 your flefh, and will give you an heart of
 flefh," Ezek. xxxvi. 26.

1.

MY heart by nature is a ftone,
 And unconcern'd can look upon
Eternal mifery,

Feels no affection for it's Lord,
Takes no impreſſion from his word,
   But lumpiſh is and dry.

2.

Some tell me, I muſt change my heart,
And undertake the Saviour's part;
   A proud and fruitleſs ſtrife!
I might as ſoon the ſeaſons change,
Or make the clouds in order range,
   Or raiſe the dead to life.

3.

My ſhoulders will not bear the load;
The work is only fit for God,
   A work of heavenly grace;
The Lord, who firſt created man
Muſt now create him new again,
   And rear the fallen race.

4.

Then unto him I lift mine eye,
My Maker, hear me when I cry,
   And give the heart of fleſh;
An heart renew'd by faith and love,
That ſeeks the joys which are above,
   And will not feed on traſh.

5.

An heart well aw'd with godly fear,
And taught to feel thy preſence near,
   And in thyſelf delight;

An

An heart, which may thine altar be,
Where facrifice devout and free
   Is flaming day and night.

6.

An heart fubmiffive, mild, and meek,
Which hears, if Jefus foftly fpeak,
   And on his word can feaft;
An heart, which prays for great and fmall,
And dearly loves thy children all,
   Yet thinks itfelf the leaft.

HYMN 213.

" Inftead of the brier fhall come up the
myrtle-tree, and it fhall be to the Lord
for a name," Ifa lv. 13.

1.

THE thorn and brier were not fet,
   Nor baneful weeds fprung up as yet,
   Till Adam brought them in;
They fhot up mainly with the curfe,
And fhew the ground itfelf grew worfe,
   Polluted by man's fin.

2.

On ev'ry foil the briers grow,
Infeft all lands, infefting too
   The ground of each man's heart;
I find them in my bofom here,
This breaft they often wound and tear,
   And caufe a fearful fmart.

A a

3..

My felf-will, pride, and peevifhnefs,
The briers are, that would diftrefs
   Myfelf and friends around;
And oft I try to root them out,
And dig and hoe them round about,
   And yet they keep their ground.

4.

Right weary of the work I am,
For nothing comes of it but fhame,
   No myrtle can I raife:
Lord Jefus, take the work in hand,
And fhew the pow'r of thy command,
   And I will give thee praife.

5.

Thy word fpoke nature into birth,
And fummon'd ev'ry creature forth,
   The nobleft and the leaft:
Thy word ftill maketh myrtles rife,
And breathe their incenfe to the fkies;
   Lord, plant 'em in my breaft.

HYMN 214.

" I will heal their backfliding, and love
   them freely," Hofea xiv. 4.

1.

WITH grief I feel a treacherous heart,
   Which daily from the Lord would
   ftart,
And leave fubftantial joys;

Forgetful of his grace and love,
It steals away, and longs to rove
  In search of gilded toys.

2.

No skill of mine this heart can hold,
It is so guileful and so bold,
  So slippery in it's ways,
With fair pretence and friendship's guise,
A thousand various tricks it tries,
  A thousand pranks it plays.

3.

But tho' my native strength is gone,
And wit or prudence I have none,
  A roving heart to heal;
I must not perish in despair,
When help is offer'd free and near,
  For Jesus says, " I will."

4.

I will both heal and love thee too,
And well and freely this will do,
  And by a pleasant way;
A golden fetter I have got,
The roaming heart to put about,
  And keep it, lest it stray.

5.

Lord, clap this fetter on my mind,
And twine it round, and firmly bind,
  And link it on thy vest:

Yet more than golden it muſt prove,
A letter of almighty love,
   And that will hold me faſt.

HYMN 215.

" Oh, that I had wings like a dove, for
then would I fly away, and be at reſt,"
Pſal. lv. 6.

1.

FULL oft I view with envious eye
   The warbling fongſters of the ſky,
   And mark their eaſy flight;
No anxious cares perplex their breaſt,
No guilty fears diſturb their reſt,
   But all is calm as light.

2.

With morning breeze they raiſe their notes,
And tune their little chearful throats,
   And found their hymns abroad;
Or perch'd, or foaring on the wing,
With all their utmoſt might they ſing,
   And praiſe their unknown God.

3.

Ten thouſand mercies cloſe me round,
Which theſe ſweet fongſters never found,
   Yet am I cold and dry;
And if I chide my drowzy heart,
And bid it riſe, and act it's part,
   It will not foar on high.

4.

In cottage coop'd of human clay,
Or fick or dull I penfive lay,
 And know not how to rife;
Dear Jefus, give me vigour meet,
Put wings upon my heart and feet,
 And bear me to the fkies.

5.

Or faft I cleave unto the earth,
Or like a fnail am creeping forth,
 And linger-langer go,
Oh, for the pinions of a dove,
Then would I fly, and foar above,
 And fing my fonnets too.

H Y M N 216.

" If the Lord (Jehovah) be God, follow
 him; but if Baal (be God), follow him,"
 1 Kings xviii. 21.

1.

JEHOVAH is the Lord indeed,
 And, like a father, loves to feed
His children on the earth:
All other gods befide are vain,
The monfters of an human brain,
 Which hatch'd them into birth.

2.

Yet, Lord, with fhame I muft confefs,
My heart would worfhip idols bafe,
 And God with Baal join;

A a 3

It would afford thee Sunday-praife,
Yet follow pleafure, wealth, and eafe,
　　And think no harm is done.

3.

I dare not take thy name in vain,
Nor would thy fabbath-days profane,
　　Nor let the needy ftarve ;
But ftill my heart would hold it right
To make the world it's chief delight,
　　And God and mammon ferve.

4.

So bafe and crafty is my heart,
It fain would act a double part,
　　And ferve the Lord by half;
The Lord of Hofts it will adore,
Yet do, as Ifrael did before,
　　Serve God, and ferve a calf.

5.

Mine utmoft fervice is thy due,
Of body, foul, and fpirit too,
　　And thine alone fhould be ;
Oh, may my heart to Jefus cleave,
And ev'ry hateful idol leave,
　　And only *follow* thee.

HYMN 217.

" And they knew that they were naked, and
sewed fig-leaves together, and made themselves aprons," Gen. iii. 7.

1.

WHEN sinners view their nakedness,
　And feel a pang of deep distress,
　　As Adam did, they do,
Some covering of their own provide,
To screen the guilty breast and side,
　Which is their apron too.

2.

To God they come and meekly bow,
And humbly weep, and proudly vow
　　To walk well in his sight;
Some sin perhaps they now forsake,
Or cover some poor naked back,
　Which sets the matter right.

3.

But sure no ransom will take place,
Except the costly work of grace,
　Which Jesus Christ has wrought:
His precious blood and righteousness
Is made our peace and glorious dress,
　And free salvation brought.

4.

The fallen pair was kindly drest
In skins of *sacrificed* beast,
　In coats by Jesus *made*;

The coats conceal their guilty fhame,
And clothe them too, and thus proclaim
   How legal debts are paid.

5.

Lord, put thy raiment on my foul,
To make me clean, and make me whole,
   And ftand in thee complete;
So fhall I free falvation know,
And love and ferve my Lord below,
   And be for glory meet.

H Y M N 218.

" Jefus found nothing on a fig-tree, but
leaves only, and faid unto it, Let no
fruit grow on thee, henceforward for
ever, and prefently the fig-tree withered
away," Matt. xxi. 19.

1.

LORD, in the gofpel glafs we fee,
   How fearful is a curfe from thee,
   How inftant is it's pow'r!
A fig-tree rears a blooming head,
Is well and drooping, fick and dead,
   In lefs than half an hour!

2.

Almighty is thy might, O Lord!
And moft effectual is thy word,
   Or when it blafts or heals!
It comes with fuch a piercing call,
It makes the trees to liften all,
   And gives them life, or kills.

3.

Let children of the houfe depend
On Jefus Chrift, a conftant friend,
   And not miftruft his care,
Yet bear in mind from firft to laft,
The chriftian life is hid in Chrift,
   And duly feek it there.

4.

And look, profeffors, to your walk,
Who learn to fing, and learn to talk,
   And learn to play by rote;
The lord will blaft a full-blown head,
And ftrike all leafy honours dead,
   Unlefs ye bring forth fruit.

5.

And, O my Lord, whate'er I am,
Or deaf or dumb, or blind or lame,
   Or poor, or fick, or worfe;
Whatever woes my life attend,
Whatever burdens thou fhalt fend,
   Oh, fend me not thy curfe.

H Y M N 219.

" By the obedience of one fhall many be
   made righteous," Rom. v. 19.

1.

THE finner's friend a furety ftands,
   Pays legal debts with his own hands,
And pays them all for me;

He perfect lives, and painful dies,
And law and justice satisfies,
    Not for himself, but thee.

2.

By Chrift's obedience fully paid,
A foul in law is righteous made;
    For what can juftice fay?
When every debt is well difcharg'd,
The debtor fure muft be enlarg'd,
    And fing and march away.

3.

Yet alfo Jefus, by his grace,
Gives meetnefs for his dwelling-place,
    And fanctifies the heart,
His peace creates the tempers kind;
And love, to all good works inclin'd,
    Fills up the chriftian part.

4.

Then let my Lord impute to me
His own obedience full and free,
    As title to his blifs,
And let his Spirit too implant
All chriftian graces that we want,
    As pledge of happinefs.

HYMN 220.

" Jesus was moved with compaſſion on them, becauſe they fainted," Matt. ix. 36.

1.

A Multitude with wonder drawn,
Had follow'd Jeſus up and down,
  And now began to faint;
The watchful Saviour quickly ſpies
Their weary limbs and languid eyes,
  And gracious pity lent.

2.

Here note the time that Jeſus will
Exert his mercy, love, and ſkill,
  To eaſe a burden'd ſoul;
When thou art ſick and weary quite,
And ſinking underneath a weight,
  He comes to make thee whole.

3.

His pow'r is then divinely ſhewn,
His mercy is completely known,
  His love exceeding ſweet;
The raviſh'd ſoul adores the grace,
And ſees it ſhine in Jeſu's face,
  And ſinks beneath his feet.

4.

With tears of love he ſoftly ſighs,
With thankful lips he ſweetly cries,
  Hoſanna to the King.

Hofannah to his deareft name,
May all his works adore the fame,
 And tafte his grace and fing.

5.

Inftruct me, Lord, in all diftrefs,
In weaknefs, darknefs, heavinefs,
 To caft my foul on thee;
Or if it fainteth under fear,
May Jefus bring his mercy near,
 And fet my fpirit free.

HYMN 221.

" Jefus faith to the man, Stretch forth thy
 (wither'd) hand, and he ftretched it forth,"
 Matt. xii. 13.

1.

HOW many haplefs fouls we fee,
 That come to wait, dear Lord, on thee,
 And cannot ftretch their hand,
They cannot pray without a book,
But wither'd are, when off they look,
 Nor can a word command.

2.

While forms *alone* direct the tongue,
And jog the coftive thoughts along,
 It feems a ftill-born pray'r,
For pluck the borrow'd helps away,
No longer can you hear 'em pray,
 But like a mute they ftare.

I

3.

Sure none but Jefus Chrift can teach
An helplefs finner how to ftretch
    A praying hand to God;
His Spirit is the gracious prop
To lift and keep the hand lift up
    Along the praying road.

4.

Not one is fit to teach but he,
And none but Jefus fhall teach me
    The work of pray'r and praife;
Lord, give devotion kindly birth,
And bid me ftretch my lame hand forth,
    And keep it ftretch'd always.

H . Y M N 222.

" Shall the throne of iniquity have fellow-
    fhip with thee ?" Pfalm xciv. 20.

1.

A Throne is planted in the heart,
    Where Satan acts a tyrant's part,
    And plays the man of fin;
Yet lurketh fo upon his throne,
Not one of all his fubjects own
    That Satan dwells within.

2.

His voice is heard in curfings loud,
In noify brawls among the croud,
    In quarrels ev'ry where;

B b

His rule is felt, when bosoms burn
With pride, and peevishness, and scorn,
   Yet none believe him there.

3.

Till Jesus casts the tyrant down,
Iniquity must rule each one,
   And rule 'em by their choice:
But God no fellowship can hold
With slaves who unto sin are sold,
   And in it's work rejoice.

4.

Professor, mark the solemn word,
No fellowship is with the Lord,
   While sin has thine embrace;
No heart can harbour Jesu's foe,
But indignation he will shew,
   And turn away his face.

5.

Oh, let my Lord his pow'r display,
And take the reign of sin away,
   And make a captive free;
To Satan I was born a slave,
A better service I would have,
   And Jesu's freeman be.

HYMN 223.

" The king of Affyria came unto Ahaz, and diftreffed him, but ftrengthened him not," 2 Chron. xxviii. 20.

1.

A Jewifh king, by war oppreft,
    Reduced much, and wanting reft,
For foreign help will fend ;
Affyria's prince an army brought,
Diftreffes him, but ftrengthens not,
    And proves a forry friend.

2.

How oft is Ahaz' cafe our own ?
How oft is Jefu's child o'erthrown,
    By feeking unto man ?
If plunged into deep diftrefs,
He flies to man for fome redrefs,
    And nothing finds but pain.

3.

With lifted voice to God we pray,
Yet look and peep another way,
    To find a creature-prop ;
And all, who look with double eye,
Nor will on Chrift *alone* rely,
    Shall find a blafted hope.

4.

That man, the Lord affirms, is curft,
Who in a creature puts his truft,
    And maketh flefh his arm ;

B b 2

His heart a wilderness shall be,
His eye no chearing good shall see,
   But shall see rueful harm.*

5.

Then give me, Lord, the simple heart,
The single eye, the childlike part,
   To rest upon thy lap,
To call when fears oppress my mind,
And leave it with the Lord to find
   A way for my escape.

HYMN 224.

" Rachel said to Jacob, Give me children,
   or else I die," Gen. xxx. 1.

1.

OR give me children, or I die,
   Was Rachel's fond and peevish cry,
   To Jacob vented forth;
Her wish was granted to her cost,
The children came, and Rachel lost
   Her life, to give them birth.

2.

Poor Rachel tells us with a tear,
How vain all earthly wishes are,
   How fatal oft they grow!
Tho' harmless things are only sought,
Yet if pursu'd with eager thought,
   Death may attend them too.

    * Jerem. xvii. 5, 6.

3.

How things may prove, or good or ill,
No man with all his wit can tell,
 And wifhes muft be vain;
What feems defirable at firft,
Of all bad things may prove the worft,
 And flay the heart with pain.

4.

This wifhing trade I fain would leave,
And learn with fweet content to live
 On what the Lord fhall fend;
Whate'er he fends, he fends in love,
And good or bad things bleffings prove,
 If bleffed by this friend.

5.

Then let no care perplex me now;
My only wifh and care be thou,
 Be thou my whole delight;
Bid ev'ry figh of rifing thought,
And ev'ry pant of breath go out,
 For Jefus day and night.

HYMN 225.

" The preparations of the heart in man, and
the anfwer of the tongue is from the
Lord," Prov. xvi. 1.

1.

THE means of grace are in my hand,
 The bleffing is at God's command,
Who muft the work fulfil;

And tho' I read, and watch, and pray,
Yet here the Lord directs my way,
   And worketh all things still.

2.

I cannot speak a proper word,
Nor think aright, but from the Lord
   Preparing heart and tongue;
In nature I can see no good,
But all my good proceeds from God,
   And does to grace belong.

3.

I see it now, and do confess
My utter need of Jesu's grace,
   And of his Spirit's light;
I beg his kind and daily care,
O Lord, my heart and tongue prepare
   To think and speak aright.

4.

Prepare my heart to love thee well,
And love thy truth which doth excel,
   And love thy children dear;
Instruct me how to live by faith,
And feel the virtue of thy death,
   And find thy presence near.

5.

Prepare my tongue to pray and praise,
To speak of providential ways,
   And heavenly truths unfold;

To ftrengthen well a feeble foul,
Correct the wanton, rouze the dull,
  And filence finners bold.

HYMN 226.

" He, that is furety for a ftranger, fhall
    fmart for it," Prov. xi. 15.

1.

FOR forry *ftrangers* fuch as I,
    The Saviour left his native fky,
  And furety would become;
He undertakes for finners loft,
And having paid the utmoft coft,
  Returns triumphant home.

2.

A judgment-bond againft me lay,
Law-charges too, which he muft pay,
  But found a fmarting debt:
The garden fcene begins his woes,
And fetcheth agonizing throws,
  And draws a bloody fweat.

3.

His back with hardy ftripes is hew'd,
Till flakes of gore, and ftreams of blood
  Befmear the frighted ground:
A fcornful and a *fmarting* crown
His holy head is thruft upon,
  And thorns begird it round.

4.

He fmarts with nails that pierce his feet,
And fmarts with hanging all his weight
  Upon the curfed tree ;
He fmarts beneath a Father's rod,
And * roars aloud, Why, O my God,
  Haft thou forfaken me ?

5.

May all my Saviour's love and fmart
Be fweetly graven on my heart,
  And with me faft abide ;
And let me fing thy praifes well,
And love thee more than I can tell,
  And truft in none befide.

H Y M N 227.

"Much food is in the tillage of the poor,
but fome are deftroyed for want of judgment," Prov. xiii. 23.

1.

SOME tillage for the poor is found,
  A little farm, a piece of ground,
  The ground of his own heart ;
It proves a rocky, barren foil,
And mocks the human tiller's toil,
  Defying all his art.

* Ἐβόησεν ὁ Ἰησῦς φωνῆ μεγάλη· " Jefus roared with a
vehement cry."

2.

No wife or wealthy men have skill,
This little human farm to till,
   Their projects all are vain;
For want of judgment in the case,
Ill-scented weeds spring up apace,
   And stifle all the grain.

3.

The poor man understanding hath,
(If poor in spirit, rich in faith)
   To occupy this farm;
He knows that human wit and might,
And human worth are scanty quite,
   And do a world of harm.

4.

He trusts the heav'nly husbandman,
To send him sun, and send him rain,
   And makes no fretful haste *
He ploughs his ground with many pray'rs,
And sows his seed with many tears,
   And reaps with joy at last.

5.

He useth means, and layeth still,
Expecting God to work his will,
   And send the promis'd grace;
And food in plenty such will find,
A peaceful and a loving mind,
   And feet that run apace.

      * Isai. xxviii. 16.

6.

I would be such a needy man,
The poorest of the Saviour's train,
   And smallest in the flock;
Then will my tillage on me smile,
And furnish corn, and wine, and oil,
   And honey from the rock.

H Y M N 228.

" Take his garment that is surety for a
  stranger," Prov. xx. 16.

1.

THRO' native pride I could not see
   My soul was banish'd, Lord, from thee,
   And in a dungeon pent;
Born like my neighbours vain and blind,
I could not view my frightful mind,
   And so remain'd content.

2.

But now thro' Jesu's help I view
My hapless state, and feel it too,
   And own my nakedness;
To screen my back, and warm my side,
No raiment can my hands provide,
   No real righteous dress.

3.

Yet some fond hope ariseth still,
That Jesus Christ in mercy will
   Relieve my ragged case;

He bids me take a surety's coat,
Who for a stranger gives his note,
  And stands in debtor's place.

4.

A friendly word the Lord has spake,
And sure I will thy garment take,
  For Surety is thy name;
Thy garment will exactly suit,
And clothe me well from head to foot,
  And cover all my shame.

5.

So clad, I shall outstrip the moon,
And shine in splendour as the sun,
  And may to court repair;
No robe like this in heav'n is seen,
No angel's coat is half so clean,
  Nor may with it compare.

HYMN 229.

" Whosoever is simple, let him turn in
  hither," Prov. ix. 4.

1.

WHEN Jesus would his grace proclaim,
  He calls the simple, blind or lame,
  To come and be his guest;
Such simple folks the world despise,
Yet simple folks have sharpest eyes,
  And learn to walk the best.

2.

They view the want of Jefu's light,
Of Jefu's blood, and Jefu's might,
 Which others cannot view,
They walk in Chrift, the living way,
And fight, and win the well-fought day,
 Which others cannot do.

3.

The fimple have a childlike foul,
Go hand in hand to Jefu's fchool,
 And take the loweft place;
Their only wifh is Chrift to know,
To love him well, and truft him too,
 And feed upon his grace.

4.

They all declare, I nothing am,
My life is bound up in the Lamb,
 My wit and might are his,
My worth is all in Jefus found,
He is my rock, my anchor's-ground,
 And all my hope of blifs.

5.

Such fimple foul I fain would be,
The fcorn of man, the joy of thee,
 Thy parlour gueft and friend;
Do make me, Lord, a little child,
Right fimple-hearted, meek, and mild,
 And loving to the end.

2   HYMN

HYMN 230.

" There is a friend that sticketh closer than
a brother," Prov. xviii. 24.

1.

THERE is a friend, who sticketh fast,
    And keeps his love from first to last,
  And Jesus is his name;
An earthly brother drops his hold,
Is sometimes hot, and sometimes cold,
  But Jesus is the same.

2.

He loves his people, great and small,
And grasping hard embraceth all,
  Nor with a soul will part;
No tribulations which they feel,
No foes on earth, or fiends of hell,
  Shall tear 'em from his heart.

3.

His love before all time began,
And thro' all time it will remain,
  And evermore endure;
Tho' rods and frowns are sometimes brought,
And man may change, he changeth not,
  His love abideth sure.

4.

A method strange this friend has shewn
Of making love divinely known
  To rebel, doom'd to die!

C c

Unafk'd he takes our humbleft form,
And condefcends to be a worm,*
　　To lift us up on high.

5.

The law demanded blood for blood,
And out he lets his vital flood
　　To pay the mortal debt !
He toils thro' life, and pants thro' death,
And cries with his expiring breath,
　　" 'Tis finifh'd," and complete.

6.

Let all the ranfom'd of the Lord
Exalt his love with one accord,
　　And hallelujah fing ;
Adore the dying friend of man,
And blefs him highly as you can,
　　He is your God and King.

H Y M N 231.

" In the light of the King's countenance is
life, and his favour is like a cloud of the
latter rain," Prov. xvi. 15.

1.

THE man, who walks a formal round,
　　And only vifits holy ground
To read or hear a pray'r ;
Can fee no light in Jefu's face,
And feel no life from Jefu's grace,
　　'Tis nonfenfe in his ear.

* Pfalm xxii. 6.

2.

But whoſo lives the life of faith,
And fellowſhip with Jeſus hath,
  Enjoys the pleaſing ſight,
A faith divine the ſoul will bring
Full in the preſence of his King,
  And ſhew the cheering light.

3.

But if believers ſaunt'ring walk,
And ſink in ſloth, or frothy talk,
  The Lord withdraws his face;
A darkneſs broodeth o'er the mind,
No light from Jeſus can they find,
  Until they mend their pace.

4.

As when ſome long expected rain
Deſcends upon a parched plain,
  The fields are gay, and ſpring;
So when the Lord his face reveals,
And paſt backſlidings freely heals,
  Believers laugh and ſing.

5.

Thine heavenly light, O Lord, impart,
To guide my feet, and cheer my heart,
  Along the wilderneſs;
So will thy pilgrim fear no toil,
But walk and pray, and ſing and ſmile,
  And Jeſus ſweetly bleſs.

H Y M N 232.

" Thy words were found, and I did eat them, and they were unto me the joy of mine heart," Jer. xv. 16.

1.

WHAT if we read and understand
   The written word of God's command,
   And give it credit meet;
The word is but a looking-glass,
And only shews a man his face,
   Unless the word we eat.

2.

It raiseth no man from the dead,
While seated only in the head,
   But leaves him dry and faint;
It maketh matter for some talk,
But cannot give him legs to walk,
   Nor make a man a saint.

3.

The word consists of letters fair,
But letters merely dead things are,
   And cannot change the heart;
The letter only bringeth death,*
Unless the Spirit by his breath
   A quick'ning pow'r impart.

* 2 Cor. iii.

4.

May thy commands obedience get,
And promiſes yield comfort ſweet,
   And threat'nings awe my ſoul;
Let exhortations ſpur me on,
And cautions make me watchful run,
   And love inſpire the whole.

5.

According as my wants require,
Adapt thy word as food and fire,
   To nouriſh and to warm;
Let ev'ry page afford new wealth,
Convey ſome life and godly health,
   And guard my ſteps from harm.

HYMN 233.

" Doth he (the Maſter) thank that ſervant
becauſe he did the things that were commanded him? I ſuppoſe not. So like-
wiſe ye, when ye ſhall have done all
things which are commanded you, ſay,
we are unprofitable ſervants; we have
only done that which was our duty to
do," Luke xvii 9, 10.

1.

A Solemn and an humbling word
   Is utter'd ſtrongly by the Lord
To all above, below;

Tho' God's commands be kept with care,
Unprofitable still we are,
   No thanks the Lord will owe.

2.

Alas! how vainly sinners talk,
Who limp and stumble in their walk,
   And yet of merit dream;
Of merit talk with lofty breath,
Whilst God declares that wrath and death
   Are only due to them.

3.

I daily feel death is my due,
And try to keep this point in view,
   To slay my pride outright:
At best, I am a sinner poor,
At worst, a hateful creature sure,
   A rebel in God's fight.

4.

And if I could perfection claim,
No thanks are owing for the fame,
   No merit would arise;
Aside all merit I must cast,
And owe my heaven to grace at last,
   And Jesu's sacrifice.

5.

Then let me learn my Lord to prize,
And view him with adoring eyes,
   Confiding in his name;

Pay chearful homage to my king,
And fweet hofannas daily fing,
 And fpread abroad his fame.

HYMN 234.

" He that is not with me, is againft me,"
  Matt. xii. 30.

1.

A Chriftian acts a foldier's part,
 And with a bold and upright heart
Anear his captain ftands;
If foes againft the Lord arife,
He neither like a coward flies,
 Nor fits with folded hands.

2.

No neuters in this holy war!
A neuter is a traitor here,
 Condemned by the word:
If I can flink my head away
In fome fad hot or rainy day,
 I am againft the Lord.

3.

Yet fmall profeffors ev'ry where
Will court the Lord in weather fair,
 And fmile, and kifs his feet;
But if he raifeth clouds and ftorms,
They creep into their holes, like worms,
 And prudently retreat.

4.

So Demas was a prudent man,
And fhuffling danger all he can,
 Leaves Paul for worldly gains :
So Judas was a prudent knave,
Yet for his prudence he muft have
 A halter for his pains.

5.

O Lord, give me an heart upright,
An heavenly courage for the fight,
 And zeal that is alert ;
Not raving mad, but meekly bold,
And not feduc'd by fear or gold
 My Saviour to defert.

6.

Such faith in Jefus fill my mind,
Such love to Jefus may I find,
 Such woith in Jefus fee ;
That I may hold his truth and name,
More dear than wealth, or eafe, or fame;
 More dear than life to me.

HYMN 235.

" He that gathereth not with me, fcattereth
 abroad," Matt. xii. 30.

1.

A Chriftian ferjeant, fent to lift,
 Muft fill his fpeech with Jefus Chrift,
And gather with his name ;

Elfe, not a foul obeys his call,
The hearers will be fcatter'd all,
　　And wander as they came.

2.

Abundance of good folks, I find,
Are gathering goodnefs for the wind
　　To fcatter it about ;
They feek with human care and fkill,
Their veffels with good wine to fill,
　　But all the wine leaks out.

3.

A fretful foul his fault may fpy,
And ftruggle much, and often try
　　Some patience to obtain ;
Yet after many toilfome years,
And many fighs, and many tears,
　　He has not got a grain.

4.

He, that with Jefus gathers not,
May plough and fow, and weed his plot,
　　But fcatters all his corn ,
No real goodnefs long can ftand,
Which planted is by human hand,
　　It dies as foon as born.

5.

They reap and fcatter all the while,
They reap and gather nought but toil,
　　'Tis labour loft I fee ;

O Lord, do thou inftruct my heart,
With my own reaping-hook to part,
 And gather all with thee.

6.

In Chrift my treafure gather'd is,
My wifdom, wealth, and might are his,
 My peace at his command;
With him is free and plenteous ftore,
And faith may have enough, and more,
 When gather'd from his hand.

HYMN 236.

" The Son of Man is come to fave that
 which was loft," Matt. xviii. 11.

1.

WHEN our firft head and nat'ral root
 Had tafted of forbidden fruit,
In that fame day he dy'd;
Of life divine he ftood bereft,
And found his only portion left
 Was wretchednefs and pride.

2.

And furely fuch a tainted fpring
Polluted ftreams can only bring,
 And fo we find they are;
No life-divine the children have,
No intercourfe with God they crave,
 Nor once about it care.

3.

By nature and by trespass dead,
His own sad ruin none can read,
  For death seals up his eyes;
No soul appears a sinner lost,
Till quicken'd by the Holy Ghost,*
  And then to Christ he flies.

4.

This truth whoever sees not well,
No hunger after Christ can feel,
  No work for Christ can find:
To save *lost* sinners Jesus came,
The spiritual deaf, and dumb, and lame,
  The wretched and the blind.

5.

All ye that weary are of sin,
And feel your natures all unclean,
  And labour under guilt;
Who find within no dawn of hope,
To Christ your weary eyes lift up,
  His blood for you was spilt.

6.

Go, sinner, go, by sin distrest,
And Jesus Christ will give thee rest,
  And act the Saviour's part;
He came to save the lost and poor,
And such are welcome to his door,
  And welcome to his heart.

* John vi. 63.——xvi. 8.

HYMN 237.

" There was a ftrife amongft them, which
of them fhould be accounted the greateft,"
Luke xxii. 24.

1.

SMALL wonder happens, when we fee
The world contend for maftery,
 It is an ufual cafe :
Yet here in Jefu's chofen band,
A ftrife enfues who fhall command,
 And take the leading place.

2.

When call'd by grace to follow Chrift,
We little underftand at firft
 The workings of our pride ;
It is a fubtle ferpent fin,
Which winds it's body fhily in,
 And it's foul head will hide.

3.

But fweetly Jefus Chrift reproves
The lurking pride of them he loves,
 And fhews the gofpel-way ;
He fhall fit foremoft in my hall,
Who can be fervant unto all ;
 The flave fhall bear the fway.

4.

This beauteous truth mine eyes difcern,
But oh. my heart will never learn,
 Unlefs my Saviour teach ;

2   My

My heart will on fubmiffion frown,
Until thy Spirit break it down,
　And well the leffon preach.

5.

Then let the Lord his grace beftow,
To make me fmall and fmaller grow,
　The fmalleft of the leaft;
Obedient run at every call,
And be that willing flave of all,
　Whom Jefus loves the beft.

HYMN 238.

"A bruifed reed fhall he not break, and
fmoking flax fhall he not quench, till he
fend forth judgment unto victory," Matt.
xii. 20.

1.

A Sinner, who can read his cafe,
　　Lament his guilt and bondage bafe,
　And view himfelf moft vile;
Behold! on fuch afflicted fouls,
And treated by the world as fools,
　The Lord will caft a fmile.

2.

A bruifed reed he will not break,
But bind up gently what is weak,
　And heal a bleeding wound;
A coftly balfam he has got,
Which oft is try'd, and faileth not
　And was at Calv'ry found.

D d

3.

The flax that fmoketh with it's fhame,
He blows up into kindly flame,
   And warms the heart with peace:
His incenfe on the fmoke is thrown,
And then the flame is quickly blown,
   And kindles heavenly blifs.

4.

Afflicted fouls muft not defpair,
But truft in Jefu's love and care,
   To give the weary reft;
His words are gentle, meek, and kind,
A picture of his loving mind;
   Believe, and you are bleft.

HYMN 239.

" In Jefu's name fhall the Gentiles truft,"
       Matt. xii. 21.

1.

A Gentile is an earthly man,
   Who follows paftime all he can,
   Nor loves a praying-place;
A Gentile has an earthly heart,
And cares not with his lufts to part;
   And is not this thy cafe?

2.

I own it, Lord, and feel with fhame,
Born with a heathen heart I am,
   A Gentile true by birth;

No good in me by nature dwells,
No good my heart defires or feels,
   But what the world brings forth.

3.

Yet, O my Lord, if Gentiles be
Allow'd to put their truft in thee,
   To thee I lift mine eyes;
Thou canft my heathen lufts fubdue,
And change my heart, and make it new,
   And train it for the fkies.

4.

My heart with weeds is overgrown,
And oft is lifelefs as a ftone,
   Nor careth for thy ways;
Yet, Lord, this Gentile heart infpire
With holy love, and heavenly fire,
   And it will fing thy praife.

HYMN 240.

" Jefus faid unto him, What wilt thou that
  I fhould do unto thee?" Mark x. 51.

1.

A Beggar poor had loft his eyes,
   And unto Jefus Chrift applies
   With loud and fervent pray'r;
Tho' charged much to hold his peace,
He louder begs for Jefu's grace,
   And Jefus lends an ear.

2.

He comes conducted to his Lord,
And Jesus drops a chearing word,
   What wilt thou have me do?
A word, which has a further look,
A word, to Bartimeus spoke,
   And yet is meant for you.

3.

Art thou arriv'd at Jesu's door,
Exceeding blind, exceeding poor,
   And mighty wretched too?
Fear not, he loves a beggar's knock,
And softly says, at every stroke,
   What wilt thou have me do?

4.

The Lord upbraids no guilty heart,
But makes the conscience act this part,
   And pierce a sinner thro',
And when the sinner pours a pray'r,
Sweet Jesus whispers in his ear,
   What wilt thou have me do?

5.

However sad be our complaint,
Or blind or lame, or sick or faint,
   To Jesus we may go;
And when we raise a faithful cry,
His mercy drops a sweet reply,
   What wilt thou have me do?

6.

Well, fince the Saviour is fo free,
Two eyes I beg that well can fee,
   And tongue that well can pray;
A loving heart, well wafh'd from fin,
With hands that bounteous are and clean,.
   And feet that will not ftray.

HYMN 241.

" In the mount the Lord will provide,".Gen.
xxii. 14. See the margin of the Bible.

1.

SEE Abram walking up the hill,
   With Ifaac fondling by him ftill,
    And prattling in his ears,
At length the lovely child is bound,
The hand is ftretch'd, the knife is found,
    And then the Lord appears.

2.

If thou art fprung from Abram's ftock,*
A fheep of Jefu's little flock,
   For trials arm thy mind;
Temptations will befet thy feet,
A thoufand dangers thou fhalt meet,,
   A thoufand ftruggles find.

3.

As every trial paffeth o'er,
Expect another full as fore,
   Perhaps a forer yet;

* Gal. iii. 7..

Dd 3

And when the clouds begin to rife,
They blacker grow, and fill the fkies,
   And threaten ruin great.

4.
Perhaps the Lord with-holds his light,
And keeps his help far out of fight,
   Thine utmoft faith to try;
Yet this remember, O my friend,
When thou art brought to thy wit's-end,
   That Abram's God is nigh.

5.
On danger's brink when thou art brought,
In fad perplexity of thought,
   Then Jefus draweth near;
He fpeaks a word divinely mild,
And chears the poor diftreffed child,
   And fcatters all his fear.

H Y M N 242.

" That which is born of the flefh, is flefh,
   and that which is born of the Spirit, is
   fpirit," John iii. 6.

1.
THE man, that's only born of man,
   Is only flefh, and only can
Defire the flefh to pleafe:
He courteth riches, honours, fame,
And follows pleafure as his game,
  -And ftudies well his eafe.

2.

Much nobler birth a few receive;
Of Spirit born, believers live
   With new and spiritual pow'r;
A seed they have of heavenly birth,
Which brings a spiritual service forth,
   Delightsome more and more.

3.

The Spirit brings the grace of pray'r,
And bids a new-born child go near,
   And Abba, Father, cry;
Reveals the way of grace and truth,
Inspireth hope, and worketh faith,
   With peace, and love, and joy.

4.

Much intercourse they have with God,
They hear his voice, and fear his rod,
   And love him kindly too;
On wings of strong desire they fly,
And train'd up sweetly for the sky,
   Their heav'n begins below.

5.

Such noble seed of spiritual plant,
Is what an earthly heart will want
   To raise it up to God;
Such noble seed sow in my breast,
And keep, O Lord, the plant well drest,
   And water'd with thy blood.

HYMN 243.

"Of Chrift's fulnefs have all we received,
even grace for grace," John 1. 16.

1.

OUR father was completely dreft
With heavenly robes around his breaft,
And Adam was his name;
But all the gracious dowry lent
Was by the father quickly fpent,
And nothing left but fhame.

2.

And if the Lord could place no truft
In creatures formed wife and juft,
Much lefs in them that fell;
If upright man his birthright fold,
The froward children would be bold
For trafh the fame to fell.

3.

Now Jefus takes the whole command,
And lays the ftock up in his hand,
To fave from future harms;
He will for his own flock provide,
But keeps them hanging on his fide,
And living on his alms.

4.

A foul, that hungry is and poor,
May find in Jefus precious ftore,
All fulnefs dwells in him;

His royal grace, a fweet fpring-head,
An empty conduit-pipe will feed,
   And fill it to the brim.

5.

As from the father fons receive
The fundry features which they have,
   And limb for limb we trace;
So from the Lord his children find
The features of their heavenly mind,
   Receiving grace for grace.

6.

Upon thy fulnefs let me feed,
And fend me ftore of heavenly bread,
   And heavenly comforts give;
My famifh'd foul thy gueft would be,
Receiving all fupport from thee,
   And only in thee live.

HYMN 244.

" Behold, I am vile, what fhall I anfwer
   thee? I will lay my hand upon my
   mouth," Job xl. 4.

1.

OF Job we read, he perfect was;
   And God himfelf relates his cafe,
   A faithful witnefs fure;
Job guides his fteps with holy care,
His houfehold trains in godly fear,
   And clothes and feeds the poor.

2.

I wonder not in Job to find
A much too much complacent mind,
    His conduct was upright,
And if, as vainly think the moft,
A finner were allow'd to boaft,
    Of all men fure he might.

3.

Some rods are fent with ftinging fmart,
To empty Job of his defert,
    Yet rods are fent in vain :
Some friends, with arguments prepar'd,
Accufe him much, and prefs him hard,
    Yet Job replies again.

4.

When Jefus fpeaks, he will o'ercome;
And Jefus brings the matter home,
    Job liftens all the while,
A naughty heart he now can read,*
And crieth out, amaz'd indeed,
    " Behold, Lord, I am vile !"

5.

So let me always read my heart,
And act the penitential part,
    Be vile in my own eyes,
Count all defert as gaudy drofs,
And mourning at the Saviour's crofs,
    Truft in his facrifice.

* Jer. xvii. 9.

HYMN 245.

" And when they had nothing to pay, he frankly forgave them both," Luke vii. 42.

1.

MEN owe the Lord a different score,
Some owe him less, some owe him more,
   Yet none can pay his debt;
No man can wipe his conscience clean,
For death is due to every sin,*
   The small as well as great.

2.

No room for merit can appear;
She must not thrust her visage here,
   Where all are doom'd to die;
Of mercy much we stand in need;
By mercy only are we freed,
   And should for mercy cry.

3.

If stinging debts the conscience wring,
Go, take them, sinner, to the King,
   Where mercy may be found ;
His look is sweet, approach him near,
His heart is kind, thou need'st not fear,
   His mercy has no bound.

4.

What if thy guilt should reach the sky,
His mercy reacheth twice as high,
   And over it will soar;

* Rom. vi. 23.

Or if thou sink in Jonah's hell,*
His mercy deep can reach thee still,
 And draw thee safe on shore.

5.

This mercy unto Christ we owe;
He bought the pearl, and dearly too,
 And now bestows it free;
A vast redemption-price he paid,
Himself a sacrifice was made,
 To buy the pearl for thee.

HYMN 246.

" The devils cried out, What have we to
do with thee, Jesus, thou Son of God?"
Matt. viii. 29.

1.

JESUS, thou Son of God most High,
 We know thy name, the devils cry,
No Saviour thou for us !
They lodged in a human breast,
And gave the frantic man no rest,
 But set him raving thus.

2.

And where the fiends possess a heart,
They always act this frenzy-part,
 And roar at Jesus Christ :
While men lay in the wicked one,†
The same reviling work goes on,
 And Jesus they resist.

 * Jonah ii. 2. † 1 John v. 19.
2

But

3.

But Jesus casteth devils out,
And then poor sinners turn about,
   And Jesus Christ adore;
They feel the virtue of his death,
And being taught to live by faith,
   They love him evermore.

4.

Well, since the world will shew it's spite,
And Satan roar with all his might,
   Hosanna let us cry;
Hosanna to the Son of God,
Who lov'd and wash'd us in his blood,
   Amen, Amen, say I,

HYMN 247.

" His brethren come to Jesus, but could
   not get near him for the croud,"
Luke viii. 19.

1.

IF unto Jesus thou art bound,
   A croud about him will be found,
   Attending day and night;
A worldly croud to din thine ears,
And crouds of unbelieving fears
   To hide him from thy sight.

2.

Yet all the vain and noisy croud
Is but a thin and low'ring cloud,
   A mist before thine eyes;

E e

If thou prefs on, the crouds will fly,
Or if thou faint, to Jefus cry,
   And he will fend fupplies.

3.

This only way can pilgrims go,
And all complain, as thou wilt do,
   Of crouds that daily come;
Yet, tho' befet by crafty foes,
And paffing thro' a thoufand woes,
   They get fecurely home.

4.

And fuch as feem to run the race,
And meet no croud to check their pace,
   Are only rambling ftill;
Not fairly enter'd on the lift,
The gate and narrow way they mift,
   Which lead to Sion's hill.

5.

O Lord, a chearing look beftow,
Or lend a hand to help me thro',
   And draw me up to thee;
And when thro' fear I only creep,
Or dare not move a fingle ftep,
   Yet thou canft come to me.

HYMN 248.

" Enoch walked with God, and he was not found, for God took him," Gen. v. 24.

1.

OF Enoch we read,
   He walked with God ;
True pilgrim indeed,
Few fuch on the road !
Kept up his communion
   Full three hundred years,
And after fuch union
   No more he appears.

2.

No pattern more plain
Or ftriking than this,
To fhew unto man
What godlinefs is,
Not merely rehearfing
   A hymn or a pray'r,
But with God converfing,
   And feeling him near.

3.

Oft roving aftray,
My fancy has been ;
Lord, fhew me the way
That Enoch walk'd in ;
With good faith abounding,
   And acting it's part ;

And Jesus surrounding
  And warming my heart.

4.

No more I would grieve
For empty things here;
'Tis time to take leave
Of vanity fair;
Be thou my heart's-longing,
  And make my soul blest,
Nor let idols throng in,
  And rifle my breast.

5.

Wherever I rove,
On thee I would rest,
And carry thy love
About as my guest;
Fix'd in meditation
  While running my race,
And sweet contemplation
  On Christ and his grace.

6.

In all my affairs
I beg I may see
Thy fatherly cares
Employed for me;
And for ev'ry blessing
  I thankful would prove,
And pray without ceasing
  Till call'd up above.

HYMN 249.

" Hold thou me up, and I shall be safe,"
Psalm cxix. 117.

1.

THE wisdom of man
  Rejects offer'd grace,
And fancies he can
  Be brisk for the race;
By shrewdness discover
  Mount Sion's fair town,
And trip the road over
  By strength of his own.

2.

But David, who knew
  Himself and the road,
Cries out, as I do,
  For help to his God;
He dare not confide in
  Weak nature's effort,
But seeks better guiding,
  And stronger support.

3.

Such succour is meet
  For cripples like me;
Lord, hold up my feet,
  And safe I shall be;
Thine arm be thrust under
  The folds of my heart,

To bear up my ſhoulder,
    And ſtrengthen each part.

4.

All weakneſs I am,
Unfit for a fight;
Decrepid and lame,
And cowardly quite;
Unable to wreſtle
    With fiends or with men;
And if they but whiſtle,
    I ſhudder again.

5.

But Jeſus is bold,
And ſtronger than hell;
This Satan has told,
And ſaints too can tell;
His arm has been glorious
    In beating down foes,
And proveth victorious
    Wherever he goes.

6.

His arm be my prop,
And buckler and ſhield,
To bear my ſoul up
For fight in the field;
And when I can reſt in
    His promiſed word,
My ſoul is much bleſt in
    The joy of the Lord.

HYMN 250.

" The Lord is nigh unto them that are of
a broken heart, and faveth fuch as be of
a contrite fpirit," Pfalm xxxiv. 18.

1.

YE broken hearts all,
    Who cry out, Unclean,
And tafte of the gall
Of indwelling fin ;
Lamenting it truly,
    And loathing it too,
And feeking help duly,
    As finners fhould do.

2.

The Lord, whom ye feek,
    Is nigh to your call,
Attends when you fpeak,
    Nor lets a word fall ;
Your forrow and fighing
    Are felt in his breaft ;
He pities your crying,
    And will give you reft.

3.

If often he hides
His face from his friends,
And filent abides
For merciful ends,

At length he uncovers
   Himfelf from his cloud,
And fweetly difcovers
   His face and his blood.

4.

All penitent cries
   His Spirit imparts,
And fetcheth out fighs
   From fin-feeling hearts;
He puts you in mourning,
   The drefs that you want,
A meek fuit adorning
   Both finner and faint.

5.

A time he has fet
   To heal up your woes,
A feafon moft fit
   His love to difclofe,
And till he is ready
   To fhew his good-will,
Be patient and fteady,
   And wait on him ftill.

HYMN 251.

" I will inftruct thee, and teach thee in the
   way which thou fhalt go," Pfal. xxxii. 8.

1.

OH, where fhall I find
   A guide to direct,

Right fkilful and kind,
And brave to protect?
To lovely Mount Sion
My heart is now bound,
But many a lion
Is in the way found.

2.

Our Jefus will teach
The way ye fhould go,
And out his arm reach
To help you on too.
The doubts that perplex you,
The fears that diftrefs,
The tempers that vex you,
His grace will redrefs.

3.

Then let the Lord give
Me faith in his name,
A faith that will live
In water and flame;
A faith that endureth,
And feafts on his blood;
A faith that enfureth
My fonfhip with God.

4.

Yet teach me to love
Thy perfon moft fweet,
Nor let my heart rove,
But keep at thy feet;

Be with thee delighted,
    And clasp thee and twine,
Most firmly united
    To thy living Vine.

5.

And further I seek
The charms of thy mind,
The grace to be meek,
And lovely and kind,
Forbearing, forgiving,
    And loving always,
And only be living
    To publish thy praise.

HYMN 252.

" Make haste, my Beloved," Cant. viii. 14.

1.

WHY, sure I must love
    Christ Jesus, my Lord;
His grace I approve,
His worship and word;
I mourn for him absent,
    And can have no rest;
And when he is present,
    I feel myself blest.

2.

These are the out-lines
Of inward respect,
And such gracious signs
I must not reject;

Why should I be moved
    With perplexing doubt?
He is my Beloved,
    I will speak it out.

3.

Yet still I do find
A sinful *self* too,
Which steals on my mind,
Wherever I go;
A fiend, very hateful
    In Jesus his eyes,
And sure the most fretful
    Thing under the skies.

4.

I seek, but in vain,
    To banish this guest;
He hears me complain,
    Yet lurks in my breast;
Oh, let him not grieve me
    By bearing the sway;
Make haste to relieve me,
    Dear Jesus, I pray.

5.

Thou hast a full right
    To all my poor heart,
Yet creatures invite
    And scramble for part;
The world too would teaze me
    And draw me away;

Oh, let 'em not feize me,
And worry their prey.

6.

When heavenly blifs
Flows into my foul,
And Chrift, with a kifs,
Poffeffeth me whole,
My tongue crieth ever,
O Lord, quickly come,
Make hafte, my dear Saviour,
And carry me home.

H Y M N 253.

" Though all be offended, yet will not I,"
Mark xiv. 29.

1.

HOW eafily man
Miftakes his own heart,
And fancies he can
Act up to his part,
Has no apprehenfion
Of weaknefs within,
But thinks good intention
Will guard him from fin.

2.

So Peter once thought,
And honeftly fpake,
But quickly was brought
To fee his miftake;

I   His

His valour was tried
   And cowardice prov'd,
He stoutly denied
   The Master he lov'd.

3.

In Peter I see
My nature display'd,
High-minded to be,
   Yet quickly dismay'd :
Presuming on valour,
   And wisdom, and strength,
We tumble the souler
   And faster at length.

4.

Enfeebled we are,
Yet stout in self-will ;
No strength for the war,
   Yet confident still ;
Ashamed to tarry
   When call'd to the fight,
Yet sure to miscarry
   When left to our might.

5.

If Peter could fall,
And fall such a length ;
Then woe be to all
That trust in their strength,
     F f

The ftrength of their nature,
 Or ftrength of their grace;
They fooner or later
 Will fuffer difgrace.

6.

No more I would walk
In fuch empty fhew,
No more I would talk
Of feats I can do;
But build a fafe neft in
 The Saviour's own tow'r,
And put my whole truft in
 His mercy and pow'r.

H Y M N 254.

" Serve God acceptably, with reverence
 and godly fear," Heb. xii. 28.

1.

O Lord, thou art great,
 And worthily fear'd;
By all at thy feat
Ador'd and rever'd;
The higheft in graces
 With fhame-blufhing heart,
Do cover their faces,
 So holy thou art!

2.

Thy faints upon earth,
Tho' bid to draw near,
Yet fing thy praife forth
With reverent fear;

Thy greatnefs adoring
  With hearts that will bend,
And mercy imploring
  Thro' Jefus their friend.

3.

What faints of thee knew,
  Lord, make to me known,
And let my eyes view
  A glimpfe of thy throne ;
Thy glory difcover,
  As mortals can fee,
And all my foul cover
  With fweet awe of thee.

4.

Such fear may I prove,
  As fuiteth a child,
Arifing from love,
  Obedient and mild ;
A fear of offending
  The Father of grace,
And pleas'd with attending
  And feeking his face.

HYMN 255.

" I will fay of the Lord, he is my refuge.'
Pfalm xci. 2.

1.

WHILST other men boaft
  Of merit and might,

And fail on the coaft
Of legal delight;
I will fay of Jefus,
My refuge he is,
None other can eafe us
And fave us but this.

2.

To thee will I fly
When confcience is fare,
And each guilty cry
Will bring to thy door ;
My wounds fhall be healed
With thy precious blood,
And all my peace fealed
By Jefus, my God.

3.

When evil defire
Is fpringing within,
And nature on fire
Grows wanton for fin ;
Thy grace and thy Spirit
The flame fhall fubdue,
And thou fhalt inherit
The praife of it too.

4.

If fcorners arife,
For mifchief prepar'd,
And hate me becaufe
I truft in the Lord ,

I need no direction
  From lawyers or law,
But all my protection
  From Jesus will draw.

5.

If famine would stare
  Me thro' with distress,
Or sickness would scare
  Me by it's pale face,
Or death hurry fast on
  With painfullest grief,
To Jesus I'll hasten
  And look for relief.

6.

My hope he shall be,
  Whilst drawing my breath;
A refuge for me
  In life and in death;
I give up all other
  And take him alone;
He is a try'd brother,
  To rest my heart on.

HYMN 256.

"What will ye see in the Shulamite? As it were the company of two armies," Cant. vi. 13.

1.

NO beautiful form
  In Jesus was seen;

He feemed a worm,
    Much fcorned of men;
And daughters of Salem
    Hence Shulamites call'd,
Find many revile 'em,
    As Jefus of old.

2.

No gallant outfide
    The Shulamite bears,
No trappings of pride,
    Thefe are not her wares;
Her wifh and her charm is
    In love to abound,
Yet war-waging armies
    Within her are found.

3.

Fall'n nature and grace
    Are ever at ftrife,
And can have no peace,
    Tho' linked for life,
With fixed intention
    Seek each other's death,
Nor drop the contention
    Till dropping their breath.

4.

Old nature thinks hard
    To be a down-caft,
She play'd the firft card,
    And would play the laft;

But grace, tho' the younger,
　　Comes down from the fkies,
And proveth the ftronger,
　　And carries the prize.

5.

This ftruggle within
　　Rafh finners deride;
A warfare with fin
　　They cannot abide;
Two armies are truly
　　In Shulamites found,
But nature does wholly
　　Take up the world's ground.

6.

Such warfare is right,
　　And marketh a faint;
-Lord, help me to fight,
　　And never to faint;
My fhield of faith lengthen,
　　My helmet fecure,
My heart and feet ftrengthen,
　　And make me endure.

HYMN 257.

" It is enough for the difciple to be as his
　　Mafter," Matt. x. 25.

1.

OUR Mafter was born
　　Where oxen are fed,

No houfe of his own
To cover his head;
Content, tho' he lived
As mean as you can;
Then why art thou grieved
To be a poor man?

2.

Soon did he begin
The carpenter's trade,
And drudged therein,
Of toil not afraid;
He never was fretful
At earning his bread:
Then think it not hateful
To work as he did.

3.

He travell'd on foot
When preaching of peace,
And carefully fought
Poor finners to blefs,
Went with an heart cheary
At any one's call,
Then why am I weary
To wait upon all?

4.

Ill was he repaid
For bleffings he gave;
Reviled as mad,
Blafphemer and knave;

His perfon they flighted,
And fpat on his face;
Then why am I frighted
At fcorn and difgrace?

5.

The Mafter in chief
A mourner appears,
And verfed in grief
A daily crofs bears;
Each night and each morrow
Some frefh trouble came,
Then why do we forrow
To fuffer the fame?

6.

I fee it right clear,
And good is the word,
That fervants fhould fare
As fareth their Lord;
Yet nature is feeble,
And prefently trips;
O Lord, make me able
To tread in thy fteps.

HYMN 258.

" Give ear, O Shepherd of Ifrael,"
Pfalm lxxx. 1.

1.

LOOK down from above
Kind Shepherd and Friend,

And tell us thy love
Which never shall end;
Supply us with manna
And streams from the Rock,
And daily hosanna
Shall come from the flock.

2.

Watch over the sheep
By day and by night,
And teach 'em to keep
Their Shepherd in sight;
With silence attending
Upon his soft voice,
And hear him commending
The flock of his choice.

3.

Where pasture is best
Incline 'em to lay;
And guard off each beast
That watcheth for prey;
The foxes who chatter
With craftiest note,
And wolves who would scatter
And take by the throat.

4.

To shepherd dogs give
Intelligent skill,
Thy word to receive,
And bark at thy will;

Right patient and heedful,
　And fond of their care;
Yet ready, if needful,
　To lug by the ear.

5.

Give peace in the fold,
　And fellowfhip fweet,
And make young and old
　Lay down at thy feet;
The elder ones bleating
　With luftieft praife,
And lambkins repeating
　The wonders of grace.

6.

Some ftrays we yet lack,
　Which in the world roam;
Lord, whiftle them back,
　And fetch 'em fafe home;
And thoufands which loft are,
　And never yet found,
Allure 'em to feaft here
　On mercy's fair ground.

HYMN 259.

" Who is this that cometh up from the wildernefs, leaning upon her Beloved?"
Cant. viii. 5.

1.

A Virgin appears
　Of comelieft hue,

Uncumber'd with cares,
    And raiment all new ;
Some daughter of Zion,
    Her fteps tell her name,
As bold as a lion,
    Yet meek as a lamb !

2.

A friend fhe has got
Who keeps at her fide,
And fays he has fought
Her out for a bride :
She leans on his fhoulder
    And hangs her head down ;
And thrufts her arm under
    The fold of his gown.

3.

Whenever he fpeaks
Or looks in her face,
Her filence fhe breaks
    And fings with all grace ;
Her heart is foon moved,
    Her eyes are foon wet,
She calls him Beloved,
    And finks at his feet.

4.

He raifeth her up
And draws to his breaft ;
Sweet pillar of hope !
And there fhe finds reft ;

I   And

And while she is trusting
    His love and his pow'r,
No sorrow can roost in
    Her heart for an hour.

5.

The world in her view
    A wilderness seems,
Where sorrows are true,
    And joys are all dreams;
So up she is hasting
    To Sion's fair hill,
In joy true and lasting
    To take her whole fill.

6.

A virgin so rare,
    Dear Lord, I would be,
And scatter my care
    By leaning on thee;
Indulge me thy bosom,
    And farewel all woes;
My desart shall blossom
    And smell as the rose.

HYMN 260.

" I am the door," John x. 9.

1.

AN insolent thief
    Most sure I have been,
A villain in chief,
A traitor in sin;

For glory I panted
    And deathlefs renown,
And truly I wanted
    To fteal the King's crown.

2.

His palace I view'd
    And batter'd it round,
The ftones and the wood,
    The roof and the ground;
I dug and expected
    To break up the floor,
And nothing neglected
    Excepting *the door*.

3.

One day the King's Son,
    A wonderful man!
Who faw what was done,
    And knew of my plan;
Steps forth a right time in,
    And foftly drew nigh,
Juft as I was climbing
    A window full high.

4.

Ah, villain! he cry'd,
    Yet fmil'd as he fpoke,
The neck of thy pride
    Shall furely be broke;

Thou needeſt a halter,
　So knaviſh thou art,
But Jeſus can alter
　And vanquiſh thy heart.

5.

See, there is the door,
　Without any lock ;
A gate for the poor !
　Go to it and knock :
The *door* gives a paſſage
　Into the Lord's room ;
Go there with thy meſſage,
　And wait till I come.

6.

The *door* is the way
　Into the King's court ;
There honeſt men pray
　And daily reſort ;
But thieves put a hope in
　A fooliſh attempt,
To break my houſe open,
　And bring me contempt.

7.

From Jeſus, a Friend,
Expect to receive
What mercy can lend,
Or majeſty give :

I'll feed thee, and clothe thee,
　　And wash thee all o'er,
And kindly betroth thee
　　In love evermore.

8.

A crown, I perceive,
　　Would suit you right well;
And freely I give
　　What you may not steal,
But wear it in honour
　　Of Jesus his grace,
And worship the donor,
　　And love him and praise.

9.

O Jesus, my Lord,
A rebel I am,
Yet grace be ador'd,
　　Still sav'd by the Lamb!
Hosanna to Jesus
　　Who came to redeem,
And loveth to bless us;
　　Hosanna to him!

10.

I never could guess
This passage to life;
But now *the door* bless,
　　Which endeth my strife;

" Lord, faften my ear in
    " The poft of thy door,"*
That I may dwell therein,
    And ramble no more.

H Y M N   261.

" I am the true vine," John xv. 1.

1.

IN Jefus I fee
    The growth of my wine,
Defirable tree,
    A true living vine !
Not lofty as cedar,
    Nor ftubborn as oak,
But humble and tender,
    And bends to my look.

2.

This plant of renown
    May boaft of it's birth,
From heaven came down,
    And rooted on earth :
It grew, and was running
    With fhoots† on it's fide,
Till thro' Pilate's pruning,
    It bled till it dy'd.

3.

The life was refign'd,
    But caught a new flame;

* Exod. xxi. 6.   † The twelve apoftles.

It's ftem * was refin'd,
　The root † was the fame;
And now it is growing
　In each humble dale,
And freely beftowing
　It's wine to regale.

4.

Whoever fhall tafte
A fip of this wine,
Will think it the beft,
And call it divine;
It certainly healeth
　All guiltieft fmart ;
And fweetly revealeth
　All joy to the heart.

5.

A graff in thy ftem,
Sweet Vine, I would be ;
Bear fruit in the fame,
And bear it for thee :
Thine arms be my fhelter,
　Thy bark be my coat,
And let the graff welter
　In fap from the root.

* The earthly nature,
† The divine nature.

HYMN 262.

" Jesus was made a surety of a better covenant," Heb. vii. 22.

1.

A Debtor I am,
I very well know;
And all of our name
Have ever been so:
Deriv'd from a father,
Old Adam we call,
Who broke altogether,
And ruin'd us all.

2.

Arrested he was
In body and soul,
For breaking the laws
He should have kept whole;
And now we inherit
His debts and his pride,
His high and hot spirit,
With bondage beside.

3.

Unable to dig,
So lame in each part!
Ashamed to beg,
So lofty in heart!
Past debts are all charged,
Which we cannot pay;
And these are enlarged
By new ones each day.

4.

Each debt is for hell,
Sad durable woe!
It's dole who can tell
But fpirits below?
Who roar with diftraction
Of horror and pain;
Feel what is damnation,
And roar out again.

5.

But, lo! a kind Lord
Has pity'd our ftate,
Who pledged his word,
And paid off the debt;
'Tis Jefus, the furety,
That friend of our race,
Who made a fecure tie
Of heaven thro' grace.

6.

Go, poor finner, go,
His mercy intreat,
Thy broken heart fhew,
And fall at his feet:
He calleth for debtors,
As many as lift;
Go, carry thy fetters,
And wait upon Chrift.

7.

With chearfulleft words
He will thee receive,

And loosen the cords
Which Moses did weave:
Thy legal obedience
In life he has paid,
And thy legal vengeance
In death he was made.

8.

As surety, he stands
Engaged on high
To bring to thy hands
The pearls he did buy;
To set thee a grieving,
And help thee to pray,
To teach thee believing,
And how to obey.

9.

From first unto last
The work is his own;
He calls the outcast,
And puts on the crown;
From Egypt to Canaan
The leader and rock;
Sends first and last rain on
His pastures and flock.

10.

Then lift up thy voice
In lustiest praise,
And learn to rejoice
In Jesus always;

He fhould have thankfgiving
   Again and again
From all that are living,
   Amen and Amen.

HYMN 263.

" They that are whole need not a phyfician,
   but they that are fick," Matt. ix. 12.

1.

FULL many a year
   I feem'd to be found,
Was lighter than air
   And fprung on the ground:
I trod on a mountain,
   And lofty was feen,
And wanted no fountain
   To wafh my heart clean.

2.

But now I am fick,
   And full of complaint,
Exceedingly weak,
   And ready to faint;
My heart an old den is *
   Of filth and deceit;
And all it's revenues
   Spring out of conceit.

3.

By breaft is a cage
   For birds of all note,†

* Jer. xvii. 9. Matt. xv. 19. † Rev. xviii. 2.

Where anger may rage,
  And fulkinefs bloat,
Where envy repineth,
  And flander will hifs,
And flattery joineth
  Them all with a kifs!

4.

My ftomach would feed
  On afhes and earth,*
Rejecting the bread
  Of heavenly birth!
A palfy perplexeth
  My tongue when it prays;
And goutinefs vexeth
  My ankles always!

5.

Right forry indeed
  I am in each part:
Oh! fick is my head,
  And faint is my heart;
So bad my condition,
  So rooted my woe,
None other phyfician
  But Jefus will do!

6.

He loveth us much,
  And dealeth in grace;
And heals by a touch
  The worft evil cafe;

* Ifai. xliv. 20.

He only wants notice,
  A tap at his door,
And then bringeth gratis
  His balms to the poor.

7.

An hospital croud
Attend on his gate,
Who keep knocking loud,
Both early and late;
And while they are preffing
  Him much to draw nigh,
He comes with a bleffing—
  " Hofanna they cry!"

8.

He drops a fond fmile,
And whifpers, All hail!
They blefs him the while,
And fing a love-tale;
All honours deck his head
  The dear Lamb of God,
" Who loved and wafhed
  " Us in his own blood!"*

9.

" Amen," fay the fkies,
And warble the found:
" Amen," earth replies,
Let bleffing go round:

* Rev. i. 5, 6.

I   And

And then trumpets blew a
Full chorus above,
" Amen, hallelujah," *
For Jesus his love.

HYMN 264.

" Thou art the King of Israel," John i. 49.

1.

WE joyfully sing
With angels above,
Of Jesus our King,
His power and love;
His look, full of greatness,
Commandeth the sky;
His heart, full of sweetness,
Relents at our cry.

2.

He suffer'd our pain,
And took up our curse;
And dying to reign,
He triumphed thus ·
Death-conquering Jesus
Our king we proclaim,
He reigneth to bless us,
And bless we his name.

3.

A lion thou art, †
Yet gentle as brave;

* Rev. xix. 4.   † Rev. v. 5

H h

And right free of heart
A captive to fave;
He bringeth a ranfom
For any that pleafe;
And does it fo handfome,
He winneth our praife.

4.

My wifh is to be
A fubject of thine,
Triumphantly free
From bondage of fin,
Releafed from forrow,
And chearful as May,
No thought for the morrow,
But happy each day.

5.

Thy kingdom of grace
Set up in my breaft,
Affording me peace
And fanctify d reft;
Bid all my affection
Cry out for the Lord,
And bring in fubjection
My will to thy word.

6.

Yea, cover the earth
With knowledge and truth,
And fpread the new birth,
And raife up thy youth;

As dews of the morning,
   So many be they;
A multitude born in
   The course of a day.

HYMN 265.

"I will betroth thee unto me for ever,"
        Hosea ii. 19.

1.

YE maidens, who want
   Rich husbands and fair,
Nor can be content,
   Till wedded ye are;
Mark, how I miscarry'd,
   As many have done,
And after was marry'd
   Unto a King's Son.

2.

Much kindness I had
For Moses indeed,
And suit to him made,
And thought I should speed;
You know he is noted
   "For beautiful mein;"*
And on him I doted,
   As plainly was seen.

     * Acts vii. 20.

H h 2

3.

His fnarling I bore
For many a year,
Which grieved me fore,
And drew a fad tear.
One folly committed
No pardon will find;
And tho' much intreated,
He ftill is unkind.

4.

My forrowful cafe
A neighbour did fpy,
Who look'd on my face,
And caft a fweet eye;
He faw me perplexed,
He heard me complain,
And faid, be not vexed
At Mofes' difdain.

5.

His Mafter I am,
The Lord of the houfe,
My name is the Lamb,
I feek for a fpoufe;
Come hither, come fafter,
Thy hand let me have;
Take Jefus the Mafter,
Not Mofes the flave.

6.

Ah, Lord, I am fick,
And ugly, and poor,

No coat on my back,
But ragged all o'er—
He smil'd, and replied,
'Tis all very true;
Yet is my heart tied
Most strangely to you.

7.

Bad health I repair,
Bad debts I will pay,
And make thee all fair
And blooming as May;
A robe of my linen
Shall gird thee about,
And thou shalt be seen in
A vest without spot.

8.

Your Moses of life
Will prattle, and health;
And talk to his wife
Of honours and wealth;
And more than a little
His merit displays,
Yet ne'er does a tittle
Of all that he says.

9.

My truth from my word
Shall never depart;
Believe a kind Lord,
Who pledgeth his heart:

H h 3

My honours I give you,
 My name you shall take ;*
I cannot deceive you,
 And will not forsake.

10.

The duty you owe
For offers this day,
My teaching shall shew,
And help you to pay :
Well ; are you contented ?
 What says the poor maid ?
He kist ; I consented,
 And so we were wed.

H Y M N 266.

" Thou art a priest for ever," Psalm cx. 4.

1.

WHEREWITH shall I come
 Before the Most High,
Who am but a worm,
 And doomed to die ?
My nature unholy
 Was tainted in birth ;
And nursed by folly,
 Brings all evil forth !

2.

Whatever I do,
Some baseness appears ;

  * Jer. xxxiii. 16.

2

Wherever I go,
    It rings in mine ears;
Pursues me and rages
    With fulsomest breath,
And tells me it's wages
    Are hell after death.

3.

No labours of mine
    With fasting and tears,
Can purge away sin,
    Or shorten arrears;
One only sweet fountain
    Of blood that was spilt,
Can loosen the mountain
    Of high-crying guilt.

4.

O Jesus, my Priest,
    And sweet Lamb of God,
No balm bringeth rest
    But that of thy blood!
This *only* is pleasing
    In thy Father's sight;
This *only* is easing
    A sinner outright!

5.

All thanks to thy love
    And pity and grace;
Which could thy heart move
    To die in our place!

We fet thee a grieving,
    Yet fuch was thy choice ;
Set us a believing,
    And we fhall rejoice.

6.

Thy wonderful crofs
With pleafure we trace ;
It's blood be on us,
And all of our race ;
A fpring to refrefh us
And nourifh the foul,
A Jordan to wafh us
And make lepers whole.*

H Y M N. 267.

" I perceive thou art a prophet," John iv.
    19.—Acts iii. 22.

1.

A Prophet we want
    Of delicate fkill,
Our nature to paint,
    Juft as it looks ill,
To fhew us our blindnefs,
    And woful bad cafe,
And fet out the kindnefs
    Of God in his grace.

2.

Deceitful and vile
And helplefs we are !'

* 2 Kings v. 14.

Yet finners will fmile
Such tidings to hear;
Difdaining to read it,
They call it abfurd;
And cannot give credit
To God in his word.

3.

I was of their mind
To cover my fore,
And thruft it behind
The back of my door;
I would not hear of it,
But now I perceive
Chrift is a true prophet,
And him I believe.

4.

He probed my foul,
And lanced my fkin;
And fhew'd I was foul
Without and within:
He, like a phyfician,
With wonderful art,
Difclos'd my condition,
The plague of my heart.*

5.

All thanks to my Lord
For giving this light;

* 1 Kings viii. 28.

His Spirit and word
Have cleared my fight;
I fee ev'ry feature
Diftorted indeed!
I am a loft creature,
And Jefus I need!

6.

Now fhew me thy face
In fmiles from above,
And help me to trace
The depths of thy love;
Be evermore healing
My wounds in each part,
And fweetly revealing
Thy love to my heart.

HYMN 268.

" A wife man built his houfe upon a rock,"
Matt. vii. 24. " And that rock was
Chrift," 1 Cor. x. 4.

1.

MY heavenly hope
I built on the fand;
And rear'd my houfe up,
And thought it would ftand:
Without it was painted,
And feem'd a neat fort;
Within it was fainted
With worth of all fort.

2.

But lo, a ftorm fell,
    A terrible blaft,
With thunder and hail,
    And down my houfe caft!
It ftagger'd and cracked,
    And broke with the fhock,
And out I ran *naked*,
    And crept to a rock.

3.

No fooner my arm
    Was on the Rock laid,
But vanifh'd the ftorm,
    And vanifh'd all dread!
My bofom was cheared
    And felt a new blifs;
My feet were up-reared,
    And walked in peace.

4.

All clamorous ftrife
    Is banifh'd from hence;
And waters of life *
    Are flowing from thence;
And combs full of honey †
    From all the fides drop;
And oil without money ‡
    Is bought on it's top!

* Exod. xvii. 6.　　† Pfalm lxxxi. 16.
‡ Deut. xxxii. 13.

5.

O Rock of delight,
On thee may I ftand,
And view from it's height
The promifed land :
Thy ftrength I would reft in,
And with thee abide,
And build a fafe neft in
The cave of thy fide.

6.

Thy honey refrefh
And fweeten my foul;
Thy purple ftream wafh
And make my heart whole;
Thy pure oil of gladnefs*
My fpirit anoint,
To drive away fadnefs,
And fupple each joint.

7.

Here build me a tent
For prefent abode,
A dwelling-place lent,
An inn for the road :
And let me be viewing
Thy love, a fweet ftock;
And good works be doing,
Yet reft on my rock.

* Ifai. lxi. 3.

HYMN

HYMN 269.

"Behold the Lamb of God!" John i. 36.

1.

THE sweet Lamb of God
  Comes forth to be slain,
And offers his blood
To purge off our stain;
With bitterest anguish
  And groans on the tree,
The Saviour did languish
  For sinners, like me.

2.

Look on him, my soul,
  And gaze on his smart;
His cries may control
  The lusts of thy heart;
His blood has set often
  The worst broken bones,
His love too can soften
  Hearts harder than stones.

3.

Right worthy indeed
He is of high fame;
And saints have all need
To trust in his name;

I i

Not feed on their graces,
 Nor ſtrut with a frame,
But fall on their faces,*
 And worſhip the Lamb.

4.

Lo, here is a feaſt
Of delicate food,
 For prodigals dreſt,
 Yet coſtly and good!
Our Father provided
 This Lamb for a treat;
And if you are minded,
 You freely may eat.

5.

None other repaſt,
 My ſpirit would have;
Thy fleſh let me taſte,
 Sweet Lamb, and yet crave;
Thy blood ever flowing
 My pleaſant cup be;
Thy fleece on earth growing
 Make clothing for me.

6.

Thus cover'd and fed
At thy proper coſt,
The path I would tread
Which pleaſeth my hoſt;

* Rev. vii. 9, 10, 11.

Thy patience inherit,
Thy lowliness prove,
-Catch all thy sweet spirit,
And burn with thy love.

HYMN 270.

" Unto you that fear my name, shall the
Sun of Righteousness arise with healing
in his wings," Mal. iv. 2.—Psalm lxxxiv.
11.

1.

THE spiritual lame
And spiritual poor,
Who fear the Lord's name,
And dwell at his door ;
With darkness are frighted,
And storms in the skies,
Nor can be delighted
Until the sun rise.

2.

And while a black night
Drags heavily thro',
They cannot strike light
By all they can do ;
But joy is returning
To visit their heart ;
A smile of the morning
Bids sorrow depart.

3.

Thou heavenly Sun,
True light of the world,*
Moſt fair to look on,
Thy beauties unfold;
Step forth from thy chamber †
And ſhew thy ſweet face,
With locks bright as amber,
And ſparkling with grace.

4.

Enlighten me well
With heavenly truth,
And fairly reveal
The weeds of my growth;
My boſom uncover,
My nakedneſs ſhew,
And kindly diſcover
The depths of my woe.

5.

Yet comfort me too
With beams from above,
And let my heart know
The depths of thy love;
With mercy ſurround me,
Too ſweet to be told,
To ſhew thou haſt found me
And brought to thy fold.

* John viii. 12.   † Pſalm xix. 4, 5.

6.

One other requeſt,
And then I have done ;
Let Sion be bleſt
With rays of thy Sun ;
Grow modeſt and wealthy
In gifts and in grace,
And teem with an healthy
And numerous race.

HYMN 271.

" Chriſt is the head of his body, the
church," Col. i. 18.

1.

THE carcaſe of man,
Disjoin'd from it's head,
With limbs may be ſeen,
But all of them dead ;
The foot or the finger
No motion can have,
And only can linger
Awhile in a grave.

2.

So dead is the ſoul
Disjoined from Chriſt !
No light in the whole,
Nor hunger nor thirſt ;

No fpiritual feeling,
 Difcernment or tafte;
It looks for no healing,
 Nor fees itfelf loft.

3.

But Jefus fupplies
His body right well;
As *head*, he brings eyes,*
And hearing, and fmell;†
Brings palate for manna,
 Frefh palate each day;
Lips finging hofanna,
 And tongue that can pray.

4.

And thus the church ftands
Upheld by clofe ties,
Redeem'd by Chrift's hands,
And near his heart lies;
With him it has union
 Thro' faith in his blood,
And thereby communion
 In fpirit with God.

5.

Then, Lord, let me be
Supply'd from thy head;
A fmall limb of thee,
Yet quicken'd and fed;

* Prov. xx. 12. † Ifa. xi. 3. Bible-margin.

The foot or the shoulder,
   It matters not much;
And as I grow older,
   Still closer thee touch.

HYMN 272.

" Where a testament (or last will) is, there
must be the death of the testator; for a
will is only of force, after men are dead,"
Heb. ix. 16, 17.

1.

THE first of our race
   Was comely and good,
Yet fully'd his face,
   And tainted his blood;
Of glory bereaved,
   He fell into thrall;
And dying, bequeathed
   A curse to us all.

2.

Thus ruin'd I am,
   Yet often thro' pride
Would cover my shame,
   As Adam first did;
Well pleased to swagger
   And prate of my worth,
Tho' born but a beggar,
   And blind from my birth.

I

3.

Condemned to die
We ſtand on record,
A voice from on high
Hath utter'd the word;
To vanity given,
We fret and complain;
And whilſt we are living,
And living in pain.

4.

But lo! a kind friend,
Beholding our caſe,
His love to commend,
Steps into our place,
Takes on him our nature
In lowlieſt form,
And God in the creature
Appears like a worm.*

5.

Tho' ſhrunk to a reed,
And mournful in mein,
The Godhead indeed
Was thro' the vail ſeen;
Winds, waters, and devils,
Submit to his nod,
And healing all evils
He ſhews himſelf God.

* Pſalm xxii. 6.

6.

With ferventeſt zeal
He acted and ſpoke,
And well did fulfil
   The law that we broke ;
Then, little bewailed,
   Hung on a ſad croſs,
And faſt to it nailed
   Our ſhame and our curſe.

7.

Let mountains and hills
A lofty ſong raiſe,
And vallies and rills
   Re-echo his praiſe ;
Shout, all the creation,
   Below and above,
And ſing of ſalvation
   From Jeſus his love.

8.

And now his will ſtands
In force after death,
Conveying good lands
   To men full of faith;
Arrears are forgiven,
   And ſinners find peace,
With title to heaven,
   And meetneſs thro' grace.

HYMN 273.

" He retaineth not his anger for ever, because he delighteth in mercy. He will
turn again, he will have compassion upon
us, he will subdue our iniquities, and
cast all our sins into the depths of the
sea," Micah vii. 18, 19.

1.

ART thou a sad soul,
  Surrounded with fears,
Whose heavy days roll
 In sighing and tears,
Bemoaning the hidings
 Of Jesus thy Lord,
And hearing no tidings
 Of joy from his word?

2.

Mark what the Lord says
 To men of sad heart,
Who love the Lord's ways,
 Yet under sin smart;
" Mine anger for ever
 " I will not retain,"
No, no, the kind Saviour
 Will heal up thy pain.

3.

" Sweet mercy I love,"
 And mercy will shew;
And mercy shall prove
 A balm for thy woe;

Fair mercy fhall bloffom
   And fmile on thy face;
And ent'ring thy bofom,
   Thy heart fhall embrace.

4.

" I will turn again,"
   And gladden thy days;
My fun and my rain,
   An harveft fhall raife;
Thy peftilent nature
   My grace fhall fubdue,
And alter each feature,
   Creating it new.

5.

The fins which are paft,
   And clamour at thee,
Thy Jefus will caft
   Them into the fea;
Thy fins fhall all under
   The deepeft wave pafs;
And caufe thee to wonder,
   And love me and blefs.

6.

Then let us proclaim
   Chrift's love to our race,
And honour his name,
   His mercy and grace;
His mercy enduring,
   And never to ceafe;
His grace well infuring
   Our health and our peace.

HYMN 274.

" Thy love is better than wine," Cant. i. 2.

1.

OUR Jefus beftows
  Good cheer on his friends;
What in his land grows,
He bleffes and fends;
Pure love is a bloffom
  Of heavenly birth,
And thro' the Lord's ranfom
  It blooms upon earth.

2.

Love from his pierc'd heart
Does pleafantly fpring,
And water each part
And plant of the King;
All heaven it filleth
  With joys ever new,
And here it diftilleth
  In fweet honey-dew.

3.

The Comforter brings
This joy to the foul,
At which the heart fprings,
And feels itfelf whole;
Love fummons all graces,
  And kindles all praife,
And fweetens all faces,
  And gladdens all days.

Hofannas

4.

Hosannas they send
To Jesus on high,
And follow their friend
With shouts to the sky;
His blood's precious merit
They boldly proclaim,
And thro' his good Spirit
Can trust in his name.

5.

No cordial on earth
Heart-grief will remove;
No wine has the worth
Of Jesus his love;
This banisheth sorrow
From ev'ry sad breast,
And welcomes the morrow
With joy for it's guest.

6.

This pilgrimage feast
For Sion below,
Lord, give me to taste,
My pilgrimage thro';
So shall I unceasing
Attend to my race,
And live and die blessing
The riches of grace.

Kk

HYMN 275.

"I am black, becaufe the fun hath looked upon me," Cant. i. 6.

1.

NO wifdom of man
    Can fpy out his heart,
The Lord only can
    Shew this hidden part;
Nor yet are men willing
    To have the truth told,
The fight is too killing
    For pride to behold.

2.

A *look* from the Lord
    Difcovers our cafe,
And bringeth his word
    Attended with grace;
The man is convicted
    And feeleth his hell,
And groweth afflicted
    More than he can tell.

3.

If once the fun fhines
    Upon a foul clear,
He reads the dark lines
    Which fin has wrote there;
Begins to difcover
    His colour and make,
And cries, I'm all over
    As any fiend black.

4.

But when the Lord fhews
  A reconcil'd face,
And buries our woes
  In triumphing grace,
This bleffed look ftilleth
  The mourner's complaint,
And with a fong filleth
  The mouth of the faint.

5.

Sweet love and fweet fhame
  Now hallow his breaft;
Yet black is his name,
  'Tho' by his Lord bleft;
I am, he fays, homely,
  Deform'd in each part,
All black, and yet comely,
  Thro' Jefu's defert.

6.

A look of thy love
  Is all that we want;
Ah, look from above,
  And give us content:
Looks fet us adoring
  Thy perfon moft fweet,
And lay us abhorring
  Ourfelves at thy feet.

K k 2

HYMN 276.

" Jefus faid, I am the refurrection and the
life; he, that believeth in me, though he
were dead, yet fhall he live," John. xi. 25.

1.

A Soul dead in fin,
Muft fleep in his grave,
Till Jefus begin
The finner to fave:
His word is with power,
And opens blind eyes;
He calls at his hour,
And up the dead rife.

2.

In Laz'rus we view
A finner's fad cafe,
Bound hand and foot too,
And bound on his face;
No arm may releafe him,
And give a new birth,
Till Jefus fays, " Loofe him,"
And then he comes forth.

3.

But all the life ftill
Is drawn from his aid;
Or vain were his will
To quicken the dead:

For never can flourish
  The spiritual flame,
Unless the Lord nourish
  And fan up the fame.

4.

The body and soul
  Herein well agree,
That life in the whole
  Depends not on thee;
Thy skill cannot save it,
  Tho' means are all try'd;
He only, who gave it,
  Can make it abide.

5.

O thou, who dost keep
  Death's key in thine hand,
Behold how men sleep,
  And hard at hell stand;
We call, but they slumber,
  And hear not our word;
They are a great number,
  Oh, waken them, Lord.

6.

On Sion send peace,
  Distilling like dew;
Their graces increase,
  Their comforts renew;

K R 3

In faith and love build up
    Thy family here,
And keep the folds fill'd up
    With lambs of each year.

HYMN 277.

" Without me, ye can do nothing,"
    John xv. 5.

1.

WITHOUT thee, O Lord,
        I nothing appear,
No will for thy word,
    No liking to pray'r;
No heart to adore thee,
    No feet for the race,
No thirst for thy glory,
    No hunger for grace.

2.

Of honour bereft
    By nature I am,
And nothing is left
    But limping and shame;
Yet, with an high spirit,
    And frothy delight,
We boast of our merit,
    And wisdom, and might.

3.

I zealously fought
To keep my own heart,
And verily thought
It was my own part;

But as I grow older,
   Am learning at length
To borrow Chrift's fhoulder,
   And walk in his ftrength.

4.

And now I confefs
   His word to be true,
Apart from his grace
   I nothing can do;
My wifdom is folly,
   My arm utter weak,
My heart is unruly.
   My ftomach quite fick.

5.

Lord, bid me renounce
   This pride of my will,
And give up at once
   Myfelf to thy fkill,
No longer rely on
   My watch and my ward,
But truft in the Lion
   Of Judah to guard.

6.

Such royal faith give,
   As honours thy throne,
A faith that will live
   On Jefus alone,
Thy arm my protection,
   Thy labours my reft,
Thy word my direction,
   Thy Spirit my gueft.

HYMN 278.

"Thy Maker is thine husband," Isai. liv. 5.

ith   1.

THE Lord of the earth,
    To Adam ally'd,
Sends messengers forth
To fetch him a bride;
To many he chuseth
    His love to impart,
And none he refuseth
    Who give him their heart.

2.

Strange marriage indeed
    For heaven's fair King,
Yet Jesus will wed
With any poor thing;
He liketh the maimed,
    The halt and the blind,
The poor and defamed,
    The lowest in kind.

3.

So after the banns
Are publish'd below,
Comes joining of hands
With joined hearts too;
Then debts are discharged,
    Tho' heavy they be,
And she is enlarged,
    From bondage set free.

4.

A rich wedding-fuit
Is to the bride brought,
Of love the fweet fruit,
And by the King wrought;
With this he does cover
 Her nakednefs quite,
And deck her all over
 As fair as the light.

5.

 A ring for the bride
 Is from the King fent,
With jewels befide
To deck her heart meant;
With thefe fhe grows loving,
 And modeft, and mild,
In good works improving,
 And feemeth a child.

6.

Now Chrift is her joy,
Her fong, and her hope;
She for him will figh,
And long to go up;
And he, from his tower
 Peeps on her e'erwhile,
And tells his love to her,
 And drops her a fmile.

7.

At length the approach
Of wedding is come,

And, lo, a ſtate-coach
To fetch the bride home :
Kind angels are bringing
Her faſt as ſhe liſt,
And up ſhe goes ſinging
Hoſanna to Chriſt.

HYMN 279.

" All thy ſaints ſhall bleſs thee, they ſhall
ſpeak of the glory of thy kingdom,
and talk of thy power," Pſalm cxlv.
10, 11.

1.

A Ranſomed race
The Saviour ſhould bleſs,
And ſing of his marvellous power and grace,

2.

He gave us a birth,
And formed the earth,
And feedeth us kindly with all it brings
forth.

3.

He makes the heart warm,
Defends it from harm,
And holds up our ſteps with a fatherly arm.

4.

He bids the ſun riſe
To gladden our eyes,
And calls up night-watches to ſpangle the
ſkies.

5.

His provident eye
Is watchfully nigh,
To guide us, and guard us, and bring us
      fupply.

6.

But grace is the thing
That makes the heart ring,
And fetcheth out luftieft praife to the King.

7.

Sweet mercy comes here
To fcatter our fear,
And bowels of love in the Godhead appear.

8.

A ranfom has been
Concerted for men,
And God in our nature the ranfom is feen.

9.

Blood only was meet
To cancel our debt,
And bleeding moft freely he cancell'd it quite.

10.

And thus a new road
Is found unto God,
Offenfive to nature, thro' faith in his blood.

11.

His Spirit prepares
The ranfomed heirs
For kingdoms of glory, eternally their's.

12.

Hearts changed and new
Are ready for you;
The grace of our Jesus all things can subdue.

13.

He stilleth all wants,
And husheth complaints,
Oh, sing him hosannas becoming the saints.

HYMN 280.

" And David brought forth the Ammonites, and put them under saws and
harrows of iron, and axes of iron,"
2 Sam. xii. 31.

1.

STRANGE tidings I hear,
Which grate on mine ear,
King David from outrages cannot forbear.

2.

Tormenting his foes,
No pity he shews,
But heaps upon Ammonites wonderful woes.

3.

He saweth their necks,
And ploughteh their backs,
With axes he choppeth, with harrows he
    rakes.

I   4. Yet

4.

Yet here I may view
My lovely Lord too,
Who Ammonites fpares not in me or in you.

5.

Whenever a child
Is running quite wild,
Our David will fmite him, tho' loving and
mild.

6.

Brifk rods he will fend,
Until the child mend,
Saws, axes, and harrows, and plagues with-
out end.

7.

He fpareth no luft,
The leaft or the worft,
But chops, till he layeth it's head in the duft.

8.

Ye children, beware
Of fin and it's fnare,
With watchfulnefs walk, and with diligent
pray'r.

9.

And woe to the man
That fins without pain,
Who feels no correction, but fins on again.

10.

By feeling no fmart
He cheers up his heart,
But Paul tells him roundly, a baftard thou
    art. *

11.

Much thanks to the Lord
We owe for his word,
And for the inftruction his harrows afford.

12.

When thee I neglect,
And wifdom reject,
Correct me, O Lord, but in mercy correct.

HYMN 281.

" The Lord thy God led thee thefe forty
years in the wildernefs, to humble thee,
and prove thee, and make thee know
what was in thine heart," Deut. viii. 2.
" Who led thee through that great and
terrible wildernefs, wherein were fiery
ferpents, and fcorpions, and drought,
that he might humble thee, and prove
thee, to do thee good at thy latter end,"
Deut. viii. 15, 16.

1.

BEHOLD the Lord's plan
    Of dealing with man,
Thro' all generations repeated again.

* Heb. xii. 8.

2.

His people of old
To Pharaoh were fold,
A notable tyrant, in wickednefs bold.

3.

He binds heavy bands,
And wearies their hands;
To Jefus they cry, and falvation he fends.

4.

The fea is pafs'd o'er;
They fing and adore,
And view all their enemies dead on the fhore.

5.

With chearfulleft praife
They trip up fteep ways,
And hope to fee Canaan in fix or ten days.

6.

All evils now feem
Quite vanifh'd from them;
Of milk and fweet honey they only can
dream.

7.

But, lo, a fad thirft
Diftreffes them firft;
And now their fine fong, and brave courage
is loft.

8.

Then quickly we read
A murmur for bread,
A figh for old Egypt, a wifh to be dead.

9.

No end of complaint!
More water they want,
And now would kill Mofes in fad difcontent.

10.

And thus the Lord fhews,
By bringing frefh woes,
The horrible evils, which in the heart grows.

11.

Where faith is not right,
It never can fight;
The wildernefs trials will flay a man quite.

12.

But if the Lord's grace
A finner embrace,
The wildernefs proveth a bloffoming place.

13.

The heart is well read,
While under the rod,
And learns to walk humbly and clofely with
    God.

14.

So may I be found,
When trials abound,
And learn to walk fteady on wildernefs-
    ground.

HYMN 282.

" Come unto me, all ye that labour and are
heavy-laden, and I will give you reft,"
Matt. xi. 28.

1.

GOOD tidings I bring
From Judah's fair King,
To cheer up a mourner and make his heart
fing.

2.

The Lord his love fends
To all his fad friends,
And much his grace to them and truth re-
commends.

3.

His love is to all,
The great or the fmall,
Who weary of fin are, and come at his call.

4.

True mourners he makes,
Invites 'em, and takes
With lighter or heavier load on their backs.

5.

His bofom has room
For all that will come,
And early or late you may find him at home.

6.

He knoweth your cafe,
How wretched and bafe,
And yet he fays, Come, and be faved by
grace.

7.

No fury he hath,
Come to me, he faith,
Come lowly in prayer, and boldly in faith.

8.

Tho' fadly diftreft,
Come to me for reft,
And Jefus will wafh the guilt out of your
     breaft.

9.

Tho' wholly unclean,
Come loathing of fin,
And grace will not fuffer corruption to reign.

10.

Come juft as you are,
Without any fear,
And come at all feafons my mercy to fhare.

11.

The call, that I read,
Is chearing indeed,
And juft fuch a Saviour a finner does need.

12.

I come to thy door,
Am weary and poor,
Relieve me, and ufe me, as thine evermore.

HYMN 283.

" Thou haft played the harlot with many lovers, yet return again to me, faith the Lord," Jer. iii. 1.

1.

HEAR what the Lord fays,
And turn from your ways,
Ye lovers of mammon, and pleafure, and
praife.

2.

Tho' idols befet
Your wandering feet,
And harlots encompafs your heart in a net :

3.

Though folly beguile
Your heart with a fmile,
And courting damnation, you laugh all the
while:

4.

Yea, tho' you have gone
In bafenefs long on,*
Committing all evils that can be well done:

5.

Or if growing flack,
You have flidden back,
And turned from Jefus, and caft off his yoke:

6.

To you a kind word
Free grace can afford,
"Return yet again unto me, faith the Lord."

* Jer. iii. 5.

7.

Return unto me,
Tho' late it now be,
And mercy, rich mercy is ready for thee.

8.

To Jesus return,
And tenderly mourn,
And he will receive thee among his new-born.

9.

Thy peace he will seal,
And pardon reveal,
Thy bent to backsliding he also will heal.

10.

Then let us proclaim
His merciful name,
And sing of his grace, and accept of the same.

11.

Return we now may;
Yet turn us, we pray,
Or still we shall wander, and further shall stray.

HYMN 284.

"If any man desire to be first, the same
shall be last of all, and servant to all,"
Mark ix. 35.

1.

AMBITION we find
In every mind;
Yet earthly ambition is paltry and blind.

2.

Each man would excel;
So far it is well,
Yet each pushes foremost, and so is last still.

3.

Our Jefus did fhew
Where honour will grow,
But rough is the path, and untrodden we
know.

4.

Who feeks to be firft
Muft rank himfelf laft,
And learn with complacence to wait on the
leaft:

5.

He muft become fmall,
And run at each call;
As Jefus, the higheft, was fervant of all.

6.

So angels, that fit
The foremoft in ftate,
On heirs of falvation moft chearfully wait.

7.

Thefe patterns are true,
Tho' notic'd by few,
And fhould be held evermore up to our view.

8.

Here honour is found
Upon it's own ground,
Not empty and flafhy, but noble and found.

9.

Dear Jefus, impart
A fpice of thy heart,
To feafon us well for this fervant-like part.

10.

Make others appear
Deserving our care,
How low in their station soever they are.

HYMN 285.

"Whither I go, thou canst not follow me
now, but thou shalt follow me afterwards,"
John xiii. 36.

1.

GOOD tidings I hear
Saluting mine ear,
A word from the Saviour to rid us of fear.

2.

An honey-comb sweet,
And savoury meat,
To cheer up a pilgrim, and quicken his feet.

3.

Rough Peter ador'd
His Master and Lord,
Believ'd in his name, and regarded his word:

4.

He could suffer loss,
And hardy he was,
Yet courage he wanted to die on a cross.

5.

But Jesus has grace
For such a sad case,
And Peter's sweet promise a saint should
embrace.

6.

The way that I go,
Is hard for thee now,
But shall be made easy for Peter and thou.

7.

'Tho' like a young tree,
Unstable thou be;
A reed groweth lusty, when grafted on me.

8.

By grace a poor worm
Can weather a storm;
And what I command thee, my grace shall
perform.

9.

Keep on in thy way,
Trust in me and pray,
And strength shall be suitable unto thy day.

10.

Such aid we implore,
Nor need we ask more
Than suitable help for the feeble and poor.

HYMN 286.

" Thy daughter is dead, why troublest thou
the Master any further? Jesus saith, Be
not afraid, only believe," Mark v. 35, 36.

1.

OR sooner or late,
Diseases will wait
On every houshold, and knock at the gate.

2.

A ruler in chief,
Much laden with grief,
From Jesus seeks for his sick daughter relief.

3.

But news very sad
He meets on the road,
" Cease troubling the Master, thy daughter
    is dead."

4.

Such news I oft hear
Assaulting mine ear,
When unto my Saviour I come with a pray'r.

5.

Mine enemies flirt,
And make me their sport,
And unbelief crieth out after this sort.

6.

Thou poor silly fool,
Sad dunce of Christ's school,
Cease troubling the Master, thou art a dead
    soul.

7.

Long hast thou laid in
A grave full of sin,
Dead prayers, dead praises, and all dead
    within.

8.

Such news I receive,
And listen, and grieve,
Till Jesus says, " *Fear not, but only believe.*"

I   9. His

9

His pow'r is then known,
And sweetly is shewn
To heal a sick sinner, or raise a dead bone.

10.

Lord, give me such faith,
As fetcheth it's breath,
And hopes against hope in the feelings of
death.

11.

So will my short race
Be passed in peace,
Not resting on feelings, but leaning on grace.

HYMN 289.

" I pray thee let me go over, and see the
good land," Deut. iii. 25.

1.

THERE is a good land,
And layeth at hand,
Yet little sought after, and few on it stand

2.

A land of free grace,
Abounding with peace,
And many fine clusters of sweet righteous-
ness.

3.

Saints, dwelling below,
It's blessedness know,
And here they find Jesus, and feast on him
too.

M m

4.

Near Jordan it lies,
Well water'd with joys,
An image, tho' faint, of the land in the fkies.

5.

And wouldft thou it fee?
Put Mofes from thee,
And let the Lord Jefus thy forerunner be.

6.

Yet reckon it good
To wafh in his blood,
This bringeth thee peaceably nigh unto God.

7.

So when thou haft found
This wonderful ground,
Be watchful and prayerful all the year round.

8.

For many a beaft
The country infeft,
And, if you are dronifh, will mangle your
    breaft.

9.

Walk well upon guard,
For battle prepar'd,
And truft in your Captain all danger to ward.

10.

With Jefus in fight
All matters go tight,
His whiftle puts all the foul monfters to
    flight.

OCCASIONAL HYMNS.

HYMN 290.

" The clouds poured down water; thy thunder was in the heavens; the lightnings flashed through the world, the earth trembled and shook," Psalm lxxvii. 17, 18.

To be sung in a tempest.

1.

HOW awful art thou seen, O God,
 When lightnings issue forth,
And rattling thunders roll abroad,
 To shake and rend the earth.

2.

If here we dread thy fiery breath,
 Nor scarce with it can dwell,
O Lord, how dreadful is thy wrath,
 Which blazeth out in hell?

3.

The forked lightnings know thy will,
 And mark thy beck'ning hand,
They harmless pass, or blasting kill,
 As thou dost give command.

4.

Thou only art our fence and tow'r,
 Our help is in thy grace;
Preserve us in this awful hour,
 And guard our dwelling-place.

5.

Such tempefts, like the fiery law,
　Thy majefty proclaim,
Oh, may we learn with rev'rent awe
　To glorify thy name.

HYMN 291.

" There was a marriage in Cana, and Jefus
　was invited to the marriage," John ii.
　1, 2.
　　　　　At a chriftian wedding.

1.

OUR Jefus freely did appear
　　To grace a marriage-feaft;
And, Lord, we afk thy prefence here,
　To make a wedding-gueft.

2.

Upon the bridal pair look down,
　Who now have plighted hands;
Their union with thy favour crown,
　And blefs the nuptial bands.

3.

With gifts of grace their hearts endow,
　Of all rich dowries beft!
Their fubftance blefs, and peace beftow,
　To fweeten all the reft.

4.

In pureft love their fouls unite,
　And link'd in kindly care,
To render family burdens light,
　By taking mutual fhare.

5.

True helpers may they prove indeed
  In pray'r, and faith, and hope;
And fee with joy a godly feed
  To build the houfehold up.

6.

As Ifaac and Rebecca give
  A pattern chafte and kind;
So may this new-met couple live
  In faithful friendfhip join'd.

H Y M N 292.

" I will fing of thy mercy in the morning,"
Pfalm lix. 16.

A Morning Hymn.

1.

THRO' Jefu's watchful care
    I fafely pafs'd the night!
His providential arm was near,
  And kept off every fright.

2.

No pains upon my bed
  Prevented my repofe;
But laying down my weary head,
  Refrefh'd with fleep I rofe.

3.

And here I ftand poffeft
  Of ftrength and vigour new;
And with my limbs and fenfes bleft,
  Another morn I view.

M m 3

4.

From thee my mercies flow,
In pearly drops they fall;
But give a thankful bosom too,
The sweetest pearl of all.

5.

Be thou my guide to day,
My arm whereon to rest,
My sun to cheer me on the way,
My shield to guard my breast.

6.

From Satan's fiery dart
And men of purpose base,
And from the plague within my heart,
Defend me by thy grace.

H Y M N 293.

"Praise the Lord likewise at evening,"
1 Chron. XXIII. 30.

An Evening Hymn.

1.

THE Lord's almighty arm
Has been my shield to-day,
He watcheth every rising harm,
And thrust it far away.

2.

Nor sick I am nor lame,
My limbs and senses sound,
Supported is my feeble frame,
And mercies close me round!

3.

Along with mercies kind,
A thankful fenfe impart,
To raife fweet wonder in my mind,
And melt and tune my heart.

4.

Be thou my guard to-night,
And fafe my dwelling keep,
Defend my heart from every fright,
And fend refrefhing fleep.

5.

No teafing care moleft,
Nor wanton thought intrude,
And harmlefs keep my dozing breaft
From fancy's idle brood.

6.

Or fleeping or awake,
Do thou furround my bed,
And with thy peace a pillow make
To reft my weary head.

HYMN 294.

" Servants, obey your mafters, and pleafe
them well, not anfwering them again, nor
pilfering, but fhewing all good fidelity,"
Titus ii. 9, 10.

A Morning Hymn for an houfehold fervant.

1.

TO Jefus, my dear Lord, I owe
The reft I had this night;

By him preferv'd from every woe,
   I wake to view the light.

2.

Accept, O Lord, my early praife,
   It is thy tribute due;
And let the morning-fong I raife,
   Rife with affection too.

3.

My dear Redeemer, while on earth,
   A fervant was to all;
With ready foot he ftepped forth,
   Attentive to each call.

4.

If unto labour I am bred,
   My Saviour was the fame;
Why then fhould I a fervice dread,
   Or count it any fhame?

5.

Yet, Lord, I need a patient mind,
   And beg a ready will,
To pay my *mafter* fervice kind,
   And every tafk fulfil.

6.

No faucy language I would ufe,
   Nor act a treacherous part,
But ferve *him* with the pureft views,
   And work with freeft heart.

HYMN 295.

" Servants, be subject to your masters with
all reverence, not only to the good and
gentle, but also to such (masters) as are
froward," 1 Pet. ii. 18.

An Evening Hymn for an houshold servant.

1.

ACCEPT, O Lord, an evening song,
    And sure it need be warm;
For mercy watch'd me all day long,
    To screen me well from harm.

2

Sound limbs and senses I possess,
    Nor food or raiment want;
Good cause I have the Lord to bless,
    And should be well content.

3.

While some with hunger pine and starve,
    And feel a thousand cares,
The *master*, whom I daily serve,
    My daily food prepares.

4.

His just commands may I fulfil,
    His person kindly treat,
His substance never waste or steal,
    Nor wink when others cheat.

5.

Or if ungentle he should prove,
    And treat me with disdain,
May yet no wrath my bosom move,
    To answer pert again.

6.

Lord, fend me quiet reft to-night,
  And fafe the houfehold keep,
Preferv'd from all alarming fright,
  And bleft with kindly fleep.

☞ Obferve, if the fervant waits on a miftrefs, then *miftrefs* muft be faid inftead of
mafter, and *her* inftead of *him* or *his*.

H Y M N 296.

" In the fweat of thy face fhalt thou eat
  bread, till thou return to the ground,"
Gen. iii. 19.

Morning Hymn for a chriftian labourer.

1.

I Thank my Lord for kindly reft
  Afforded in the night ;
Refrefh'd, and with new vigour bleft,
  I wake to view the light.

2.

What need I grieve to earn my bread,
  When Jefus did the fame ?
If in my Mafter's fteps I tread,
  No harm I get, or fhame.

3.

Oh, let me blefs, with thankful mind,
  My Saviour's love and care,
That I am neither fick, nor blind,
  Nor lame, as others are.

4.

A trufty workman I would be,
  And well my tafk purfue,
Work when my mafter does not fee,
  And work with vigour too.

5.

And whilft I ply the bufy foot,
  Or heave the labouring arm,
Do thou my withering ftrength recruit,
  And guard me well from harm.

6.

To fweeten labour, let my Lord
  Look on, and caft a fmile;
For Jefus can fuch looks afford,
  As will the hours beguile.

HYMN 297.

" The fleep of a labouring man is fweet,"
Ecclef. v. 12.
Evening Hymn for a chriftian labourer.

1.

THE Lord be prais'd for labour done,
  And ftrength to work this day;
The clock has ftruck, the time is gone,
  And calls from work away.

2.

When all my rolling years are paft,
  And labouring days fhall ceafe,
Then let my foul have reft at laft
  In thy fweet world of peace.

3.

And whilſt I dwell on earthly ground,
    And toilſome work purſue;
Preſerve my limbs and ſenſes ſound,
    And daily ſtrength renew.

4.

May Jeſus on my labour ſmile,
    And each day's earning bleſs;
Then, like the widow's meal and oil,*
    It yields a daily meſs.

5.

Direct my feet in wiſdom's ways,
    And keep my heart from care,
Refreſh it with thy love and praiſe,
    And guard it with thy fear.

6.

My humble cottage ſafely keep,
    It will not move thy ſcorn;
And let thy labourer have ſweet ſleep,
    And riſe refreſh'd at morn.

HYMN 298.

" This is the day, which the Lord hath made,
    we will rejoice in it," Pſal. cxviii. 24.

Lord's-day morning.

1.

ON this ſweet morn my Lord aroſe,
    Triumphing o'er the grave!
He dies to vanquiſh deadly foes,
    And lives again to ſave!

* 1 Kings xvii. 12, &c.

2   2. I

2.

I blefs my Lord, and hail the morn,
  It is my Lord's birth-day;
And faithful fouls will furely fcorn
  To doze the houre away.

3.

A day for holy joy and reft,
  Yet clouds will gather foon,
Except my Lord become my gueft,
  And put my harp in tune.

4.

No heavenly fire my heart can raife
  Without the Spirit's aid;
His breath muft kindle pray'r and praife,
  Or I am cold and dead.

5.

On all the flocks thy Spirit pour,
  And faving health convey;
A fweet refrefhing Sunday fhow'r
  Will make 'em fing and pray

6.

Direct the fhepherds how to feed
  The flocks of thy own choice,
Give favour to the heavenly bread,
  And bid the folds rejoice.

HYMN 299.

" A day (ſpent) in thy courts, is better
than a thouſand (ſpent elſewhere),"
Pſalm lxxxiv. 10.

Lord's-day Evening.

1.

HOW lovely are thy courts, O Lord,
  How ſweet thy dwelling-place,
When thou doſt bleſs the goſpel-word,
  And ſhew thy gracious face!

2.

While Jeſus in his chariot rides,
  And truth and mercy brings,
My heart will taſte no joy beſides,
  And nauſeates earthly things.

3.

One ſavoury day in his houſe ſpent
  More ſweetneſs yieldeth far,
Than thouſands paſs'd in merriment,
  Or than whole ages are.

4.

The goſpel word may Jeſus bleſs,
  To quicken ſinners dead,
To give the children growth in grace,
  And raiſe the mourner's head.

5.

Refreſh my ſoul with thy ſweet love,
  Well water'd let it be,
And, ſoaring up to things above,
  Cry out and thirſt for thee.

6.

Let each new fabbath bring new reft,
  New faith and love impart,
Croud fweeter praife within my breaft,
  And hallow more my heart.

H Y M N 300.

" Glory to God in the higheft, peace on eaith,
  good-will towards men," Luke ii. 14.

On the birth of Chrift.

1.

A N heavenly hoft triumphant bing
  The news of Jefu's birth,
They fing and fay the heavenly King
  Is come to dwell on earth.

2.

Is come to fave a guilty race,
  By opening mercy's door;
Is come to purchafe ftores of grace,
  To fet up finners poor.

3.

So God's good-will to man is told,
  And friendfhip is begun:
What can the Father now with-hold,
  Who freely gave his Son?

4.

Lift up a fong to God moft High,
  For love fo free, fo dear;
Exalt his praife above the fky,
  And make his angels hear.

5.

And thou, moſt precious Prince of Peace,
   Accept my homely heart;
Thy name I love, thy feet I kiſs,
   For pleaſant ſure, thou art!

6.

A manger I have got for thee,
   It is my boſom, Lord;
And if the Lord, can dwell with me,
   It will be richly ſtor'd.

H Y M N 301.

" Great is the *myſtery* of godlineſs; God
manifeſt in the fleſh!" 1 Tim. iii. 16.

On the birth of Chriſt.

1.

O Sweet myſterious grace
   On mortal man beſtow'd !
My God comes down with human face,
   To fetch me home to God !

2.

Tho' might was all his own,
   And boundleſs too his ſway,
He vails his glory, quits his throne,
   And takes an houſe of clay.

3.

From everlaſting ſure;
   Yet of a mortal ſpan !
And will from age to age endure,
   Yet proves a dying man !

4.

He formed man and beaft,
And rear'd the worlds around;
Yet fuckled at a creature's breaft,
And in a manger found!

5.

Myfterious love indeed!
Who can it's depth explore?
Yet as it fuits my faddeft need,
It's depth I muft adore!

6.

The wonders of his birth
An heavenly fong could raife,
And fure the ranfom'd fons of earth
Should fing and fhout his praife.

HYMN 302.

" Is it nothing to you, all ye that pafs by?
Look and fee, if there be any forrow
like unto my forrow, wherewith the
Lord has afflicted me, in the day of his
fierce anger," Lam. 1. 12.

On the crucifixion of Chrift.

1.

YE fons of mirth, and fons of pride,
  Caft here a penfive eye;
Behold the Saviour crucify'd,
  Nor pafs him heedlefs by.

2.

With kind concern he says, " Look up,
  " Behold, I die for you ;
" The sorrows in my deadly cup,
  " O sinner, were thy due !

3.

" For thee my back is lash'd and torn,
  " With thorns my head is crown'd;
" For thee I hang a wretch forlorn,
  " Fast on a gibbet bound !

4.

" Thy guilt brings all my sorrows down,
  " More sad than I can tell ;
" And now my God begins to frown,
  " And sure his frown is hell !

5.

" O Father dear, some pity take,
  " And ease my tortur'd breast ;
" O God, my God, do not forsake,
  " I sink, I sink opprest !"

6.

And were these pangs, dear Lord, for me,
  These cries and deadly smart ?
And by thy bonds am I set free ?
  Then take my ransom'd heart.

HYMN 303.

" Jefus faid, It is finifhed : and he bowed
his head, and yielded up his Spirit,"
John xix. 30.

On the crucifixion of Chrift.

1.

THE dreadful fcene is paft;
  " 'Tis finifh'd," Jefus cries:
Redemption's work is done at laft;
  He bows his head, and dies.

2.

" 'Tis finifh'd;" Mark it well!
All legal debts are paid :
He freely took our curfe, our hell,
  And full atonement made.

3.

The law he magnify'd,
  And gave it honour due;
Complete obedience he fupply'd,
  Not for himfelf, but you.

4.

His *life* a title brings
  To glory, full and fair;
His *death* robs death of all it's ftings,
  And fets the guilty clear.

5.

The Father reconcil'd,
  No frowning vengeance fhews,
But hafting to a weeping child,
  A pardoning kifs beftows.

6.

Thy crofs be all my boaft,
  Thou bleeding love divine!
Redeem'd I am, and at thy coft,
  Oh, take and keep me thine.

H Y M N 304.

" Jefus is not here, he is rifen : come, fee
  the place where the Lord lay," Matt.
  xxviii. 6.

On the refurrection of Chrift.

1.

AT length the joyful morn is come,
    A triumph o'er the grave ;
The ftone is rolled from the tomb,
  And Jefus quits his cave.

2.

An angel, with commiffion fent,*
  The Saviour fets at large ;
To fhew that juftice was content,
  And gave a full difcharge.

3.

Eternal laurels gird thy brow,
  And grace thy temples well!
All hail, my Lord, triumphant now
  O'er fin, and death, and hell !

4.

The battle thou haft nobly fought,
  The wine-prefs trod alone ;

* Matt. xxviii. 2.

Thy single arm salvation brought,
  The glory all thine own!

5.

With songs exalt the Prince of peace,
  And give a joyful shout;
His love we must arise and bless,
  Or will the stones cry out.

6.

Within his cave I would abide,
  And bid the world good night,
There bury all my guilt and pride,
  And soar to endless light.

HYMN 305.

"If ye be risen with Christ, seek those things
which are above," Col. iii. 1.
On the resurrection of Christ.

1.

IN vain the sealed cave,
  In vain the Roman guard,
My Lord will quit his silent grave
  Just at the time prepar'd.

2.

An earthquake tells the hour,*
  Of Jesu's second birth,
An angel opes the prison-door,
  And lo! he springeth forth!

3.

All hail, my risen Lord,
  Triumphant Saviour now!

      * Matt. xxviii. 2.

Sin, death, and hell, with one accord
  Before thy footstool bow.

4.

The fight is bravely fought,
  The work is nobly done,
A full salvation thou haft bought,
  And endless honour won.

5.

Oh, bid thy little flock
  Their rifen Lord pursue,
Gaze after him with wishful look,
  And warm affections too.

6.

Instruct the faints below
  To feek the things above,
And foaring upwards, fweetly grow
  In light and heavenly love.

H Y M N 306.

" While Jefus bleffed them, he was parted
  from them, and carried up into heaven:
  and they *worshipped* him," Luke xxiv.
  51, 52.

On the afcenfion of Chrift.

1.

AND now the Saviour goes,
  The parting hour is come,
A parting bleffing he beftows,
  Then mounts triumphant home!

2.

With eafy flight he soars
Beyond our feeble ken:
Unfold, unfold, ye heavenly doors,*
And let the Saviour in.

3.

Amaz'd the fkies reply,
Who is this mighty-Lord?
The King of glory, angels cry,
By all but fiends ador'd!

4.

'Tis Jefus from the dead,
Who lives to die no more!
Bow down, ye gates, your lofty head,
And hail him, and adore!

5.

Now girt with glory round,
With praifes ever bleft,
My King on Sion's hill is crown'd,
Where none can break his reft.

6.

He fits and rules on high,
And fends his heralds forth,
Who run to raife a gofpel-cry,
And fpread his fame on earth.

* Pfal. xxiv. 7.

HYMN 307.

" They were all filled with the Holy Ghoſt,
and ſpake with *other* tongues, as the
Spirit gave them utterance," Acts ii. 4.

On the pouring out of the Spirit at Pentecoſt.

1.

BEHOLD! the promis'd help is come,
And holy fire ſent down at laſt!
The heralds are no longer dumb,
When warmed with the Holy Ghoſt.

2.

With *other* tongues they freely ſpeak,
And blow the goſpel-trumpet loud,
Proclaim the word to Jew and Greek,
And much amaze the liſt'ning crowd !

3.

So now, when heralds come abroad,
With goſpel on their boſom ſeal'd,
And full commiſſion feel from God,
With *other* tongues their mouth is fill'd.

4.

A ſon of *thunder* firſt appears,
To ſhake the earth, and plough the ground,
To wake the dead with guilty fears,
And make a ſinner feel his wound.

5.

But when the lofty cedars bow,
And ſink and fall at Jeſu's feet,
A Son of *conſolation* now,
His lips, like honey-combs, are ſweet!

6. If

6.

If peace salute the guilty mind,
And faith'has found the joyful rock,
An *other* voice the shepherds find,
On Jesus Christ to *build* the flock.

7.

Such tongues the heralds now receive,
Not such as in the *Acts* we read,
Yet such as God alone can give,
And suited well to every need.

HYMN 308.

" Jesus shall baptize you with the Holy
Ghost," Mark i. 8.
On the baptism of the Spirit.   A Pentecost
Hymn.

1.

BAPTISMAL water I have had,
And hold the water needful too;
Yet sure I need the Spirit's aid
To wash my heart, and make it new

2.

No spark of spiritual life I find,
Without the Spirit's quick'ning breath,
Supine and earthly is my mind
And slumbers in the arms of death.

3.

Come, breathe thine influence, Holy Ghost,
And light and heavenly love impart;
Bring down a gracious Pentecost,
And kindle fire in every heart.

O o

4.

Without thy breath we are but clay,
Our harp is on the willows hung,
Devotion droops and dies away
On fainting heart, and faultering tongue.

5.

Thy heavenly unction let us feel,
And give us faith, and faith's increafe;
The bleffings of the covenant feal,
And bring the year of fweet releafe.*

6.

Our fpirit unto God unite,
And keep us meekly in his fear;
Thy holy law within us write,
And make the treacherous heart fincere.

H Y M N   309.

" Lord, behold, he whom thou loveft, is
fick," John xi. 3.
For a believer in ficknefs.

1.

FROM thee, O fin, our forrows flow,
    Our fhort and painful years!
And life becomes a fcene of woe,
    A mournful vale of tears!

2.

No fooner is one ficknefs paft,
    But others quickly come;
They break the earthly cafe at laft,
    And lodge it in the tomb.

* Deut. xv. 1, 2.

3.

O Jesus, thou the healer art
 Of human pain and grief;
Thy balms alone asswage the smart,
 And bring us kind relief.

4.

See, Lord, thy servant here is sick!
 We trust, beloved well,
Yet pray thou wouldst in mercy speak,
 And all thy kindness tell.

5.

In every faint and trying hour,
 Thy arm be round *his* bed,
Supporting by thy secret pow'r
 His droop'ng heart and head.

6.

With heavenly peace refresh *his* mind,
 And keep the bosom still,
To live or die alike resign'd,
 As suits thy holy will.

HYMN 310.

"Whom the Lord loveth, he correcteth,"
   Prov. iii. 12.

For a believer in sickness.

1.

OUR heavenly Father must correct
 A well-beloved child,
Or sure he would his will reject,
 And wanton grow, and wild.

O o 2

2.

He knows how apt we are to ftart,
  And caft his fear afide;
And by his rod's inftructive fmart,
  He brings us near his fide.

3.

O Father, make thy love appear,
  But every doubt remove,
By whifpering in the fick child's ear,
  " I fmite, becaufe I love."

4.

While rods are in the Father's hand,
  A father's heart reveal,
And teach the child to underftand
  Thy loving-kindnefs well.

5.

Support *his* heart, and hold *his* head,
  And fanctify the rod;
Purge out the drofs which health has bred,
  And draw *his* heart to God.

6.

Beftow a calm and patient mind,
  With ftrength to fuffer pain,
And in the furnace let *him* find
  Some rich and folid gain.

HYMN 311.

" The Lord will be thine everlasting light,
and the days of thy mourning shall be
ended," Isa. lx. 20.

For a believer in much weakness of body.

1.

AFFLICTED soul, lift up thine eyes
To Jesu's glorious throne,
Thy mourning days, and pensive sighs,
Will all be quickly gone.

2.

The Shepherd, while on earth, did weep
A thousand tears for thee;
Nor can his lambs, nor can his sheep
From grief exempted be.

3.

Beset we are with sins and fears,
Our peace they much annoy;
But they that sow awhile in tears,
Shall reap with endless joy.

4.

The loving Saviour has prepar'd
A rest for all his saints;
And when he brings the rich reward,
Farewel to all complaints.

5.

There sin and pain are banish'd quite,
And mourning fled away;
The Lord will be thy glorious light,
And make eternal day.

6.

Such heavenly peace he will impart,
    As here we cannot prove;
And fill up well thy ravish'd heart,
    With endless joy and love.

HYMN 312.

" Look upon my affliction and my pain,'
      Psalm xxv. 18.

For a believer in strong pain.

1.

O Lord, bow down thy gracious ear,
    And listen to our grief;
Look on a child afflicted here,
    And send *him* some relief.

2.

With pain and anguish sore opprest,
    He makes a piteous moan;
Behold the torture of *his* breast,
    And mark each labouring groan.

3.

Thou knowest well our feeble frame,
    The house is built of clay;
And if thou only crush the same,
    It moulders fast away.

4.

Some pity take, O Lord, relieve
    His agonizing pain;
And bid the aching limbs receive
    Some chearing rest again.

5.

But if thy hand renew *his* smart,
　And grant him no release ;
Yet let thy hand uphold *his* heart,
　And yield it heavenly peace.

6.

And if the house, which tottering stands,
　Should make the tenant fly ;
A better house not made with hands,
　Provide *him* in the sky.

HYMN 313.

" Why art thou cast down, O my soul?
hope thou in God, for I shall yet praise
him," Psal. xlii. 5.

For a believer in great darkness and distress.

1.

WHY so cast down, dejected soul?
　A loving Christ is near ;
Thy broken bones he can make whole,
　And drooping spirit cheer.

2.

If guilty stings thy conscience feel,
　And pierce thee thro' and thro',
Yet past backslidings Christ can heal,
　And love thee freely too.

3.

If justice draw it's flaming sword,
　And seems intent to kill ;
On Jesus call, and trust his word,
　And thou shalt praise him still.

4.

Thy foul with tempeft may be toft,
    And Satan forely thruft,
Yet fure no foul fhall e'er be loft,
    Who makes the Lord his truft.

5.

Dear Jefus, fhew thy fmiling face,
    And Calvary's peace impart,
Difplay the pow'r of faving grace,
    And cheer a troubled heart.

6.

Refrefh *his* eye with fweeter light,
    And whifper in *his* ear,
" Thy foul is precious in my fight,
    " No need thou haft to fear."

H Y M N 314.

" Bleffed are the dead, who die in the Lord;
they reft from their labours," Rev. xiv. 13.

On the death of a believer.

1.

O Happy foul, who fafely paft
    Thy weary warfare here,
Arriv'd at Jefu's feat at laft,
    And ended all thy care !

2.

No more fhall ficknefs break thy reft,
    Or pain create thee fmart,
No more fhall doubts difturb thy breaft,
    Or fin afflict thine heart.

3.

No more the world on thee shall frown,
  No longer Satan roar,
Thy *man of sin* is broken down,
  And shall torment no more.

4.

" Adieu, vain world, the spirit cries,
  " All tears are wip'd away ;
" My Jesus fills my cup with joys,
  " And fills it every day.

5.

" A *taste* of love we get below,
  " To chear a pilgrim's face ;
" But every saint must die to know
  " The feast of heavenly grace.

6.

" Delightful concord always reigns
  " In Jesu's courts above !
" There hymns are sung in rapt'rous strains,
  " With ceaseless joy and love !"

HYMN 315.

" O death, where is thy sting ?" 1 Cor.
xv. 55.

On the triumphant death of a believer.

1.

AT length *he* bow'd *his* dying head,
  And guardian angels come ;
The spirit dropt it's clay and fled,
  Fled off triumphant home.

2.

An awful, yet a glorious fight,
  To fee believers die!
They fmile, and bid the world good night,
  And take their flight on high!

3.

No guilty pangs becloud the face,
  No horrors make them weep;
Held up and chear'd by Jefu's grace,
  They fweetly fall afleep.

4.

On death they caft a wifhful eye,
  When Jefus bids 'em fing,
" O grave, where is thy victory,
  " O death, where is thy fting?"

5.

Releas'd from fin and forrow here,
  Their conflict now is o'er;
And feafted well with heavenly cheer,
  They live to die no more.

6.

So may I learn by grace to live,
  And die in Jefus too;
Then will my foul that reft receive,
  Which all his people do,

HYMN 316.

"Duſt thou art, and unto duſt thou ſhalt return," Gen. iii. 19.

A funeral hymn.

1.

PRAY, caſt a look upon that bier,
 A corpſe muſt preach to day,
It tells the old, and young, and fair,
 Their houſe is built of clay.

2.

The ſtrong may think their houſe a rock;
 Yet ſoon as Jeſus calls,
Some ſickneſs brings a fatal ſhock,
 And down the building falls.

3.

The limbs, now lifeleſs, only crave
 A coffin for their bed,
With leave, to find a ſilent grave,
 And lodge among the dead.

4.

The funeral knell, you heard to day,
 By tolling tells your doom;
The hours are poſting faſt away,
 To lodge you in the tomb.

5.

But are you waſh'd in Jeſu's blood,
 And thus prepar'd to die?
His blood alone gives peace with God,
 And ripens for the ſky.

6.

The Saviour yet invites you all
 To knock at mercy's gate;
Arise, arise, for mercy call,
 Before it be too late.

HYMN 317.

" While the child was yet alive, I fasted and
wept; but now it is dead, why should I
fast or weep?" 2 Sam. xii. 22, 23.
 On the death of a child.

1.

AN early summons Jesus sends
 To call a child above,
And whispers o'er the weeping friends,
 'Tis all the fruit of love.

2.

To save the darling child from woe,
 And guard it from all harms,
From all the griefs you feel below,
 I call'd it to my arms.

3.

Ah, do not rashly with me strive,
 Nor vainly fast or weep;
The child, tho' dead, is yet alive,
 And only fall'n asleep.

4.

'Tis on the Saviour's bosom laid,
 And feels no sorrow there;
'Tis by an heavenly parent fed,
 And needs no more your care.

2   5. To

5.

To you the child was only lent;
    While mortal, it was thine;
But now in robes immortal pent,
    It lives for ever mine.

6.

Arise and run the heavenly road,
    Nor in dumb mourning fit;
Look up toward the child's abode,
    And haste to follow it.

HYMN 318.

" What is your life? It is even a vapour,
    that appeareth for a while, and then va-
    nisheth," James iv. 14.

A Funeral Hymn.

1.

AS vapours, issuing from the earth,
    Dance in the liquid air,
But when the sun is peeping forth,
    March off and disappear:

2.

So frail is man, so fleet his age,
    A floating vapour true!
A while he danceth on the stage,
    Then bids the world adieu.

3.

A thoughtless creature sure he seems,
    And roams about to-day,

P p

And in the midſt of earthly dreams,
　Is check'd and ſnatch'd away.

4.

Or full of mirth, or full of care,
　And heedleſs of his doom,
Till ſickneſs ſtops his wild career,
　And drops him in the tomb.

5.

One drops, and ſtraight another falls,
　And raiſe a paſſing-bell;
We ſtartle at the ſolemn calls,
　Yet ſoon forget the knell.

6.

Awake, O Lord, our drowzy ſenſe,
　And rouze the ſoul at laſt
To ſeek in Chriſt a ſure defence,
　Before the doom is paſt.

HYMN 319.

" Prepare to meet thy God," Amos iv. 12.

A Funeral Hymn.

1.

AN awful work it is to die!
　A work we all muſt do;
And every day is creeping nigh,
　More nigh to me and you.

2.

Diſeaſe will ſhake our houſe of clay,
　And make it reel and fall;
The ſpirit will be forc'd away,
　When Jeſus gives a c

3.

Before his awful judgment-feat
   Each mortal muft appear;
And Chrift will fix their doom complete,
   In joy or fad defpair.

4.

And are you deck'd in heavenly drefs,
   Prepar'd to meet your God;
Array'd in Jefu's righteoufnefs,
   And wafh'd in Jefu's blood?

5.

Does heavenly love infpire your breaft,
   And find you fweet employ?
Is God's dear word your favoury feaft,
   And Chrift your fong and joy?

6.

Be wife before it be too late,
   And ferze your gofpel-day;
The Lord yet waits at mercy's gate,
   Awake, arife, and pray.

SACRAMENTAL HYMNS.

HYMN 320.

1.

THE table now is fpread,
   With guefts around the board;
Dear Jefus, blefs the wine and bread,
   And heavenly peace afford.

2.

Yea let the Lord appear
With looks divinely mild,
And whisper in each humble ear,
" I love thee well, my child."

HYMN 321.

1.

DEAR Jesus, end our legal strife,
And send the Spirit down,
Breathe on our souls the breath of life,
And seal us for thine own.

2.

Our little grain of faith increase,
Our feeble hope improve,
Refresh us with thy crofs's peace,
And ground us well in love.

HYMN 322.

1.

MY Saviour would become
A man of griefs for me,
My guilt he bury'd in his tomb,
To set the sinner free.

2.

No longer I would rove
In sin or folly's ways;
Henceforth may all my heart be love,
And all my life be praise.

HYMN 323.

1.

DEAR Jefus, come and grace thy board,
  And peep on every mourning gueft;
The table now with food is ftor'd,
But thy fweet prefence makes the feaft.

2.

Come in, thou bleffed of the Lord,
And bring the gofpel-banquet here,
Thy prefence and thy peace afford,
And feaft our fouls with heav'nly cheer.

HYMN 324.

" They fhall look on me, whom they have
  pierced, and mourn," Zech. xii. 10.

1.

DEAR dying friend, we look on thee,
  And own our foul offences here;
We built thy crofs on Calvary,
And nail'd and pierc'd thy body there.

2.

Yet let the blood, our hands have fpilt,
Be fprinkled on each guilty heart,
To purge the confcience well from guilt,
And everlafting life impart.

3.

So will we fing thy lovely name
For grace fo rich and freely giv'n,
And tell thy love, and tell our fhame,
That one, we murder'd, bought our heav'n.

P p 3

HYMN 325.

1.

THE Lamb of God flain
    We love and adore,
Now rifen again
To reign evermore;
All riches poffeffing,
    And wifdom and might,
All honour and bleffing,
    And in his own right.

2.

While feraphs beftow *
Their loftieft praife,
His people below
Hofannas fhould raife;
And glory to Jefus
    We chearfully fing,
His honours well pleafe us,.
    All joy to our King.

HYMN 326.

SPIRIT of glory come
   And light of life impart; †
Bring Jefu's bleffings home,
And feal 'em on each heart;
Well hallow every humble breaft,
And make it thine eternal reft,

* Rev. v. 11.   † John viii. 12.

HYMN 327.

1.

FATHER, we adore thy grace,
  Bleſs the love ſo richly ſhown,
Shown to an apoſtate race,
Up in arms againſt thy throne.

2.

Long we did thy Spirit grieve,
Now we humbly ſue for peace,
And a bleſſing would receive,
Sealed with a Father's kiſs.

3.

Shew thy heart is reconcil'd,
Call us ſons and daughters dear,
Give us tempers of a child,
Godly love, and godly fear.

HYMN 328.

MOST holy, holy, holy Lord,
  The Three-One God, by ſaints ador'd!
Whoſe mercy ſhewn in covenant grace,
Reſtores a vile apoſtate race.
We bleſs the grace, and thankful own
Salvation is from God alone.*

HYMN 329.

1.

BOUGHT I am, and dearly too,
  Jeſus paid my ranſom due, †

* Pſalm iii. 8.   † 1 Cor. vi. 20.

Freely paid it with his blood,
Tells me I am bought for God.

2.

Lord, my all I would refign,
Soul and body now be thine,
Take and ufe me as thy own,
Let thy holy will be done.

HYMN 330.

1.

DEFIL'D I am indeed,
    Defil'd throughout by fin ;
Thy purple fountain, Lord, I need,*
    To wafh a leper clean.

2.

The fountain open ftands,
    Yet on it's brink I dwell ;
Oh, put me in with thy own hands,
    And that will make me well.

HYMN 331.

1.

ATONEMENT Jefus made,
    For he our furety ftood,
The ranfom-price he fully paid,
    And paid it with his blood.

2.

His blood for mercy cries,
    And bids the finner come.

* Zech. xii. 1.

To feaft upon the Sacrifice,
  And whifpers, " There is room."

3.

I blefs thee, dying Friend,
  For making my curfe thine:
Such pity none but God could lend,
  Such love is all divine.

HYM'N 332.

1.

OUR Father has prepar'd a feaft,
  Where prodigals may come and dine;
Each hungry foul may fuit his tafte,
Who wants to feed on food divine.

2.

Here kind repentance is beflow'd,
And precious faith is freely giv'n,
With bofom pray'r to fuit the road,
And grace to train us up for heav'n.

3.

" All things are ready," you are told,*
A gracious God waits on you ftill,
And grace is not for merit fold,
But free for whofoever will.†

HYMN 333.

1.

O Love divine, fweet Lamb of God,
  Our fins are fwallow'd up in thee;

* Matt. xxii. 4.   † Rev. xxii. 17.

The cleanfing virtue of thy blood
From bondage fets believers free;
Thy blood's fweet voice, thro' earth and fkies,
For mercy, boundlefs mercy cries.

2.

O let me plunge into this fea,
Which drowneth guilt, and bringeth reft;
And if a billow threat'neth me,
I'll dive into the Saviour's breaft;
And viewing mercy all wrote there,
Will fing away my grief and care.

HYMN 334.

1.

A Monthly feaft we keep,
Where hungry fouls may come;
Kind Shepherd, gather in more fheep,
For in thy fold is room.

2.

Thy table would provide
For many a twenty more;
No bread we lack, nor wine befide,
Send guefts, a precious ftore.

HYMN 335.

1.

THRO' Jefu's death we live,
Upon his crofs we reft;
And faithful fouls receive
What makes a finner bleft;

The Father's love, the Spirit's grace,
And Jesu's legacy of peace.

2.

Eternal love and praise
To Jesus Christ are due;
And ransom'd souls may raise
The new song, ever new;*
A song, which from redemption came,
The song of Moses and the Lamb.

HYMN 336.

1.

THE flocks of Jesu's choice
The Shepherd's love should praise;
He chears them by his voice,
And guards them in their ways;
He hears and heals their sad complaints,
Hosanna to the King of saints!

2.

His precious name we bless,
His person we adore;
And what can saints do less
Than love him evermore?
Our souls and bodies are his due,
Our highest love and service too.

HYMN 337.

1.

NOT worthy, Lord, we must confess,
That we of children's bread should taste,

* Rev. xiv. 3. xv. 3.

Yet trufting in thy righteoufnefs,
We venture to the gofpel feaft;
The bread we afk which comes from heav'n,
And let fome bleffed crumbs be giv'n.

2.

Lord, fet thy crofs before our eyes,
With all it's wond'rous toil and fmart,
And feaft us on the Sacrifice,
And fhew our names upon thy heart;
Till faith cry out, I Jefus view,
I truft him now, and feel him too.

HYMN 338.

1.

POOR forrowful foul,
To Jefus repair,
He makes finners whole,
That broken heart are;
Whatever their plight is,
No matter for that,
He healeth all gratis
That come to his gate.

2.

No cafe is too hard,
So great is his fkill;
No one is debarr'd,
So kind is his will;
Come fooner or later,
You find him at home;
The fooner the better,
Yet knock till he come.

2   AFTER

AFTER SACRAMENT.

HYMN 339.

TO Father and Son
And Spirit of grace
Full honour be done
By Adam's loft race;
And may a free blessing
Come down from above,
While we are rehearsing
Their covenant-love.

HYMN 340.

ERE we leave thy table, Lord,
Drop us down a pledge of peace;
Give us all a parting word,
Sealed with a parting kifs.

HYMN 341.

HOLY, holy, holy Lord,
Ever live by us ador'd;
Ever should a sinner cry,
Glory be to God moft High.

HYMN 342.

THE Lord of the feaft
We folemnly blefs,
And pray that each gueft
May grow in his grace:

Q q

Thanks for his preparing
This banquet of love;
Oh, may we all share in
The banquet above.

A N

AN
INDEX OF THE TEXTS

BELONGING

TO THE HYMNS.

Q q 2

INDEX.

INDEX.

Q q 3.

I N D E X.

I N D E X.

INDEX.

INDEX.

F I N I S.

Ingram Content Group UK Ltd.
Milton Keynes UK
UKHW050643270623
424112UK00008B/329